Caucus Chaos
Trump

DAVE PRICE

Thanks for reading!

Dave Price

Cover by Jiaff Design

Cover Illustration by Akinshin, istockphoto.com

Edited by Mark Hostetter

ISBN-13: 978-0-578-46047-5

Library of Congress Control Number: 2019901616

CONTENTS

INTRODUCTION

Months before Iowa Governor Terry Branstad (far right) joined Lt. Governor Kim Reynolds (center) and candidate Donald Trump (far left) on stage on November 6, 2016, in Sioux City, Iowa, Branstad had already decided that he should help Trump become president.

Photo by Dave Price

Make America great again! Drain the swamp. Build a wall. Fake media. Travel ban. Impeachment. Russian collusion. Staff turnover. Drama. Chaos. Tweets. So. Many. Tweets. So. Much. Controversy.

Indictments. Guilty pleas. Resignations. Blue Wave. Record midterm turnout. Congressional investigations.

Donald John Trump: 45th President of the United States of America.

It's been quite a first term so far for President Trump. He has shocked people in ways that no politician who came through Iowa ever has.

Republican presidential candidates like Ted Cruz, Marco Rubio, Jeb Bush, Rand Paul, Carly Fiorina, Jim Gilmore, Mike Huckabee, Rick Santorum, Ben Carson, Chris Christie, George Pataki, Lindsey Graham, Rick Perry, Scott Walker, Bobby Jindal and John Kasich felt that shock.

So did Democratic presidential candidates like Hillary Clinton, Bernie Sanders, Martin O'Malley, Jim Webb and Lincoln Chafee.

Republican-turned-Independent presidential candidate Evan McMullin did as well.

As did the Green Party's nominee, Dr. Jill Stein, and the Libertarians' choice, Gary Johnson. They all tried to beat Trump to become president. They all failed. Many still can't believe that happened.

Trump shocked the political system then. He continues to shock it now. Trump has shocked America. "Shocked" seems like the appropriate word to me.

- *He **shocked** people with his words.*
- *He **shocked** people with his tweets.*
- *He **shocked** people with the intensity of his followers.*
- *He **shocked** people with his refusal to adhere to political norms.*
- *He **shocked** people by the manner he trashes the media.*
- *He **shocked** people with his views of the facts.*
- *He **shocked** the political system.*
- *He **shocked** people by becoming president in the first place.*
- *He has **shocked** people ever since.*

One of the most fascinating things to me about this seismic level of shock in this country is the completely different, polar opposite, extremely passionate views people have about it.

"Donald Trump is **saving** this country."

and

"Donald Trump is **ruining** this country."

Saving vs. ruining. When has a president ignited such deep disagreement? Every modern-day president divides people on some level, right? Let's just consider the last two, for simplicity's sake.

Republican George W. Bush won over Americans with his "compassionate conservative" mantra (of course, Democrat Al Gore won the popular vote in that 2000 election but lost the electoral count. In 2016, it was Trump who became president despite Clinton winning the popular vote).

"I call my philosophy and approach 'compassionate conservatism.' It is compassionate to actively help our fellow citizens in need. It is conservative to insist on responsibility and results. And with this hopeful approach, we will make a real difference in people's lives."

President George W. Bush--April 30, 2002 (White House archives)

But President Bush later divided people with his war on Iraq that he sold to the public based on stunningly inaccurate intelligence that falsely claimed Iraq's leader, Saddam Hussein, had weapons of mass destruction. It also didn't help that Bush turned a projected surplus of trillions of dollars into a realized deficit of trillions (thanks to massive tax cuts without offsetting spending cuts, along with the wars in Iraq and Afghanistan). The "compassionate conservatism" that he championed as a candidate did not include compassionate budgeting as president.

His successor, Democrat Barack Obama, galvanized voters in 2008 with soaring rhetoric that could make a small-town preacher envious.

"The same message we had when we were up and when we were down; the one that can save this country, brick by brick,

block by block, calloused hand by calloused hand, that together, ordinary people can do extraordinary things. Because we are not a collection of red states and blue states. We are the United States of America. And in this moment, in this election, we are ready to believe again."

Barack Obama--Iowa Caucus victory party, January 3, 2008

However, Obama couldn't keep some in those red and blue states believing in his mission. Some progressives lost faith in his anti-war message as the U.S. involvement in other countries' conflicts dragged on. And some previous Republican optimism in a truly united, United States of America soon faded as the Democratic-driven Affordable Care Act (not the bipartisan compromise that idealists may have hoped after listening to candidate Obama's speeches on the stump) proved not to be the panacea for the healthcare system that advocates hoped. And yes, I agree that Obama doesn't deserve all the blame for failing to unite the country. Surely, he could have done better in this regard, but Republican-determined opposition, cable news and social media furor all deserve blame for further separating our country, too.

Obama championed change. But that change resulted in outcomes that he couldn't have imagined after he got elected as Democrats' power disintegrated all over Iowa and across the country.

But Trump's degree of division within our neighbors feels so much deeper than either Obama or Bush. Trump's true believers are incapable of doubt, no matter their leader's inconsistent policy positions, struggles with sticking to the facts, questionable ties with Russia, secrecy with his tax returns and propensity for juvenile name-calling and insults.

His vague promises to "drain the swamp" in Washington, D.C., have instead led to dozens of staff departures. That included U.S. Secretary of Health and Human Services Tom Price (criticisms of his spending/use of taxpayer-funded charter flights), Environmental Protection Agency Chief Administrator Scott Pruitt (criticisms of improper spending, conflicts of interests with a lobbyist and using staff to carry out his personal errands), U.S. Attorney General Jeff Sessions (fired after disagreements with Trump), U.S. Secretary of State Rex Tillerson (fired after disagreements with Trump), United Nations Ambassador Nikki

Haley (resigned to pursue other interests), White House Counsel Don McGahn II (resigned after successfully getting Brett Kavanaugh confirmed to the U.S. Supreme Court), Federal Bureau of Investigation Director James Comey (fired after disagreements with Trump), U.S. Secretary of Veterans Affairs David Shulkin (Shulkin said Trump fired him; White House said he resigned), plus numerous other staff departures, including two National Security Advisers (Lt. General H.R. McMaster and Lt. General Michael Flynn), Chief of Staff Reince Priebus and various other positions.

That doesn't include far more headline-grabbing scandals due to Special Prosecutor Robert Mueller's investigation into whether the Trump campaign colluded with Russia during the 2016 presidential election. By the 2018 midterm elections, the investigation already resulted in about three dozen indictments, along with guilty pleas by some prominent figures in Trump's orbit, including his former campaign manager Paul Manafort, longtime attorney Michael Cohen, National Security Adviser Flynn and campaign adviser George Papadopoulos.

Aside from all that, Trump's detractors seem incapable of holding out any hope a non-politician, a man who claims to have made billions in business, could take a CEO's private sector approach to a bloated, inefficient, debt-drowning federal government to make it a leaner, nimbler, better functioning, economic igniter for those seeking a more stable future, while also torpedoing the modern two-party political system and mainstream media...both of which elicit such disappointment and frustration with his fervent fan base.

A Quinnipiac University study laid out the divide among Americans about four months into the Trump presidency. By 2018's end, I don't think things had changed much.

Here was the question, followed by the ten most popular responses:

"What is the first word that comes to mind when you think of Donald Trump?"

Idiot = 39 responses
Incompetent = 31 responses
Liar = 30 responses
Unqualified = 25 responses
Leader = 25 responses

President = 22 responses
Strong = 21 responses
Businessman = 18 responses
Ignorant = 16 responses
Egotistical = 15 responses

Put together the most mentioned negative responses and you get:
Donald Trump, an **incompetent idiot** who **lies**.

Put together the most mentioned positive responses and you get:
Donald Trump, a **strong leader, president** and
businessman.

*(From May 4-9, 2017, Quinnipiac University surveyed 1,078 voters nationwide with a
margin of error of +/- 3 percentage points. Live interviewers call landlines and cell phones.)*

Welcome to Trump's America.

It seems so deeply divided. And Trump is historically unpopular. Nate Silver, the blogger/statistician/numbers guru and founder of FiveThirtyEight.com, the website of all things poll-related, compiled the numbers to show how Trump's negatives rate.

Trump is the most unpopular president at the 1-year mark

Approval, disapproval and net approval ratings of presidents since 1945
after 364 days in office, according to the FiveThirtyEight aggregate

PRESIDENT	INAUGURATION YEAR	APPROVE	DISAPPROVE	NET APPROVAL
John Kennedy	1961	79%	10%	+69
George W. Bush	2001	81	13	+68
George H.W. Bush	1989	78	11	+67
Lyndon Johnson	1963	74	15	+59
Dwight Eisenhower	1953	71	18	+53
Richard Nixon	1969	60	23	+38
Jimmy Carter	1977	55	27	+28
Bill Clinton	1993	57	34	+22
Harry Truman	1945	50	35	+15
Ronald Reagan	1981	49	40	+9
Barack Obama	2009	50	43	+7
Gerald Ford	1974	44	39	+5
Donald Trump	**2017**	40	55	-15
Average without Trump		62	26	+37

All numbers rounded

(Chart source: FiveThirtyEight.com)

In his first year in office, President Trump failed to favorably change his standing with the population. He didn't in his second year either.

Republicans don't quite know what to make of it all. Some believe Trump is just what their party needs and what the country wants. Trump can rebuild their party and remake their party in his image. He can connect with a part of the population that has been disconnected from traditional Republicans. Trump can grow their support in ways that no other Republican can do. Maybe no other Republican ever. Remake the courts. Remake the tax structure. Remake the country's image before the world on our military, trade and economic policies. Show other countries that without a doubt the United States of America is a force no one should ever f$#k with.

Others are nothing short of disgusted with the spectacle Trump has made of the American presidency. They don't consider Trump to be a Republican, moral or honest, not the leader that anyone should emulate. He is a national embarrassment to them, like no other president in history...a man spewing lies, deception and division.

Democrats can't believe that anyone on the face of the earth would support Trump. They are falling over themselves to show they can stop him. Beat him. Impeach him.

But regardless of whether they are looking to get behind him or defeat him, we must first understand how and why Trump is where he is and why he is in a position few thought possible.

Lee and Jody Rouse of Des Moines figured it out long before most. That's because they were listening.

"People are pissed." It was both a statement of the day and a conclusion of the times from Lee Rouse. I have worked with Lee for my entire career at WHO-TV. I don't think I've ever worked with anyone quite like him.

Lee has been a television news photographer for a quarter of a century. He has a unique ability to connect with people. It's an essential trait for someone in our business.

It doesn't matter if Lee is interviewing the president of the United States (we get to do that a lot in Iowa), a mother who just lost her husband in a car crash (we have to do stories like these too often) or a five-year-old who just sat on Santa Claus' lap (we can't EVER do too many of these!), Lee can talk to anyone. And he can relate to *everyone.*

Lee is never intimidated by anyone--not even the sleazy business owner who, along with a few of his strippers, jumped him one night because of the umpteenth news story about a crime at his club.

Maybe it's Lee's upbringing. He grew up in Grundy Center, a rural community of 2,700 people about 90 minutes northeast of Des Moines.

His dad owned Rouse Motors for years. Maybe that experience of talking with potential customers from all walks of life--farmers looking to spend big on a new truck during a particularly good year or the down-and-out family hoping to scrape together enough for a clunker to get them by until the finances hopefully get better--maybe that's what taught him how to relate to people. I really don't know, to be honest. But whatever it was, he is remarkable at it. And that makes people comfortable talking to him.

Lee told me that he sense how upset people were early in 2015 at the Cottontail Lounge in the Des Moines suburb of Urbandale. It's a neighborhood bar with a good mix of people from different backgrounds, but mostly every day, middle-class Iowans.

"People were just getting fed up with everything," Lee told me after thinking about the conversations he heard that night. "They're mad about how their raises at work suck, wonder how they're going to afford to send their kids to college...whether their kids will ever move out of their basements, mad at rich people...everything!" Lee recalled.

"People are just pissed off," he said. Lee couldn't really remember a time where so many people were mad. Neither could I.

Let's be honest: people are always upset about something. But come election time, it's primarily one major party or the other. Democrats couldn't stand George W. Bush. But they couldn't beat him. Republicans found little to like in Barack Obama. They couldn't beat him either. And I must point out that both men won twice. So anger apparently only gets you so far.

But when have we had a presidential campaign where it seems like a good chunk of followers in *both* parties are ticked off like this?

None that I can remember over the past three decades, at least.

I moved to Iowa in 2001, so I've witnessed Bush-Kerry, Obama-McCain, Obama-Romney and Trump-Clinton general election contests. Iowa, fortunately for political reporters, is always considered a battleground state, a "purple" state. The majority of voters may go for a Democrat (blue) or a Republican (red). It just depends on the candidate. It just depends on the year. That's why we're purple here. It's a mix. Registered Independents ("non-party," technically) make up the largest bloc.

Having painted that picture, I still feel like red was the more appropriate color of the 2016 cycle and it's not because of the Republicans. Red for anger. I just never anticipated the anger of the electorate as this race shaped up early. I don't think many others did either.

Lee had great insight on what fueled that anger: "People are pissed!"

I wanted more observations. And I found plenty of them.

I tried a little experiment. I went to the place where people so frequently express their anger: social media. I posted this question on Facebook:

"I keep hearing so many times how angry people are right now and its impact on the election. But WHY is there so much anger? Tell me what frustrates you most right now."

And to get things going, I offered my own rant:

"The country is nearly $20 trillion in debt. I'm amazed how few politicians seem to work on this. Where's the progress? Republicans want tax cuts but don't making the offsetting spending cuts. Democrats expand government programs but don't raise taxes or find other ways to make up for the costs. Is no one looking at the long-term future of this country?"

That got us going. Actually, it got us arguing. Perhaps that was fitting.

> **Mark Cullen**: *Is the dollar figure the real issue? Isn't the more important number the percentage of debt to GDP?*

> **Claire Celsi**: *People are confused about the difference between the debt and the deficit. The U.S. Budget deficit has gone down more than 2/3 under Obama.*

> **Tom Grady**: *SOME people are confused, Claire. Others understand. We still have a $20 trillion dollar debt.*

> **Claire Celsi**: *How would you solve the problem, Tom?*

9

> ***Tom Grady:*** *I think most people are tired of being labelled by the other side, and I think most people are tired of being ridiculed for one belief or another. I think a candidate who understands this would be well-received. In this day and age of political gamesmanship, I don't see very many who seem to understand. But it would be a good start.*

Mark, Claire and Tom sparked the conversation. Others stoked the flames. Fire away! And, yes, I realize this goes on for a while. Quite a while. But it's worth it to show how many issues out there have people upset.

> **Jeff Burkett**: What angers me most is the number of people relentlessly complaining about politics on Facebook when the majority of them can't identify their elected officials. Let alone what bills they may be working on or what their stance is. But they can tell you who won the Super Bowl, who the last Bachelor was or the lyrics to the most recent Taylor Swift song.

> **Mike Lose**: Why Hillary isn't in jail if I did what she has I would be locked up.

> **Liz Adrian**: Trump . . he falls in the category of "too big to fail", and has the $$$ to pay powerful lawyers who stomp on the little people and bribe him out of troubles. That leads to the feeling of "helplessness" which I think is part of the problem. On some level, most people recognize that all citizens are NOT equal in this county.

> **Mike Lose**: You may be right but her lies and cover ups are what is making people mad. Look at what she has done criminally and gotten away with. Too many things for me to overlook. Trump may be rich and powerful but I think he would put America first. I don't think Clinton would.

> **Waneta Hailey Knudsen**: My greatest grief is what is at the core of what really matters in this country, what is in people's hearts. Hatred is the killer. The answer is an easy fix. Each one take responsibility for fixing our heart and that means truly living by the Golden Rule.

Michael Demastus: Our turning our hearts away from God. Proverbs 14:34.

Brian Cox: Amen.

Misti Johnson Craig: The magnitude of the frustration can't be a Facebook comment Dave. I'm angry at so many different things that can all be directly related to the fact that our whole political system is corrupted by business, with complete disregard to the real effects to the people. Pick a topic, follow the money.

Bill Strike: The debt, health care and SS.

Lance Peterson: Everyone is so mad at Obamacare, but nobody was addressing the issue of affordable health care until President Obama, so I applaud him for bringing attention to the problem.

Brian Cox: Obamacare is the anger.

Mike Lose: Also I can speak for law enforcement and someone who has been shot by an illegal (or undocumented) person that Trump wants to do something about both. Misti is right it would take too long to type it all out.

Albert Bregar: While I am angry that our politicians act like that, I am more angry that voters keep re-electing them. Until the American voter gets their collective head out of their nether regions nothing will change. We as voters need to hold our elected officials accountable.

Gayle Goble: Totally agree Albert, sadly, too many are dumbed down and ignorant of history. They speak in propaganda lines… talking points.

I told you that went on for a while. There were actually at least 10 times that many comments that I didn't include here.

But that not-so-little exchange between a few dozen people on Facebook on a Wednesday afternoon showed me two things:

1. There wasn't just one main issue of unhappiness for the campaign cycle, no matter how the media sometime try to put everything into a one-size-fits-all category (And don't even get us Midwesterners started about how the coastal media pretend like they know how everyone here in "Flyover Country" thinks about things). No, there were numerous issues that riled people up and talking about these issues can bring out a lot of energy and emotion. Sometimes it's in passionate dialogue; other times it's not nearly as polite.
2. The anger wasn't just directed at one party. It was directed at all parties and all people in power, both in politics and business. Too many Iowans felt like they were no longer making progress economically and they were anxious about their jobs, retirement, education and kids. Politicians weren't listening or, if they were, they just weren't doing anything to help, the electorate felt. And big business took care of the superrich, not those who wore out their backs, knees and minds making them all that money.

It was time for a revolution. An uprising. Time to put the "establishment" in its place.

But that's what made this interesting. Democratic power brokers were already behind that "establishment" on their side: Former U.S. Secretary of State Hillary Clinton, as Vermont Senator Bernie Sanders and former Maryland Governor Martin O'Malley found out.

Republicans had plenty of establishment choices, too. They had current and former governors like Florida's Jeb Bush, Ohio's John Kasich, Texas' Rick Perry, New Jersey's Chris Christie and Louisiana's Bobby Jindal. And if they wanted D.C. experience, they had senators like Florida's Marco Rubio and South Carolina's Lindsey Graham.

But Republicans also had a slate of "outsider" choices. Texas Senator Ted Cruz worked in Washington but liked to rip on those he considered the establishment. Former neurosurgeon Ben Carson and business executive Carly Fiorina both hadn't served in public office before, so they clearly brought the outsider perspective. And, of course, there was Donald Trump. Oh, Donald Trump.

Iowa Gov. Kim Reynolds casts her kernel during the 2018 Iowa State Fair.

Plenty of options out there. But the pissed off outnumbered them. That had been simmering for the past several years under the summer sun in Des Moines.

"Can we pick none of the above?" I hear that countless times every year at the Iowa State Fair. But in 2016, that question grew far more frequent.

Every year, my TV station asks fairgoers to "Cast Your Kernel." A former colleague of mine, Jeff Felton--one of the most talented photojournalists I know--and I came up with the concept about a decade ago. We ask people to come by our booth and drop a piece of corn (this is Iowa, after all!) into a Mason jar of their preferred presidential candidate.

Before I go on, let's get a few things out of the way:

> *Question: Is the poll scientific?*
> *Answer: Of course, not. It's corn, for crying out loud.*

Question: Is it accurate?
Answer: We don't have poll watchers or security guards monitor the votes and we weigh the corn, rather than count each kernel individually. So I'll say it's "sort of" accurate.

Question: Are they registered voters?
Answer: We don't ask. We just ask that they are at least 18 years old. I do think our voters skew Republican, since so many rural folks typically come to the State Fair.

Question: Is it a predictor of the real winner?
Answer: Remember, we do this in August, months before an election. And polls change. Although, in 2008, Democrat Barack Obama beat Republican John McCain. I mentioned the right-leaning skew of our poll. So that vote told me Obama may be on his way to doing something special and, obviously, he was.
In 2010, Republican (former governor) Terry Branstad clobbered the Democratic incumbent Governor Chet Culver in our poll. Branstad also won easily in the November general election.

Question: Can you eat the corn?
Answer: We re-use the corn year after year. But some people do try to eat it. Although, I wouldn't advise it.

We don't have a "none of the above" choice for the voters, much to some people's chagrin. And invariably, I hear pretty spirited complaints about that. But this time in August of 2016? Oh, my!

Here's a sample of what I heard in about 10 minutes when people found out they had to choose between Clinton and Trump, the two most unpopular nominees in modern times:

"That's scary as hell."
"I don't like my choices."
"Not those two."
"Both of them I see integrity as an issue."
"Scoundrels."

"Scoundrels" was Asa Cope's description of choice for those options. Cope and his wife, Jennifer, of Oskaloosa, stopped by with their young boys.

"We don't believe either one of them stand up for our values...or God, really," Jennifer said, "That's the most important thing."

Asa picked up the thought from there with barely a second's pause between the two of them. "Our convictions," he said, "Pretty hard to have a clear conscience when both of the people there are scoundrels."

To be fair, the Copes' words were from the vocal minority that day. Maybe many others thought them and just didn't say it? I don't know. Again, we didn't have a "none of the above" jar, so there really is no way to know for sure. All I can go by is what I saw and heard. I saw people coming up to me more than I can ever remember telling me that they didn't like Trump or Clinton. And I heard the disappointment in their voices. Sometimes, it was just anger.

"This is the best we can do?" more than a few people rhetorically asked me. The best? Probably not, when you figure that we have 325 million people in this country. But these were the two people willing to run, the ego to do it, capable of winning their party's primary and crazy enough to withstand the scrutiny that comes with wanting to become the next president of the United States.

People were more vocal about their disgust of those two options (more than any previous year) but, of course, most people picked one or the other.

Trump beat Clinton in our Cast Your Kernel contest. It wasn't close, actually: Trump 56 percent, Clinton 44 percent.

Iowans saw this matchup coming actually. In 2015, when we included the full slate of current Republican and Democratic candidates on each side, Trump and Clinton came out on top.

This was the Republican top five:

- Trump 36%
- Ben Carson 19%
- Carly Fiorina 8%
- Ted Cruz 6%
- Marco Rubio 5%

And here was the Democratic top five:

- Clinton 57%
- Bernie Sanders 37%

- Martin O'Malley 4%
- Jim Webb 1%
- Lincoln Chafee 1%

Democrats were content--according to the corn kernels--to go with the establishment choice, Clinton (although, conversations with some of them indicated a discontent with leaders of both parties in Washington, D.C.). Republicans already knew that they wanted something and someone far different: Trump. The corn didn't lie.

All of that anger--some at the choice of candidates, some at the overall perception of politicians--provided the backdrop for the campaign. Not everyone was walking around in a foul mood, to be sure. But that anger, frustration, unhappiness, discontent, yearning for something better seemed everywhere.

That's what made this campaign so different from others I remember. So different. There's been unhappiness before, of course.

- In 1980, Ronald Reagan became president because of the public's discontent with the President Jimmy Carter economic malaise and the inability to free the hostages held at the U.S. embassy in Iran.
- In 1992, Billionaire businessman Ross Perot galvanized voters who weren't thrilled with President George H.W. *"read my lips, no new taxes"* Bush's time in office (Bush later agreed to raise taxes) and weren't sure about Arkansas Governor Bill *"I didn't inhale"* Clinton (claimed that he used marijuana but didn't inhale) and his womanizing ways. But, of course, Clinton still won and became a two-term president, despite his philandering and lying about it. Perot likely helped.
- In 2000, Bush's son, George W., took advantage of Clinton fatigue and came out on top over Clinton's Vice President Al Gore.

I guess there is always some unhappiness from voters. But add that unhappiness to all the other factors people were experiencing and that is why 2016 was so unique for me and so telling of the future.

Democrats had such an obvious and overwhelming front runner in Clinton. But she wasn't something new and different to many voters, not like Obama was. Clinton tried to sell herself as something different, though. So did her husband. He called her a "change-maker" at the 2016 Democratic National Convention in Philadelphia. "She's the best darn change-maker I've ever met in my whole life," the former president said of his wife.

Hope and change, Part 2 ("Hope and change" was Obama's central campaign theme). But, it turned out voters hoped for a change in ways the Clintons didn't expect.

In 2016, Hillary Clinton was almost like the vice president of her party running after a two-term president, Obama. That's how expectations were for her. Other Democrats would be just token opposition. She was expected to become the nominee.

Because of that, much of the anticipation in the media focused on the Republican side. It helped that the field included 17 legitimate candidates. And that large field was diverse. I must say when I say 17 candidates, it makes me doubt that using the word "large" properly sums up how vast the field was. How about massive field? Humongous field? Holy crap, that's-a-lot-of-people field?

Regardless, it was more diverse than the previous cycles. Remember 2012? Activists pointed out that Republicans didn't just have a bunch of white guys running. The field then included Herman Cain, the African-American former Godfather's Pizza CEO. And it included Michele Bachmann, the Congresswoman from Minnesota.

That diversity meant that the party that gave us Ronald Reagan, George H. W. Bush and George W. Bush over the past three decades could break the older white male streak. It didn't, of course. Mitt Romney became the party's nominee as Cain and Bachmann both withered in the spotlight on a national stage. It didn't help that seemingly half the women in Georgia alleged Cain had made unwanted advances on them in one way or another. And Bachmann didn't seem ready for prime time.

The field in 2016 offered even more diversity. Again, it had a woman in Carly Fiorina, the former Hewlett-Packard CEO. And once more the Republican field had an African-American possibility: famed neurosurgeon Dr. Ben Carson.

But diversity didn't stop there. There were two Cuban-Americans with Florida Senator Marco Rubio and Texas Senator Ted Cruz. Plus, Louisiana's Governor Bobby Jindal meant an Indian-American in the race. Overall, it was a far bigger and much more heterogeneous set of choices for voters.

But, of course, in the end, a white man continued the Republican tradition for nominees. Trump became president. Two years into his term, Democrats rallied voters who strongly disagreed with what Trump had done as president.

CHAPTER 1

PRESIDENT DONALD J. TRUMP, AKA BATMAN

"You see the love. I mean this is love!"

Donald Trump summing up the crowd he attracted at his first Iowa State Fair visit in Des Moines on August 15, 2015.

Photo by Dave Price

"I thought it would be easier."

President Donald Trump said that to Reuters on April 27, 2017, 97 days after taking office. Critics went nuts. I actually thought that admission by Trump--while such a simple statement, even if by a man who doesn't seem to admit mistakes or show much humility--demonstrated the divide of feelings about him.

Those who can't stand Trump think the statement shows how this narcissistic, arrogant, incompetent man assumed he could breeze through the job with his self-professed greatness as a business icon. And then he realized he couldn't.

But others think Trump's statement reflects just a moment of honesty. And that's how I took it. Maybe Trump realized how hard the job was, how difficult it is to get Congress to do what he wants (even when his Republican Party held majorities in both the U.S. House and Senate) and how challenging it is to make major changes in a country and in an economy many times larger than any company he's ever led.

Maybe that statement reflected how the enormous magnitude of actually working as the president of the United States was settling in to this man, even one with an ego this YUUUUGGGE (to borrow his phrase).

Since Trump became president, it has been...well...one-of-a-kind. Did Iowa Senator Chuck Grassley see it all coming? "No," he smiled and shook his head.

Grassley has seen many, many things during his past seven decades in politics. It's difficult to find an Iowan--ANY Iowan from ANY party--who has been around politics longer than Grassley.

Charles "Chuck" Grassley Bio

Corn and soybean farmer
1959: Elected to Iowa House of Representatives
1975: Elected to U.S. House of Representatives
1981: Elected to U.S. Senate
Political Party: Registered Republican

"No. No," Grassley repeated to me about not initially seeing Trump's rise as we sat in a golf cart to escape the bright sun on a warm day at the Iowa State Fair in August of 2017.

(Side note: The golf cart, by the way, is not to play golf in this case. Rather, it's a reasonable way to try to maneuver your way through the mass of people, food vendors, security and occasional

White House aspirant at the State Fair. And I say "reasonable," because you must understand that guiding a golf cart through this mass of people--many of whom are either too oblivious or just don't care that they are in your way--without hitting anyone and actually making better time in the cart than you would be just walking...well, it's quite an accomplishment.

The senator and I just sat parked in the cart. We didn't have to worry about pedestrians, only those who kept interrupting our conversation so they could say hello to Grassley. And that probably happened five times during our eleven-minute conversation. Grassley's popularity is no longer what it once was, but he still largely remains a popular figure with Iowans.)

"It was hard to see how he could win," Grassley acknowledged.

Grassley knew that Trump had publicly flirted with the concept of running in the past but didn't follow through. Why would this time be any different?

Iowa Sen. Chuck Grassley shakes hands with President Trump at an Iowa event.

Photo by Dave Price

After all, Trump had an NBC reality show, *The Apprentice*. Millions of people watched each episode. NBC made millions of dollars. Trump made millions. Why would he give that up?

Back then, Grassley just didn't think he would. I wasn't sure of either of those things either. Chuck Laudner and Ken Crow were.

Laudner made a name for himself especially in the 2012 Iowa Caucus cycle. He drove around Rick Santorum in what became known as the "Chuck Truck."

Laudner's contributions to Iowa politics are far more than being a chauffeur for an unexpected winning caucus campaign.

Chuck Laudner Bio:

2002-2007: Campaign Manager, Chief of Staff to Iowa Congressman Steve King
2007-2008: Executive Director of the Republican Party of Iowa
2010: Executive Director, Iowa for Freedom
2012: State Caucus Director, Rick Santorum for President
2015: State Director, Donald Trump for President
Republican Political consultant

Santorum had very little campaign money and seemed to have just as little caucus support for most of the 2012 race. But Laudner kept driving him around all over the place in his personal vehicle, that Dodge Ram "Chuck Truck."

Laudner and his truck kept Santorum engaged with Iowans across the state, even if some of those early crowds in the cycle could have fit in the truck with them.

Other candidates had their moments of fame at the top of the public opinion polls that cycle. Former U.S. Speaker of the House Newt Gingrich did. Minnesota Congresswoman Michele Bachmann had hers. Texas Governor Rick Perry had his. So did former Godfather's Pizza CEO Herman Cain.

But Santorum had his when it really mattered: Iowa Caucus night. Thanks to Laudner, Santorum and that truck. Few saw it coming.

Trump was different in 2016. Very different. OK, that is an incredible understatement.

Santorum: little money.
Trump: had billions (or so he claimed, even though he failed to produce his tax forms of the past like he claimed he would during the campaign).

Santorum: had the "Chuck Truck."

Trump: had his own private jet. That made travel much, much easier. Obviously.

Santorum: "Who is this guy?" (Most Iowans' reaction early in the 2012 campaign).
Trump: "It's the Apprentice!" (Iowans' reaction of the reality TV star in 2016).

Santorum: former member of the U.S. House and Senate.
Trump: never elected to public office.

Laudner liked Santorum. He respected him. He shared many of his social conservative beliefs. But Santorum "fought the good fight and lost" in 2012 as Laudner would say. Santorum finished second to former Massachusetts Governor Mitt Romney for the party's nomination that cycle.

Laudner didn't want to just fight the good fight again in 2016. He wanted an entirely new type of fighter. He was convinced Iowa did, too. And the country. Laudner had already seen a bit of this in a different, previous campaign --- Congressman Steve King's. King's nearly three decade political career may have helped to lay the groundwork for the success of Trump more than any other figure in Iowa.

Steve King Bio

Founder, King Construction, an earthmoving company
1996: Elected to Iowa Senate
2002: Elected in 5th Congressional District
2012: Elected in 4th Congressional District (districts merged because of state's stagnant population, which eliminated the 5th District)

King is Iowa's most controversial member of Congress. By far. He relishes it. King represents the state's 4th Congressional District. The state's districts are largely divided into geographical quadrants. The 4th covers the northwest. Although, because of the district's sparse population, its boundary lines stretch east beginning at the western border. They go two-thirds of the way across Iowa's northern region to match the population of the other three districts (they each have approximately 500,000 registered voters). That gives King's district 39 counties, more than a third of the state's 99.

King knows how to speak to the far right bloc of Iowa, a prevalent group in his district. They cheer on his fights against abortion, same-same marriage, illegal immigration and the downfall of the country's Christian foundation.

That segment of the electorate has proven to be vital in Caucus victories for former Arkansas Governor Mike Huckabee in 2008, Santorum in 2012 and Texas Senator Ted Cruz in 2016.

However, King's comments about diversity and immigrants, in particular, repulse people across the country, including some in his party.

This comment earned King the sharpest bipartisan condemnation of his career:

"White nationalist, white supremacist, Western civilization...how did that language become offensive?"

(Source: King interview with the *New York Times*, January 10, 2019)

King claimed that people misunderstood what he was trying to say. He tried to make the case that he was really lamenting the labels that people unfairly place on others, like "white nationalist" and "white supremacist," when all he is really trying to do is stop illegal immigration. He blamed the *New York Times* for quoting him out of context. An "urgent" email he sent to supporters on January 25, 2019 blared this headline:

"The blatantly biased liberal/fake-news media complex is out of control."

King has tried to explain that when he was pontificating to the *New York Times* about language that became offensive over the years, he was only talking about Western civilization at the time, not all three of those terms. However, in a television interview with me (October 21, 2018) he did question how "white nationalism" had become a derogatory term.

Here was part of our exchange:

Me: "What is a white nationalist?"

King: "Well, I'm not sure of that. First of all, I think you have to be white...It is a derogatory term today. I wouldn't have thought so maybe a year or two or three ago. But today they use it as a derogatory term...It implies...it implies that you are a racist."

King's remarks and subsequent explanations did little to calm the rebukes from his own party. National leaders skewered him. Condemnations came from all over. Democrats mocked Republicans for finally speaking out against King this forcefully and pointing out that most had only done so following King's re-election in the 2018 midterms.

U.S. House Minority Leader Kevin McCarthy (with support of his members) stripped King of all his committee assignments, a humiliating punishment. Utah Senator Mitt Romney (the party's 2012 presidential nominee) and Wyoming Congresswoman Liz Cheney (the former vice president's daughter) were among those who called on King to resign.

Iowa Republican Senator Joni Ernst called King's comments "offensive and racist." Governor Kim Reynolds even suggested that unless King re-committed himself to the people of his district, "he needs to find something else to do."

Reynolds and Ernst joined Republican Party of Iowa Chairman Jeff Kaufmann and Senator Chuck Grassley by refusing to publicly endorse King in his Republican primary in 2020. Less than three weeks after King got sworn in for his ninth term in office, three Republicans had already announced intentions to primary him.

King could blame Democrats and the media all he wanted. But his words created the firestorm and top Republicans had had enough.

Throughout the years, Democrats detested King. They have questioned how voters in the district could back King, despite all the other previous offensive assertions that he made.

"Diversity is not our strength...Assimilation has become a dirty word to the multiculturalist Left. Assimilation, not diversity, is our American strength."--December 8, 2017, Twitter

"You cannot rebuild your civilization with somebody else's babies. You've got to keep your birth rate up and that you

need to teach your children your values."--March 14, 2017,
CNN

"For every one who's a valedictorian, there's another
hundred out there who weigh 130 pounds. And they've got
calves the size of cantaloupes because they're hauling 75
pounds of marijuana across the desert. Those people would
be legalized with the same act."--July 18, 2013, Newsmax

But Democrats have been able to do very little about King. Registered Republicans have a comfortable advantage over registered Democrats in the region and that's despite the more liberal Ames region that is in the district.

> *Democrats: 121,079 (24.7%)*
> *Republicans: 191,540 (39.1%)*
> *Libertarians 2,617 (0.53%)*
> *No Party: 174,008 (35.5%)*

(Source: Iowa Secretary of State, November 2018)

In theory, if a Democratic candidate could turn out the party faithful, as well as earn a sizeable chunk of Independents, that person could knock King out of office. But no Democrat had been able to make that anything more than just a theory.

King wins again and again and again and again and again and again and again and again and again. Nine times Iowans elected him to represent them in Congress. The man has been invincible.

Laudner witnessed that. And he knew social conservatives, King's strong base, would play a key role in choosing the next president.

In 2016, there were plenty of candidates going after those voters.

- Famed neurosurgeon Ben Carson
- Texas Senator Ted Cruz
- Former Arkansas Governor Mike Huckabee
- Louisiana Governor Bobby Jindal
- Texas Governor Rick Perry
- Former Pennsylvania Senator Rick Santorum

The other candidates would undoubtedly welcome the support of those social conservatives, too, of course. Count Trump among them. More on that later.

Laudner would end up running Trump's Iowa Caucus campaign. I would love to share Laudner's specific thoughts on Trump, how he won, what he has been like as president, etc. But, Launder declined. Trump makes staff sign confidentiality clauses that prohibit them from sharing information.

However, Laudner's presence on Trump's early Iowa visits, though, signaled to me that Trump was serious about becoming president.

"He's running. I promise you!" Ken Crow told me. It was January 24, 2015, and about an hour before I had my first television interview with Trump.

Ken Crow Bio:

Political consultant
Conservative activist
Author
Blogger/Public Speaker
Winterset, Iowa resident

Admittedly, I was skeptical of what Crow had told me outside the main doors of Hoyt Sherman Place, a stunningly impressive art gallery, historic Victorian theater and auditorium in downtown Des Moines. The masterpiece that was built in 1877 is a mix of elegance, marble and mahogany with those classically-long crimson curtains that take you back in time.

Trump was making the most of his time there that day and Crow tracked his every word and movement. "I'm serious, Dave," Crow followed up with me, underscoring that he was positive Trump would run for president.

Crow paid attention to virtually all of the speakers who also showed at the Iowa Freedom Summit. Congressman King hosted the summit.

King lives in Kiron, a rural, Swedish-settled town of fewer than 300 people in Crawford County. Never mind that Kiron is 125 miles northwest of Hoyt Sherman and that Des Moines doesn't fall in the district King represents. King knows how to get the media to pay attention. Being part of a high-profile event in Iowa's capital city is a good way to do it, even if it means playing host away from home.

Inviting Trump to Iowa, along with more than a dozen other well-known names in Republican circles, a year before the Iowa Caucuses, at a time conservatives loved to gather to bash the liberal ways of President Barack Obama...yes, King knew that would entice the media. And a crowd.

The Iowa Freedom Summit's website tallied the invited guests:

> Tennessee Congresswoman Marsha Blackburn
> Iowa First District Congressman Rod Blum
> Former U.S. Ambassador John Bolton
> Iowa Governor Terry Branstad
> Dr. Ben Carson
> New Jersey Governor Chris Christie
> Texas Senator Ted Cruz
> South Carolina Senator Jim DeMint
> California Congressman Jeff Duncan
> Iowa Senator Joni Ernst
> Businesswoman Carly Fiorina
> Former Virginia Governor Jim Gilmore
> Former U.S. Speaker of the House Newt Gingrich
> Iowa Senator Charles Grassley
> Former Arkansas Governor Mike Huckabee
> Utah Senator Mike Lee
> New Hampshire State Representative William O'Brien
> Alaska Governor Sarah Palin
> Texas Governor Rick Perry
> Iowa Lieutenant Governor Kim Reynolds
> Former Pennsylvania Senator Rick Santorum
> Businessman Donald Trump
> Wisconsin Governor Scott Walker

Quite a list, huh? That was a lot of speakers. And many of them had been part of the early conversation among politicos as possible candidates in the 2016 presidential race.

(Side note: I don't really like events like these. Actually, I should be more accurate: I have mixed feelings about these large "cattle call" events. The good thing is that it is a great way for me to get in a room full of Iowa political activists. These are the people who really care about politics and will undoubtedly show

up to the Iowa Caucuses and help select a presidential candidate. So going to a large gathering like this lets me gauge these activists' responses to the potential candidates' speaking styles, messages, personalities and interactions with the crowd, both on and off the stage.

But the part I really don't like is trying to figure out how to do a story on television that night about it. I hate basing our coverage on the perceived "front runners" in a race. I just don't feel like that is fair to anyone, not the candidates or the viewers. It's especially unfair so early in the Caucus campaign. And in this case, they were not even candidates yet. It was too early.

Another thing: I may get two minutes to tell the TV story of this all-day event with all of these people. That makes it truly impossible to include every person on that stage who wanted Iowans to know he or she was interested in becoming their president.)

But back to Crow, who has to be one of the most unique Iowa activists I know…

As he stood there with the boots, black cowboy hat and southern drawl that moved with him from Texas, Crow was thinking not just about what he would see and hear, but also what he had been reading on his blog earlier.

Crow founded "Crow's Nest Politics," which offers his take to those he calls "over 5,000 conservative political junkies."

Here's an idea of his content over the past several years. Crow's posts blare these headlines:

"DEMOCRATS ARE COMMITTING THE LARGEST SCAM IN AMERICAN HISTORY"
"THE NEUTERING OF AMERICAS (sic) MEN"
"WHY DEMOCRATS ARE HEARTLESS AND HAVE NO BOUNDARIES"
"41 & 43 NEED TO SHUT UP AND GO AWAY"

That last post is Crow's critical take after former father and son Presidents George H.W. and George W. Bush expressed their less-than-pleased thoughts on Trump.

This was part of it:

"Just as the Democrat Party wishes that Hillary would take a long walk in the woods, I'm pretty sure the Republicans wish that Bushes 41 & 43 would also take a long walk off a short pier up in

Kennebunkport. For two former Republican President's (sic) to be publically chastizing (sic) a sitting Republican President is beyond comprehension. It is nothing short of political treason in my book. These two goof-balls (sic) not only criticize the sitting President, but the elder Bush also admits he voted for Hillary Clinton in this past election. That admission speaks volumes for the former President's loyalty to the party and the nation, not to mention his level of senility... Donald Trump is a man's man and as I said earlier, POTUS 43, take your drooling father, go back to Kennebunkport and shut the hell up!"

So, yes, Crow was ready for an anti-establishment, name-calling, not-politically-correct candidate like Trump. So, too, he felt where many of his readers.

"The venom being spewed told me a lot," Crow told me, recalling the harsh tenor of his readers' words back then, "Every day, I would read the frustration in the post, and the American people were fed up with politics as usual."

Despite Crow's assurances that Trump would run for president, I figured I would try to find out for myself. I have covered dozens of presidential candidates--declared candidates and others who could only be candidates in their own minds--since I moved to Iowa in April 2001. But I have never begun an interview with a potential presidential candidate with these words:

"Some people don't really believe that you are going to run. Describe your level of seriousness."

But I said those words to Trump before he took the stage at the Iowa Freedom Summit.

I felt like I needed to do it. "I'm looking at it very seriously," were Trump's first words to me when I questioned him about his intentions.

(Literally, his first words had actually been, "Okay, let's go," as he verbally signaled to me that he was ready for me to start the interview.)

But after conveying to me that he was serious about running, Trump continued. "I want to make this country great again," he said showing his ability, when he chose to, to stick to his campaign theme. Trump knew what he was doing. He was a master at marketing himself, his brand and his message. Two sentences into our interview and he worked in that hallmark bumper sticker message of his.

With that bumper sticker message plastered up front, he was like an 18-wheeler rolling through as he worked to verbally flatten the opposition before him.

"I know the people that are running," he continued with me, "I see Jeb Bush is not going to do it (win the presidency). Mitt Romney failed miserably (as the party's 2012 presidential nominee). He failed miserably. He let us all down. He choked in the end."

Trump would not choke, was his implication. He would be the leader to save the party and the country.

Trump continued, "I'm the one that can turn the country around. I want to make America great again (there it is again!). I want to make our military strong. I want to save Social Security, Medicare and Medicaid. I want to make this country great again."

That was three times he worked in a variation of his bumper sticker message during the first 29 seconds of our interview. Master marketing.

He worked in that border wall that he would put between the southern side of the United States and the northern edge of Mexico, too, built with his verbal touch. "Building a fence," Trump told me, "It's a very simple thing to build. Believe me."

Believe him. (Although building that wall and getting Mexico or Congress to agree to pay for it proved to be much more difficult as he would later find out).

Extremely talented people were coming into the United States--legally--was Trump's argument. But those who come illegally are not those types of people, according to Trump.

"We have people (legally) coming into this country," Trump explained to me, "They go to Harvard. They go to the Wharton School of Finance (Trump earned a degree from Wharton). They're first in their class. Then we send them out and they're not allowed to stay (in the U.S.)."

So that was Trump's frustration...that we let foreigners come to this country to study but then we force them to go back to their country, instead of contributing to the future of the United States.

And even more frustrating to him, were the others who came illegally into this country from other places...those we did not force to go back home.

"People are pouring across our borders," Trump continued, "They're criminals. They're crooks. We're getting all of the bad ones. And we have to stop it. And we have to stop it fast."

I talked to him for only about three minutes. Afterwards, Trump tried to make his way through the crowd that had gathered to watch us but he got stopped numerous times by those who wanted his autograph, a selfie with him or to shake his hand.

"We're getting all the bad ones."

That is the Trump line that really stuck out to me following our brief conversation. That line resonates so loudly with people and in the unique way Trump can. For some, it emboldens their belief that this country needs to do more to protect its borders because criminals sneak across. Criminals do sneak across the border. I don't see how anyone can dispute that. Whether they are truly "pouring across our borders" may be more in dispute.

The reality is that of the estimated 11 million people in the United States illegally, most didn't "pour across" the Mexican border and sneak their way into neighborhoods across the country. Most, in fact, are in the country illegally because they overstayed whatever temporary visa they received to work or go to school in the United States. That was the case in every year between 2007 and 2014, according to the Center for Migration Studies.

(Source: "U.S. Undocumented Population Drops Below 11 Million in 2014, with Continued Declines in the Mexican Undocumented Population," Center for Migration Studies, 2016.)

Trump had acknowledged that dealing with illegal immigration was a "very, very tough situation," during our conversation.

"You're gonna have to look at how they've (undocumented immigrants) done over the time they've been here. But you have to start with the border and you have to make it absolutely stop," Trump continued about shutting off the flow of those illegally crossing.

Then, he added this part, which didn't become a fixture on his stump speeches or tweets. "You have to look at who's here, how have they done, how are they acclimated to the community, have they done a great job? And you have to make some really hard decisions," Trump said, without elaborating how he would make those decisions.

And I didn't get to ask him.

"But above all," he concluded, "You have to stop people from pouring in. The wrong people are coming into this country."

Trump can ramble, especially in front of adoring crowds as he searches for the lines that will get them to erupt. But he also can be skilled during interviews in his ability to come back to a main point and reiterate his message.

He wanted Iowans to remember that "bad" people were illegally coming into the country. He claimed that he will stop it (and he will figure out later what to do about those who already found an illegal path here).

Trump's comments sounded like a man who would run for president. And they matched what Crow and his readers yearned to hear.

They all wanted Washington stood on its head," Crow continued, "Washington is broken. We need something unique and fresh."

Trump, the billionaire, foul-mouthed senior citizen, who had threatened to run for higher office--but never had before--would bring both that uniqueness and freshness. And on that day, with Crow in the audience, Trump delivered it.

"Isn't he a great guy?," Trump began his remarks at Hoyt Sherman as he praised his host, Congressman King, before the crowd of more than 1,000 people.

Trump combined that deference to King by also ripping the media (which would become a frequent target). "He doesn't get a fair press. He doesn't get it. It's just not fair," Trump said, "And I have to tell you I'm here, and very strongly here, because I have great respect for Steve King."

Trump added some love for Iowans, too. He knows how to play to his audience. Trump reached out to the crowd, "...the people of Iowa. They have something in common" ("something in common" with King? With Trump? Perhaps, both, he was saying here?).

"Hard-working people. They want to work, they want to make the country great. I love the people of Iowa. So that's the way it is," Trump added, "Very simple."

Very simple, indeed. Trump was making a lasting connection. There would be sore hands, feet and throats afterwards from this room of Christian conservatives after clapping, standing and cheering several times throughout Trump's remarks.

And may I remind you that Trump stood before them as a twice-divorced man--accused of numerous sexual affairs and allegations of sexual improprieties--a man who had made his name and fame as a controversial businessman, far from a choir boy. Hardly a man who might sit next to them at church or come to town to speak to them in a typical campaign cycle. Of course, as we know, there was very little "typical" happening.

On stage, after Trump was finished lauding King and other Iowans who spent this Saturday taking in politics, faith and fervor, rather than sports from their couches, he tore into the current state of politicians, the political parties and whatever else he felt like through that microphone.

"Our country is really headed in the wrong direction with a president (Barack Obama) who is doing an absolutely terrible job," Trump said, "The world is collapsing around us, and many of the problems we've caused."

The speech not only riled up the activists, most of whom had never seen Trump in person before. But it also offered some themes that Trump would end up using throughout his presidential campaign and into the White House, as well. Here are some of the highlights *(transcription courtesy of Democracy in Action):*

On President Obama:

"Our president is either grossly incompetent, a word that more and more people are using, and I think I was the first to use it, or he has a completely different agenda than you want to know about, which could be possible."

(Note: It's highly doubtful that Trump was the first person to say that Obama was "grossly incompetent," but "I think I was the first to use it," or a similar phrase, is something Trump seems to like to say.)

On politicians:

"Politicians are all talk, no action. They are all talk and no action. And it's constant; it never ends."

(Note: this is a message that could have bipartisan support. Politicians from both major political parties have no shortage of campaign promises that remain unfilled, if they ever meant to fulfill them in the first place)

Selling himself as a Republican, while also ripping other politicians:

"And I'm a conservative, actually very conservative, and I'm a Republican. And I'm very disappointed by our Republican politicians. Because they let the President get away with absolute murder. You see always, 'Oh, we're going to do this. We're going to...' Nothing ever happens. Nothing ever happens."

(Note: There was great debate over whether Trump was a conservative and/or a Republican.)

On the Affordable Care Act/aka Obamacare:

"Look at Obamacare with a $5 billion website. I have many websites, many, many websites. They're all over the place. But for $10, okay?"

(Note: Trump would repeat that $5 billion cost claim at other rallies, too, although PolitiFact, the Pulitzer Prize-winning, non-partisan, truth-checking project found Trump's claim wasn't true. PolitiFact found that Trump at least more than doubles the longer-term cost of the site. And Trump's claim about using $10 websites for his business ventures? He is obviously exaggerating here to try to make a point.)

More attacks on the failures of Obamacare:

"Now everything about Obamacare was a lie. It was a filthy lie. And when you think about it, lies, I mean are they prosecuted? Does anyone do anything? And what are the Republican politicians doing about it?...It's disgraceful. It's a big, fat, horrible lie. Your deductibles are going through the roof. You're not going to get--unless you're hit by an army tank--you're not going to get coverage. And people that had plans that they loved, that they really loved, don't have those plans anymore. So it's a real, real disaster. And somebody has to repeal and replace Obamacare. And they have to do it fast and not just talk about it."

(Note: Perhaps, "somebody" could repeal and replace Obamacare. But Trump was not able to do that in his first two years as president, even though he had Republicans who held majorities in both the U.S. House and Senate, and who like himself, had promised numerous times during the campaign that they would repeal and replace.)

Building the border wall/fence between the United States and Mexico:

"Now, we have to build a fence. And it's got to be a beauty. Who can build better than Trump? I build. It's what I do. I build. I build nice fences, but I build great buildings. Fences are easy, believe me. I saw the other day on television people just walking across the border. They're walking. The military is standing there holding guns and people are just walking right in front, coming into our country. It is so terrible. It is so unfair. It is so incompetent. And we don't have the best coming in. We have people that are criminals. We have people that are crooks. You can certainly have terrorists. You can certainly have Islamic terrorists. You can have anything coming across the border. We don't do anything about it. So I would say that if I run and if I win, I would certainly start by building a very, very powerful border."

(Note: Fences may be easy in Trump's mind. But they haven't been easy for him to accomplish. However, his rhetoric did heighten awareness of the overall illegal immigration issue by having Immigration and Customs Enforcement agents take a more visible role in rounding up those people not in the U.S. legally.)

But ripping President Obama, taking on terrorists, threatening to pull the plug on Obamacare...any Republican could sound those major themes, right? Trump again reminded all of those paying attention on that January 2015 day, though, that he wasn't like those other Republicans. He wasn't like them, he didn't seem to care for them and he decided to come right after two of the best known of them.

Watch out, Mitt Romney, the former Massachusetts governor and the party's 2012 presidential nominee and Jeb Bush, the former Florida governor and President George H.W. Bush's son and President George W. Bush's brother. Trump was coming after you.

"It can't be Mitt because Mitt ran and failed. He failed. I mean I liked him...The Romneycare from Massachusetts, that's not going away. What do you think they're going to say? 'Oh, we won't bring that up this time?' He choked (in the 2012 presidential campaign).

Something happened to him in the last month. He had that election won...That election, sort of like a dealmaker that can't close the deal. I know many of those guys. They get it up to the one-yard line. They go, 'Ah, ah, I can't close it!' Or a golfer that can't sink the three-footer to win the tournament. And there are many of them. Most people are like that. I mean most people are like that. You can't give somebody another chance, 'cause actually I think this election is tougher to win than beating a failed president. I really do. I think beating Obama would have been a much easier one than the one that's coming up, which is sad to say but true. So you can't have Romney. He choked."

"You can't have Bush...The last thing we need is another Bush. Now, he's totally in favor of Common Core."

(Note: The Common Core State Standards Initiative began under President Obama and was approved by 42 states. It aimed to provide a testing mechanism to improve student performance. Obama's administration tried to incent states to participate with grants. Some Republicans grew to loathe the idea as an overreach by the federal government into areas that they felt states and local school boards should monitor instead. Source: Corestandards.org).

"That's a disaster. That's bad. It should be local and all of that. But he's totally in favor of Common Core. He's very, very weak on immigration. Don't forget--remember his statement--'They come for love.' I say, what? Come for love? You've got these people coming, half of them are criminals. They're coming for love? They're coming for a lot of other reasons, and it's not love. And when he runs, you got to remember his brother really gave us Obama. I was never a big fan, but his brother gave us Obama. 'Cause Abraham Lincoln coming home back from the dead could not have won the election because it was going so badly. And the economy was just absolutely in shambles that last couple of months. And then he appointed Justice Roberts (to the U.S. Supreme Court). And Jeb wanted Justice Roberts. And Justice Roberts basically approved Obamacare in a shocking decision that nobody believes. So you can't have Jeb Bush. And he's going to lose aside from that. He's not going to win. So Mitt and--you just can't have those two. That's it. That's it. It's so simple."

Simple. Did you follow all of that? Trump packs a lot of thoughts into a speech. Sometimes, those thoughts feel disconnected from each other. A Trump speech doesn't flow like a soothing waterfall of poetic prose like Maya Angelou or William Shakespeare.

It can be more like a machine gun, a rapid fire spray of cut downs, insults and one-liners that get his supporters on their feet and loaded for action.

Seven months later, Trump came back to Des Moines and showed just how unique he and the political environment would be.

It was August 15, 2015 (which also happens to be my birthday). Over the course of that day and the other 10 days of the annual Iowa State Fair, nearly a million people couldn't resist a 600-pound bovine made of butter, random foods impaled by a tiny wooden stick or the chance to chuck a rubber chicken as far as possible. Or maybe they just needed to unfurl their mullet to demonstrate its length, pull an outhouse across a parking lot as fast as they can or show what a chainsaw can do to a tree (yes, all of these things really happen in annual competitions).

A billionaire reality TV star, a Socialist and a president's wife couldn't resist. Now, to be fair, I doubt any of those attractions are really what brought Trump, Bernie Sanders and Hillary Clinton to the State Fair on the same day.

They came for the people. Or more realistically, the TV cameras. But they came. The campaigns for the three candidates who commanded the most attention during the presidential cycle all picked the same day to make the obligatory photo op to show they relate to the common folk in Iowa (Democratic Virginia Senator Tim Kaine and Republican Indiana Governor Mike Pence represented the nominees' tickets the following year.)

"Amazing," Connie Boesen recalled.

That is saying something for Boesen to call something at the fair "amazing." For Boesen, that August day stands out from thousands of other days she has spent at the State Fair. Yes, *thousands*. She has spent much of her 68 years at the State Fair.

Boesen actually grew up on the fairgrounds while her father, Kenny Fulk, ran the place. Fulk served as fair manager for 15 years. She sold candy, soda and cigars as a girl. Years later--and for the past 30 years--she ran her own Applishus stands, which sell all things apple...sliced caramel apples to apple pie on a stick. In 2018 her apple egg rolls got awarded the best new food at the State Fair. She has clearly figured out what people like.

Boesen met her husband at the fair, got married there and recently celebrated a half century as a fair food vendor. So when Boesen calls a day "amazing," it means something.

"Keep the line moving. Keep the line moving!" Boesen recalls a woman saying over the loudspeaker in the Agricultural Building, which housed one of her stands. It wasn't her caprese salads that were slowing down traffic (yes, she sells those, too). It was a much bigger draw: Trump.

"Donald was in," Boesen said, "The place was mobbed!"

It isn't often a presidential candidate draws more interest from passersby than the fair's iconic cow sculpted in butter. But Trump was one of those exceptions.

"His helicopter!" Boesen then remembered.

Trump made his Iowa State Fair entrance by helicopter. Of course he did. Few state fairs, carnivals or circuses have ever entertained bigger showmen than Trump. And what better way to enter the State Fair than by helicopter? Quite an entrance from the man decked out in a blazer, a French-cuffed shirt and white dress shoes. Yes, he wore white dress shoes at a place where farm animals are likely to temporarily share some of the same walkways as people and leave a trail of…well…you know what farm animals drop behind them. But he wore white dress shoes.

I'm not sure "showman" is quite the word for Bernie Sanders. He didn't arrive in his own helicopter like Trump. But Sanders, too, made quite an entrance that day. His posse of the passionate believers seemed to grow with every step.

You would expect Trump to attract the masses as he wandered about the fairgrounds. But Sanders, up until this 2016 race, was barely known outside his home state of Vermont except for his brief national bit of fame for his 2010 filibuster against President George W. Bush's tax cuts.

But Sanders was like a magnet, a magnet powered by persistence and perspiration. "I felt the energy," Boesen said. "The number of people!"

It's tough to estimate crowd size when people are constantly moving. But Sanders' throng easily reached the hundreds (same for Trump, by the way). And it might have topped 1,000 when Sanders stood on the *Des Moines Register*'s Soapbox. There isn't actually a traditional soapbox on which the candidate stands. But there is an actual stage with hay bales theatrically placed nearby. Apparently, they have to have the hay to prove that it's Iowa. It does look iconic, though.

"The hot sun," Boesen pointed out. The temperatures pushed 90 degrees that day, not including the extra discomfort of humidity.

Sanders' sweat was obvious. Just ask his blue, button-down shirt. But so was his appeal with Iowans. This day would show that unlike your deodorant after a long day at the State Fair, Sanders had staying power. Sanders would prove that months later on caucus night. Trump would, too.

Clinton, to her credit, put in some time. She spent nearly 90 minutes on the grounds (maybe half that for Trump? Sanders far more since he did the Soapbox and walked the grounds).

Clinton brought an escort: Tom Harkin, Iowa's retired, longtime U.S. Senator, who had always been popular with liberal Democrats and had already endorsed Clinton, his former Washington colleague. The two walked around together. Harkin's always been comfortable with a crowd. Maybe that would help put Clinton at ease (no one has ever accused her of having her husband's ever-flowing charm working from stranger to stranger).

Secretary Clinton did the things candidates are supposed to do (the *Des Moines Register*'s Soapbox, notwithstanding) by getting a pork chop, sipping lemonade, checking out the famed butter cow and shaking hands with people.

But it just feels differently when she does it. Maybe it's the Secret Service agents never more than steps away or the black SUV with its engine running a few seconds away, just in case she needs to make an emergency getaway. Whatever it is, it's just different.

Now, don't get me wrong: Clinton still attracted attention that most any other candidate, most any other year, would have loved to have.

But during her second run for president, she just wasn't the novelty that Trump was. He just cast too big a shadow, almost quite literally on this day. His helicopter circled overhead as Clinton walked below.

Sure could have made for an even more unbelievable day had the two run into each other.

Picture this:

- The two of them share a golf cart (maybe Clinton could drive. Apparently, she hadn't spent much time behind the wheel over the past few decades).
- They could each have a pork chop-on-a-stick in one hand and wave to the crowd with the other.
- Follow that up with some kind of fried dessert-on-a-stick.
- Then they head over to the new attraction, the 27-degree beer tent (that's some ice cold beer!).

Now that would have been a moment! Alas, no such luck. Trump did give one Iowa family an unforgettable moment, though, thanks to that helicopter.

Sarah Bowman of Clive knows politics but nothing like she experienced at the state fair that day. She had previously helped Republican candidates for years, including Senator Chuck Grassley. And she worked as a legislative clerk in the Iowa legislature.

Bowman also had a connection to a member of the Trump campaign that predated the candidate's foray into politics. She formerly served as Co-Chair of the Polk County Republicans in 2008. Ryan Keller volunteered for the party back then. Fast forward seven years: Keller was now working for Trump.

"Ryan knew my oldest son (William) was a Cub Scout and asked if they'd be willing to lead the Pledge of Allegiance at Trump's official Iowa announcement (in June 2015). My husband was the boys' den leader," Bowman told me, "and we were able to arrange for a few other boys to participate."

The Bowmans took part. They met Trump, nothing too out of the ordinary so far. Until the helicopter two months later at the state fair.

Keller told her shortly before the start of the fair that her family would be first on the list for the helicopter ride with Trump. Proof that patriotism was not the only reward when you volunteer to lead the Pledge.

The Bowmans only knew that there would be a helicopter ride but didn't know *when* it would happen. Finally, they got the word from Keller. The next day was time to fly.

Nice timing, actually. That next day happened to be the third birthday of the Bowman's youngest son, Henry. Quite a present.

"We thought it would be a memorable experience," she told me.

Oh was it!

Remember, Henry was turning three, a day past the "terrible twos," perhaps, according to the calendar of parenting, but not according to reality. The "troublesome threes" can be just as challenging, as many of us know.

Candidate Trump would find that out, in case he hadn't experienced it before with his own kids.

Bowman and her four boys boarded the helicopter. William (holding a Go-Pro camera to capture the memories for eternity, as long as that technology endures), Sean and Brandon were loving it. Henry? Not so much. "Started screaming, fussing when the engine started," his mom said.

That got Trump's attention and not in a good way. "I don't think the little guy is ready for this. He might have to get off," Trump told Henry's embarrassed mother.

"Sorry, buddy," Trump said to Henry.

Ugh.

The helicopter's pilot added to the family's awkwardness. "I can't take off if that kid is screaming," Bowman remembers him saying.

Ugh, again.

The boys' father, David, came over to the stalled helicopter waiting on the ground. He carried Henry off the chopper and some media members took the boy's place.

Sorry, Henry.

Several minutes later...

"Whoa! Whoa!" was followed by "Whoa! Whoa!"

The first exclamations came from the Bowman boys. Trump excitedly offered the response. The boys were having quite a time. All of them, including the one who was on his way to the White House.

But Bowman wanted to avoid another "Whoa! Whoa!" She was four months pregnant with her daughter, Mary Elouise, and wasn't sure how this chopper ride would go.

Pregnancy is hard enough, even for an experienced mother like Bowman. Adding a helicopter ride to it would not have been what the doctor ordered.

"Just hoping that I wouldn't get sick!" she said.

Fortunately, the ride wasn't as rough as she feared. Trump seemed to enjoy the view, too. "As we flew over the fairgrounds, he commented that he'd never seen so many trailers in one place," Bowman said.

Trailers are nothing new to Iowans, though. They are more prevalent on the fairgrounds than even presidential candidates.

Hundreds of people bring trailers, campers and fifth wheels to stay on the grounds during the fair. Plus, there are numerous other mobile units that vendors use to sell food, drinks and anything else that threatens your waistline. Add them up, and you see trailers everywhere.

So, Trump was right. There are a lot of trailers at the fair. But it wasn't the trailers or Henry's protest before the ride began that the Bowmans remember most about their encounter with Trump.

Donald Trump surveyed the view of the Iowa State Fairgrounds from his helicopter.

Photo by Sarah Bowman

It was what William said to the future president of the United States and how Trump responded. It happened on the plane. Bowman didn't understand it all until after they landed and she got an explanation from her husband.

She said her kids were talking to their dad before the flight as they waited for Trump to arrive. "The boys were asking him (her husband) if Trump was Batman," she said.

Why Batman? "He's rich, has a black helicopter," Bowman said of her kids' logic.

Their father responded, "Why don't you ask him?"

So, of course, William did.

"Mr. Trump?," he asked while recording on his hand-held camera.

"Yessss," replied the candidate.

"Are you Batman?" William asked him.

"I am Batmaaaannnnn," Trump responded to the delight of the Bowmans sitting next to him.

Quite a trip. Quite a performance. Trump may have been new to politics, but he knew theater. And he delivered his line to the kids like an experienced entertainer. But it was not enough to get the Bowmans' support in the Iowa Caucuses months later. Ted Cruz did.

The Bowmans appreciated the memories with the future president, nonetheless. Cruz wasn't on the fairgrounds that day for a helicopter ride. Just Trump, Clinton and Sanders. Oh, I just remembered Rick Santorum was there that day at the fair, too. Lincoln Chafee, also. At least I think he was.

CHAPTER 2

DONALD TRUMP, THE REPUBLICAN?

How many brothers can say they flew in Donald Trump's private helicopter? The Bowman brothers can.

August 15, 2015 at the Iowa State Fair in Des Moines.

Photo by Sarah Bowman

Donald Trump, the politician, has been so hard to define because of decades of inconsistencies on same-sex marriage, abortion, war, taxes, guns, trade, drugs and likely a few more I have overlooked.

Perhaps the easiest and most obvious factor that makes it difficult to define Trump's political position is his ever-changing political affiliation: he has been a registered Democrat, Independent and Republican at various times over the past several decades. It's like trying to put a nametag on a greased Iowa pig. Good luck making it stick.

Grassley decided, though, Trump's latest iteration brings him to Grassley's Republican Party, at least in the broadest sense.

"Right now, he's a Republican," Grassley concluded during that conversation that we had at the Iowa State Fair in 2017.

The comment struck me as a particularly striking summation from a dedicated party loyalist like Grassley about the man elected president of the United States under the Republican Party name.

"Right now, he's a Republican."

Trump may have been a Republican--at least at that moment in time in Grassley's estimation--but he and Grassley aren't really in the same party when it comes to one of the prominent issues: trade.

And that was something Grassley readily admitted. "He made big issues out of trade (ending or re-negotiating international trade deals) and jobs (during the campaign for president)," Grassley told me, and the senator's explanation came months before Trump, as president, demonstrated even more differences.

In 2018, Trump launched his trade war with other nations, particularly China, that made Iowa's agriculture community and investors everywhere squirm with anxiety. Would hiking tariffs actually prod other countries to buy more American goods? Would they force China to quit stealing American designs and research (intellectual property)? Grassley (an Iowa farmer himself) and many others were left wondering.

"Republicans tend to be more free trade," Grassley said in a simple sentence as he distilled the differences between a traditional Republican leader and Trump.

I asked for a scholarly breakdown from Dr. Kedron Bardwell, a political science professor at Simpson College--a Methodist-influenced, liberal arts college of 2,000 students about 20 miles south of Des Moines.

Kedron Bardwell Bio

Department Chair of Political Science at Simpson College
Director, "Simpson Survey" (Student-run poll of campus political
attitudes)
Started at Simpson in 2005
M.A. and Ph.D. in Political Science from University of Iowa
Grew up in Nebraska, New Mexico and Colorado

Bardwell wrote to me in an email:

"Trump's emergence as the leader of the party, fueled by a coalition of economically disaffected and strongly nativist voters, is reshaping the GOP conventional wisdom on trade and America's role in the global economic system. The Trump administration position on trade is a jarring reversal for the GOP; in recent decades, candidates from Reagan to Romney positioned the Republicans as a resolutely free trade alternative to the more protectionist or 'fair trade' Democrats.

Recall that in the 1990s, Republicans in Congress worked with a free-trade Democrat, President Clinton, to pass NAFTA (the North American Free Trade Agreement). Overall, more Republicans than Democrats in Congress voted for that landmark legislation, which opened up markets with Mexico and Canada, eliminating many tariffs and barriers to trade."

Meanwhile, Trump publicly decried NAFTA as a deal that was bad for the United States.

Perhaps Trump was ahead of his party on a change of thinking about trade (if, as Grassley surmised, Trump was actually a Republican).

Bardwell also wrote, "As recently as 2009, more Republicans than Democrats thought that free trade was 'a good thing.' By 2016, the majority free-trade position of GOP voters had evaporated, with 61 percent saying free trade is 'a bad thing.'"

If you look deeper at the Pew Research study that Bardwell cited, you see the change that occurred is pretty dramatic and rapid.

Check out the good versus bad split on how Republicans felt about free trade's impact on their country:

May 2015:   **Good: 51 percent, Bad: 39 percent**
August 2016:   **Good: 32 percent, Bad: 61 percent**

What a change and in only 15 months' time! I can't find one specific trade-related event that drastically altered views. It wasn't like every single automaker put the brakes on U.S. production and raced down to Mexico all at once. And it wasn't like the economy all of a sudden tanked, where manufacturing overall in the United States shut down.

One other significant event did happen, though. Trump happened.

"I'm a free trader," Trump said when he announced his presidential campaign from Trump Tower (his tower) in Manhattan, New York on June 16, 2015.

Trump continued:

"But the problem with free trade is you need really talented people to negotiate for you. If you don't have people that know business, not just a political hack that got the job because he made a contribution to a campaign, free trade is terrible. Free trade can be wonderful if you have smart people, but we have people that are stupid. We have people that are controlled by special interests. And it's just not going to work."

The man can turn a phrase, can't he? He also offered this one during that same speech:

"Ford announces a few weeks ago that Ford is going to build a $2.5 billion car and truck and parts manufacturing plant in Mexico. I would call up the head of Ford, if I was (sic) president, I'd say, 'Congratulations. I understand that you're building a nice $2.5 billion car factory in Mexico and that you're going to take your cars and sell them to the U.S. Zero tax, just flow them across the border.' And you say to yourself, 'How does that help us? Where is that good?'"

Trump went on to say it isn't good and then laid out what he called the "bad news" for Ford or any other automaker thinking about doing that. "Every car and every part manufactured in this plant that comes across the border, we're going to charge you a 35 percent tax," Trump said, "And that tax is going to be paid simultaneously with the transaction."

Trump's anti-trade deal refrain sounded a bit similar to the words that we heard in a campaign seven presidential elections earlier. In 1992, they came from another billionaire, non-traditional presidential candidate: Texan Ross Perot. Remember Perot's warning about a "giant sucking sound?"

"We have got to stop sending jobs overseas. It's pretty simple: If you're paying $12, $13, $14 an hour for factory workers and you can move your factory south of the border, pay a dollar an hour for labor,...have no health care—that's the most expensive single element in making a car— have no environmental controls, no pollution controls and no retirement, and you don't care about anything but making money, there will be a giant sucking sound going south." (*New York Times* transcript, October 16, 1992).

Perot, an Independent candidate, sounded that warning during a presidential debate when he made the case that America's jobs would become employment in Mexico.

How does the country stop it? Perot concluded, " ...when [Mexico's] jobs come up from a dollar an hour to six dollars an hour, and ours go down to six dollars an hour, and then it's leveled again. But in the meantime, you've wrecked the country with these kinds of deals."

It's likely too strong to say that Trump, 24 years after Perot's warnings, single-handedly changed the minds of Republicans across the country that their view of free trade plummeted 19 percent in that Pew Study. But surely he had an impact, right, likely a major one?

Self-identified supporters of the Democratic nominee, Hillary Clinton, held a 59-32 percent good versus bad view of free trade in that Pew Research poll. Remember, the split was nearly reversed for supporters of Trump: 32-61 percent.

Overall, the voters seemed split with a 45 percent good versus 47 percent bad on free trade. That is almost exactly in the middle of the two candidates' followers.

That makes me wonder whether either candidate had an advantage on this. In Jasper County, though, Trump's position on trade could have helped take a chunk of voters you might assume would have gone with Clinton.

According to the Iowa Secretary of State's office, here were the voter registration breakdowns for November, 2016, for Jasper County:

> *Registered Democrats: 8,557*
> *Registered Republicans: 7,414*
> *Registered Independents (Officially: No Party): 8,535*

But despite that 1,143 deficit that Republicans faced in registered voters in the county, Trump, the Republican, crushed Clinton, the Democrat, by a 56 percent to 38 percent margin.

That's a huge margin, no doubt. It is even more remarkable when you consider the results in Jasper County during the previous two presidential elections.

2012
Mitt Romney (Republican): 8,877
Barack Obama (Democrat): 10,257

2008
John McCain (Republican): 8,794
Barack Obama (Democrat): 10,250

In both cases, the Democrat (Obama each time), easily defeated the Republican challenger.

It is interesting to note, however, that Americans' views on trade changed substantially, again, during Trump's first term in office.

Pew Research Center's follow up study on free trade in 2018 showed that 56 percent of Americans considered it a "good thing" versus just 30 percent who thought it was a "bad thing." Whatever happened during the lead up to the 2016 election that shifted Americans' views on free trade--whether it was Trump's influence, something else or a combination of factors--largely disappeared over the next two years.

That doesn't really surprise former Newton Mayor Charles "Chaz" Allen, who said Trump's overwhelming victory in his county was about far more than trade (Newton is the county seat in Jasper).

"I think he (Trump) spoke to the people who had been unemployed," Allen told me.

Allen would know. His job got cut when in 2009, Arkansas-based Windstream Corporation announced plans to buy Iowa Telecom, a rural provider of broadband, internet and digital TV for 450 smaller communities.

Charles "Chaz" Allen Bio

2004-2012: Mayor of Newton
2015-2019: State Senator
Director, Jasper County Economic Development Corp.
Tow truck operator
Race car driver

Allen had worked for more than a decade as Iowa Telecom's billing operations manager before becoming the government and community affairs director/lobbyist.

"Yep, I'm out," Allen recalled of what he was thinking when the sale got announced.

So much for company loyalty, although loyalty doesn't mean much when your company gets bought out by another company and "restructuring" of the workforce soon follows. Allen said most of the 800 Iowans working for Iowa Telecom got to keep their jobs. He just wasn't among the lucky ones.

Company loyalty also didn't mean much to many of Allen's other friends and neighbors a few years earlier in a much more devastating and painful period for Newton.

Newton, which is about 30 miles east of Des Moines, served for generations as the headquarters of the Maytag Corporation, a longtime, internationally-respected producer of household appliances.

Maytag had been anchored in Newton since 1893. Over the years, the company sold ovens, ranges, irons, refrigerators and even military aircraft components during World War II. But it was best known for its washers and dryers. And its mascot.

"Ol' Lonely," was the face of the company for half a century in television and print advertisements. Actor Gordon Jump (who starred in the 1970s sitcom "WKRP in Cincinnati") was the best-known actor to portray "Ol' Lonely," the character dressed as a Maytag repairman who had nothing to do, since the products were marketed as being so reliable that you didn't need to call for service to fix anything. "Ol' Lonely" even had a sidekick, a dog named Newton. Yes, Newton.

About 15,000 people live in the town of Newton. In its heyday, Maytag employed more than 5,000 people there. Incredible, huh? Not everyone who worked for Maytag lived in Newton, of course, but Maytag's presence was undeniable, unmatched and unable to be duplicated by any other company in the area.

The company not only was the area's largest employer but it invested deeply into the fabric of the community. Often something that carried the Maytag name collided with another.

- The **Maytag** Queen got crowned at the **Maytag** Bowl.
- Turophiles could nibble on some **Maytag** Blue Cheese at the **Maytag** Dairy Farms.

- The Fred **Maytag** Family Foundation supported numerous non-profit organizations.
- Visitors to Newton could take a dip in the Fred **Maytag** Pool before heading back to the **Maytag** Hotel.
- Or maybe they would prefer to check out the **Maytag** Mansion or **Maytag** Guest House or maybe the **Maytag** Event Complex.
- Company employees and their families could read the **Maytag** Bulletin before they enjoyed the **Maytag** Picnic at **Maytag** Park and looked forward to two of their favorite days of the year: the **Maytag** Day Parade and **Maytag** Winter Party.
- And if that weren't enough **Maytag** for them, they could wander around town and gaze at the **Maytag**-inspired art and statues. There were many. Newton Community Marketing Manager Danielle Roger played tour guide and assembled this list:
  - ○ "Edna, Before **Maytag**" (portrayed a hard-working woman named Edna, who struggled with those annoying washboards before Maytag saved the day with wash machines) at the U.S. Bank Plaza.
  - ○ Fred L. **Maytag** II at DMACC Newton Campus.
  - ○ Fred **Maytag** I at the **Maytag** Pool building entry.
  - ○ Fred **Maytag** II bust at Newton Municipal Airport.
  - ○ **Maytag** medallions at The **Maytag** Event Complex.
  - ○ **Maytag** repairman at **Maytag** Park (known as "Ol' Lonely").

Maytag had quite a presence in Newton, right? Maytag *was* Newton. Well, until Allen's phone rang at 10:23 p.m. on Tuesday, May 9, 2006, instructing him that it would no longer be.

"You had a feeling that it was coming," Allen told me more than a decade later in October of 2017, "But you get that call and it's a gut punch."

Maytag had been anchored in Newton for 113 years at that point. But it would eventually move much of its operations to Mexico, along with some to Michigan. That was a major kick in the "cojones" for the company town.

One of the reasons that Allen had a feeling he would get that dreaded phone call was because of something that happened six months previously. Whirlpool Corporation acquired Maytag.

Consolidation, cost-cutting, layoffs were bound to happen. They frequently do when one big company swallows up another to become even larger and eliminate some competition at the same time.

"It (Whirlpool/Maytag) was down to 1,700 people at the end," Allen said of the workforce when he got that 2006 phone call from a company representative that told him of the pending move.

It isn't the phone call any town mayor wants to get, especially one that comes as Allen and his wife were getting ready to go to bed for the night. "It's not a very good sleeping pill," Allen added with a sarcastic chuckle.

A few minutes later, the phone rang again. This time it was Iowa Governor Tom Vilsack--the state's well-respected leader and later President Barack Obama's United States Secretary of Agriculture--who had already been briefed on the decision. "We had to hold a press conference the next morning in front of city hall," Allen recalled, "...put on a good face."

Allen had a knack for that, though. Whether it was staying positive on Newton's behalf when Iowa Telecom got sold (despite losing his own job because of that sale), he did it. Whether it was dealing with the astoundingly complicated financing, public drama and squabbling with doubters on his own city council that it took to finalize the deal to build a NASCAR track on the outskirts of the city, he did that, too.

So dealing with the trickle of lost jobs at the Maytag operations that culminated with that last agonizing, late-night phone call from Whirlpool? Allen had no choice the next day. He stood in front of the microphones and laid out how his town would recover, even if he himself questioned how and when that would happen.

"We just can't put all our eggs in one basket again," Allen would say again and again, repeating Newton's mission of not again relying on a "new Maytag" to absorb the discarded workforce but rather put together a more diverse industrial economy, like the new companies that would use some of Maytag's old facilities to make new products like wind towers and turbines.

But those new industries weren't as big; neither were their staffs or paychecks. They weren't the old Maytag. Optimism wasn't its old self either.

"We lost all of our jobs...those 20 (or more) dollar an hour jobs," Allen said, "People aren't getting those jobs back."

And when those $40, 50, 60, or 70,000 a year jobs are no longer available--and even if you are fortunate enough to find a replacement, albeit far lesser-paying job--your lifestyle just can't match what it once was.

"When you're used to getting a new car every three years and now you're driving something from 2001 still...," Allen said of what became too real for too many after Maytag moved on.

"Back then (when Maytag was thriving), you could put in your 20 or 30 years...retire, have your health care and then, if you wanted to, go do construction, repair, whatever...because you didn't have to worry about health benefits," Allen said.

That meant retirees could start a second career while they were still in their 40s and 50s and end up fully retiring years later in a financially comfortable position. Although, the generous Maytag union retirement benefits often meant workers didn't have to transition into that second career.

In a further blow to the town in 2008, though, Whirlpool sued to reduce some of those previously guaranteed lifetime benefits for Maytag retirees. Another gut punch. A final blow, a final parting shot to Newton.

For all those years, Allen lamented, "It was Maytag...Now that's gone."

Also gone was some residents' faith in government and the economy. Especially, since the Great Recession was threatening the wellbeing of the country, just as the final Maytag employees in Newton cashed their final paycheck in 2007. The timing was awful for a turnaround.

Enter Donald Trump. He actually made his presence felt in Newton years before he ran for president in 2015 and 2016. In fact, it was right after CBS News' Scott Pelley came to town for a story that laid out the struggles of Newton on "60 Minutes," the revered, must-watch Sunday night news magazine show for generations.

The timing, as it turned out for Trump, was spot on. Much of Pelley's piece that aired in October 2010 read more like the town's obituary.

Here was one of the early exchanges between Pelley and business owner David McNeer:

Pelley: "What's surprised you the most about this recession?"
McNeer: "I think the depth of it and the length of it. I think what surprised me the most about this one is it doesn't wanna end."

Pelley: "You know, the economists say that the recession's over."

McNeer: "Really? They should come to Newton, Iowa."

Not exactly an infomercial for commerce in the heart of Jasper County. Pelley's piece offered a laundry list of economic stains that even one of Maytag's finest washers wouldn't be able to get clean.

- McNeer had to get rid of 10 of his 22 employees at his advertising agency.
- A furniture store halved its payroll that used to have room for 60 people.
- A website developer dropped 6 of 14 employees.
- A car dealership closed.
- An elementary school had to shut down, too.
- Police officers, firefighters and hospital staff all suffered layoffs.
- And, of course, Maytag.

There wasn't much room for positive thoughts here when even the local Optimist Club closed.

"People are hurting," Allen acknowledged, himself included at the time. He hadn't found a job when the story ran, other than his part-time job as mayor that paid a meager $4,000 salary and $2,600 a year car allowance.

Allen enjoyed serving the city, mind you, but $6,600 a year wasn't going to do much to send his two daughters to college.

After the *60 Minutes* piece aired, phones across Newton started ringing. Some callers offered sympathy. Some brought questions about the shuddered Maytag facilities. A few others brought inquiries from Manhattan, New York.

Yes, that's where Trump Tower is. Or at least one of those Trump Towers.

Allen's cell phone rang. He didn't recognize the number, so he let it go to voicemail. Then, curiosity led him to immediately check the message. The message came from Michael Cohen, a longtime attorney and confidant to Trump (Cohen later pleaded guilty to lying to Congress about a business project to build a Trump Tower in Russia. Also, Cohen had been my early contact in New York when I needed to interview Trump. He and I didn't talk about that project in Russia, in case you wondered).

"I called him back after making sure it was legit," Allen said.

Cohen put Trump on the phone. "Is there anything we can do to help?" Allen recalled Trump asking him.

What would have really helped was that Trump could start, expand or relocate a company to Newton and fill the 2.5 million square feet that Maytag no longer needed.

(Note: Nearly 11 ½ years after Allen received that goodbye call from Maytag's representative, his city still hadn't filled all the space).

But Trump didn't seem to have much interest in moving anything to Newton, as Allen recollected. "Nope," Allen said, "just talked about how manufacturing was moving away from USA."

"No sh*t!" thought Allen, who didn't need a billionaire businessman to remind him what was happening.

Trump did offer to help the mayor, though, Allen said. "Offered to put money in my (mayoral) campaign," Allen explained, "...which I didn't take."

Allen wasn't easily starstruck. He might have been mayor of a relatively small town that many people in the country--outside of those who were familiar with Maytag/Whirlpool--had never heard of, but that doesn't mean that he would just melt at the offer from a celebrity. Besides, Trump wasn't the first celebrity to come calling. Remember, this is Iowa, so nearly every prominent presidential hopeful had come through town at one time or another during Allen's tenure in politics.

Also, remember that Allen helped get that NASCAR track built in Newton. And that track isn't just for racing; it also holds concerts. That means that Allen got time to chat with racing stars Danica Patrick and Dale Earnhardt, Junior, but he also got to meet Gene Simmons, the legendary rocker with Kiss.

But still, why not take some campaign cash from Trump, who seemed sympathetic to Newton's plight after seeing the *60 Minutes* story?

"Just didn't want that on my record," Allen told me.

Not just because the money would come from Trump, but rather, the rural Iowa mayor just didn't want it looking like he was yucking it up with rich out-of-staters. So, no business deal or campaign cash from Trump for Allen.

Others did get something out of it, though. And Trump got some pizza. Three pizzas, actually.

Thin crust Mediterranean Vegetarian
Original Philly Cheese Steak

Bacon Cheddar Cheeseburger

Scott Creech, a Domino's Pizza store owner in Newton, had those pizzas delivered by another store near Trump Tower. For the record, Creech isn't sure that Trump actually ever took a bite of his pizza. But he does know the pizzas arrived at Trump Tower. Either way, Creech figured he owed Trump.

Cohen had called Creech after that *60 Minutes* story, on behalf of Trump. Creech recalled, "He (Cohen) said Mr. Trump was touched by what he saw on *60 Minutes* and he wanted to send me something in the mail."

Creech thought it was a thoughtful gesture but didn't have time to think much about what could be arriving in the mail. He didn't have a lot of time to just sit around and think about much of anything, really, and hadn't for a long time.

"October 1, 1989," he said proudly of the day he opened his store.

But in 2010, keeping the pizza ovens going was a struggle. He was in real danger of losing the store. With so many people in town suffering after Whirlpool/Maytag's move, they didn't have the money to indulge in a pizza and a soda.

Creech had to slice his staff by two-thirds. But he still had to have the ability to make pizzas when customers wanted them, even if there were far fewer customers.

Creech worked to make up for the difference by being at the store full-time, and full-time again and almost full-time yet again. In other words, no 40-hour weeks for him. There were weeks he would work nearly 100 hours. (Reminder: there are only 168 hours in a week.)

This one man had to work like 2 or 2 ½ full-time workers a week. It was exhausting but necessary so the business could survive.

"It's what my mom and dad taught me," Creech said of his commitment to work.

"The strongest are going to survive. The ones who will work 100 hours a week will survive," he added.

And Creech was determined to survive.

That commitment and mentality are what he said earned Trump's praise.

"What he (Trump) saw on TV was that Scott Creech was going to bust his tush to make this work," Creech said, "And that's the attitude this country needs."

Creech shared a story of an incident with me that demonstrated that attitude. It started simply enough: a walk with his dog one day to the nearby convenience store.

"I found a receipt that showed someone bought a 20 ounce Mountain Dew (soda) and a pack of Gummy Bears," Creech said of the slip of discarded paper on the ground from a previous customer's sugar-soaked snack.

Creech is no captain of the health police. He does sell pizzas, after all. And while a few slices of a double-stacked pepperoni thick crust may taste great, they probably won't make it on the recommended list from your nutritionist (I'm a bacon and mushroom, thin crust fan myself).

But Creech was bothered a bit by that soda and candy purchase that day. The receipt also detailed how the customer used a government-issued EBT (Electronic Benefit Transfer) card, the modern-day debit card that replaced the old federal food stamps' system.

"If you're hungry, I want you to eat," Creech said, perhaps, an obvious statement from a man who sells food for a living.

It also seems to be a statement that gets to his core beliefs: help others who need the help to survive. He has done that, donating hundreds and hundreds of pizzas over the years.

But he also thinks if the government, i.e., the taxpayer, is going to help someone who is struggling, it should not be by providing that person with a soda and candy. Meat? Yes. Vegetables? Of course. But soda and candy? No.

Creech didn't get the chance to share that story with Trump. But the praise from Trump that Cohen relayed to Creech about his work ethic would have been rewarding in itself. Yet something else proved to be even more rewarding.

A few days after that *60 Minutes* story aired, Creech was bombarded with all kinds of business propositions "from all kinds of places with an idea on how to get rich," as he described it. No thanks, he figured. The deals smelled worse than burnt cheese on the bottom of a pizza oven ever could.

But along with all of those get-rich schemes in the mail, also came an envelope from Trump Tower. "I'm embarrassed about what's happening in our country," Creech said the letter from Trump read. It also contained two other things: a request and a check.

"When you get a chance, send me some pizza," Creech said was Trump's request.

So, of course, Creech figured he would honor that request, although it was miles and miles outside his normal delivery zone. He would just find another franchise that was much closer to Trump to help him with the order.

Then, there was the check. Creech never expected anything like it. He doesn't like to brag about the amount. So he keeps the dollar amount to himself. "We didn't take a vacation or anything," Creech said of the money.

But the check was big enough that this pizza owner did add a new topping to his home: a roof.

"I just thought it was so compassionate for him to send that money," Creech said, "Generous, what Mr. Trump did."

Creech got a letter and a check. But he didn't get the chance to actually talk to Trump back then. That would change several years later.

Fast forward about four years when Trump was officially a presidential candidate...

My television station held a town hall at Des Moines Area Community College in Newton in November 2015. Trump would be the special guest on stage with me to take questions from the audience. Creech made sure he got a seat. He brought along 50 pizzas, too. How did I miss 50 pizzas showing up that day? I guess I was a little busy getting ready for a live, one-hour show where the headliner, Trump, showed up seven minutes after the live broadcast began, without an apology or explanation.

Creech brought along one of Trump's books. After the town hall event finished, Creech finally got the chance to meet Trump. The conversation was very brief.

"Fourteen words," Creech joked.

But at least he got to talk to him and he got Trump to autograph his book.

That autograph later got company. Trump's running mate, Mike Pence, held an event at DMACC in October 2016. Creech asked Pence to sign the same book. And the future vice president obliged.

"I can't imagine too many people in the country have the autographs of those two men in the same book," Creech told me.

Creech knows Trump is a controversial figure. "I don't think the Trump thing affected me," Creech said when I asked him whether the publicity of the Trump letter, check and recognition helped or hurt his business.

Author Dave Price talks with candidate Trump during a commercial break of their live WHO-TV town hall in November 2015.

Photo by Emily Price

But then again, Creech said he mostly stays out of politics. "My wife is very good at keeping me out of politics," he said.

Many of his customers do talk politics, especially in this age of Trump. Most everyone has an opinion. To put it in pizza terms, Trump is like anchovies. "You either like him or you hate him. There aren't a lot of people in between," Creech explained.

Dave McNeer definitely is not in between about Trump. There is no way he could be after his experience with Trump.

"Chaz gave me the heads up," McNeer told me of the phone call Mayor Allen made to him after the *60 Minutes* piece aired.

"Chaz called me and said, 'You are going to get a call from New York,' McNeer recalled, "And I said, 'Chaz, you're full of crap!'"

Allen had already explained to McNeer that he had just talked to Trump. But McNeer didn't believe that Trump would be talking to him, too, especially not after McNeer had laid out the good, bad and ugly of life in Newton at that time on television. Why would Trump be interested? Why would he want to talk to McNeer?

McNeer had been skeptical of the entire series of recent events. He had been concerned that CBS "wanted to just put the nail in the coffin" with that prime-time story about Newton. And he would have no part of that.

He also felt like he needed to be true to the people in his town and be honest about the suffering all around him because of Whirlpool/Maytag's departure. He wasn't going to bury his town. But he also wasn't going to pretend everything was great. "I won't sugarcoat anything," McNeer said was his mindset during the interview with Pelley.

But sure enough, the day after Pelley told Newton's story on that Sunday night on television, just like Allen said, McNeer's phone rang with a New York number on the other end. It was Trump.

"Whatever we can do to help," McNeer remembers Trump saying to him.

McNeer didn't figure Trump meant that literally. He was wrong.

McNeer said the next week he found himself making a presentation in Chicago to do some promotional work for Trump's hotels. McNeer got the project. It wasn't enough to make up for the Whirlpool/Maytag-caused recession that plagued his business. But it was enough to make a difference.

Fast forward again. McNeer found himself in a similar experience that Creech had. Trump would re-emerge.

"Chaz called me and said, 'Hey, do you want to meet Mr. Trump? He's coming up to the Statehouse...coming up the backstairs and then going to meet with Republicans,'" McNeer recounts of the call.

It was Spring of 2015. Trump wasn't yet officially a presidential candidate. But he was doing the customary ritual of the seriously interested by stopping by statehouse Republicans' Caucus--the party's private meeting of elected officials and staff (no reporters allowed).

Allen was a Democratic state senator by this point. But it's not unusual for a member of one party to give a heads-up to someone from the other party when a V.I.P. guest is coming. So since Allen knew what was happening, he felt obliged to share it with his fellow Newton resident.

McNeer showed up when Trump and the entourage walked up the stairs. Here's how he told the story of their encounter:

McNeer, as he extended his hand to Trump: "Hey, thanks, for calling after that *60 Minutes* piece."

"I remember you! Hey, hey, listen up!" Trump then said to the people around them, "This is the man from Newton. If I ever run for president, we're going to do some business together."

Yeah, right. That will happen, McNeer thought to himself.

When he talked to his wife, Sandra, at home that night, McNeer told her, "I thought that was nice of him. But, hell! He's NEVER going to run."

Never say never.

A few months later, Chuck Laudner, the northeast Iowan from Rockford who headed Trump's Iowa Caucus campaign, called McNeer. Laudner said Trump wanted McNeer to know there was no more IF Trump would run for president. It was happening. Oh, and one more thing: "He needs buttons and signs," for the launch, Laudner told him.

Dave McNeer, owner of Maxim Advertising in Newton, made campaign swag for candidate Trump.

Photo courtesy of Dave McNeer

One other thing: "By Tuesday," Laudner added.

"Tuesday?!" McNeer thought.

"Chuck, It's Thursday!" McNeer pointed out.

"Yes," Laudner's response.

"Well," McNeer remembers saying, "We'll get it done."

Five days. That was all McNeer had to make good on his promise. As McNeer calls himself, he's an "idea producer." So he and his team create a concept but he seeks outside vendors to print whatever he needs. In this case, he needed to create it especially fast. And he did.

Come Tuesday, McNeer had come through.

Stacks of buttons and signs were ready for the Iowa launch of Trump's presidential campaign. McNeer also oversaw what he described as "tons of knit hats and posters" too, for the Trump movement.

Trump had his campaign swag. McNeer had a little more business flowing through his office.

Trump, regardless of whether he was a Republican, Democrat or Independent, it didn't matter either way to McNeer or Creech. Trump to them was a politician who delivered.

CHAPTER 3

PURPLE IOWA IS RED

"Generous, what Mr. Trump did."

Newton, Iowa Domino's Pizza store owner Scott Creech said of an envelope that he got in the mail from Trump, as well as the autograph for his son, Parker.

Photo by Scott Creech

The question about Donald Trump's political affiliation wasn't on Cindy Pollard's mind. Many other things were. And it's difficult to figure out what became more raw with Pollard: her knuckles, feet or feelings about Trump.

"It's been horrible. It's been depressing. Unbelievable," Pollard said of Trump as her president, "Unbelievable."

O.K., I guess it's not too hard to figure it out then. Pollard is raw, sore, pissed off that Trump won. But it wasn't for a lack of effort on her part.

That's why her knuckles and feet got sore. She knocked on so many doors in Jasper County and walked so many neighborhoods for months that she could put any door-to-door salesperson to shame.

And Jasper County wasn't even her home turf. In 2008, she was busy trying to convince her friends and neighbors in Des Moines that Hillary Clinton should be the next president of the United States.

Candidate Hillary Clinton campaigns in Iowa during the caucuses.

Photo by Dave Price

Eight years later, she was still trying to sell Clinton's candidacy but in a new area. Between Clinton's two campaigns for president, Pollard married a Jasper County woman, Gayla Snook. Snook was entrenched in Newton, so Pollard moved to her.

Pollard had retired as a nurse in Des Moines and volunteered full time and then some for Clinton. That 40-year career of 10-12 hour shifts on the hospital floors conditioned her for long stints on her feet.

Pollard's work ethic as a volunteer was unmatched. And her passion was as strong as ever. She wished she could say that for her new neighbors' feelings toward Clinton.

"She's going to take my gun!"
"She lies!"
"She's going to jail!"

Those were just some of the comments Pollard heard from people in Jasper County after she knocked on their door and tried to get them to support Clinton. And remember, this was supposed to be friendly territory where Democrats had an 1,143 registered voter advantage over Republicans in the 2016 election.

I mentioned earlier that Barack Obama won the county comfortably both times he ran for president. Second District Democratic Congressman Dave Loebsack also enjoyed back-to-back wins in the county in 2012 and 2014.

I should point out that Bruce Braley, a former Democratic Congressman, lost big in 2014 in the county--despite the advantage of Democrats--when he ran against Republican State Senator Joni Ernst for U.S. Senate. The Secretary of State's office official count showed the lopsidedness: Ernst beat him by 1,429 votes in Jasper County.

Ernst and Braley were both vying for the seat that liberal icon Tom Harkin gave up when he retired. But Braley turned out to be a bad statewide candidate. Voters turned against him all over the state, not just Jasper County. Ernst defeated him by 94,205 votes.

Two years later, Trump would be Ernst. Clinton would be Braley. Trump, like Ernst in 2014, won comfortably despite the registered party disadvantage. And Clinton, like Braley, suffered the embarrassing defeat.

Pollard's life would be painful. "People who trash Hillary on Facebook," Pollard said, "I unfriend them."

She took it all very seriously. "It's like they're saying something about your family," Pollard said.

Pollard knew that Jasper County--while it traditionally favored Democratic candidates--hadn't favored Clinton's Democratic Caucus campaign in 2008. In fact, Clinton finished third behind Obama's second and the county caucus winner, former North Carolina Senator John Edwards (this was before the world would find out that Edwards was sleeping with, and later impregnating, his campaign videographer while his wife, Elizabeth, was dying of breast cancer).

That year, Clinton didn't fare any better statewide in the caucuses. She finished third.

Nevertheless, Pollard had been convinced in 2016 that her county and country were ready for Hillary, as the campaign slogan said. "The strength," Pollard said of her political idol, "...what she does for women and little girls. Empowerment."

But the more Pollard walked those Jasper County neighborhoods, the more she grew nervous that voters were moving away from Clinton. "Voters were so confused. They were believing it," she said, "All that horsesh*t that Trump said!"

"I would go out there every day. Every day," Pollard said.

One man especially frustrated her. "He said he voted for Trump just so people couldn't come back at him later (after Clinton won) when Hillary screwed up things."

"What the hell!" she wondered.

"Why not give Clinton a chance to prove she could do the job, rather than just assuming she couldn't," Pollard wondered. But for too many of Pollard's new neighbors in Jasper County, they just weren't answering her house call. They didn't want another Clinton in the White House.

"Many people voted for him not necessarily because they liked him all that much," Tim Hagle, a University of Iowa political science professor determined, "but that they disliked Clinton more."

That was what Pollard and Clinton were up against. Hagle figured that some people just really didn't like Clinton at all. So even if they weren't so sure about Trump, they figured that he would be better than she would be.

As it turned out, Pollard's Jasper County wasn't some strange outlier in what was going on for Clinton, or for the Democrats in Iowa, for that matter. Iowa's traditional "purple hue" on election night in 2016 that represented its unpredictable battleground status was instead undergoing a remarkable Republican red makeover, led by Trump.

It was a similar story in Adair County. And Adams. And Allamakee. And Butler, Calhoun, Cass, Davis and Fremont Counties. And just about every other county in Iowa.

Iowa has 99 counties. Clinton won six of them in 2016. Six!

- Blackhawk County   Clinton 51%   Trump 43%
- Johnson County   Clinton 66%   Trump 28%
- Linn County   Clinton 51%   Trump 42%
- Polk County   Clinton 52%   Trump 41%
- Scott County   Clinton 48%   Trump 46%
- Story County   Clinton 51%   Trump 39%

(Source: Iowa Secretary of State)

Not much of a scorecard for Clinton in the state where the previous Democratic nominee for president, Obama, won in both 2008 and 2012.

Clinton did manage to win the state's most populous counties. Those are also among the most heavily Democratic counties in Iowa. But if a candidate gets annihilated in the other counties, then it doesn't matter if she carried those larger counties. That candidate has no chance to win a statewide contest in such a rural state.

There was some irony in Clinton's defeat, too. She lost the county that bears her name and borders her birth state of Illinois. She didn't win the county seat there either: the town of Clinton.

Politically speaking, Clinton County was really "Trump County" in 2016, despite its name and the traditional Democratic advantage there.

Check out the swing from 2012 to 2016:

2012   Barack Obama 60%   Mitt Romney 38%
2016   Donald Trump 50%   Hillary Clinton 44%

(Source: Iowa Secretary of State)

Clinton County was one of 27 Iowa counties that swung by at least 20 percent in 2016 compared to 2012. Fayette County in the northwest transformed by 32 percent. Astounding. A half dozen other counties swung by at least 10 percent. That means one-third of Iowa saw at least a double-digit change away from Democrats. Clinton got crushed. Her party was sinking.

Clinton wasn't Obama. Of course, Trump wasn't either. He was better. In Iowa Trump was better than Obama was in 2012 and just as good as Obama in 2008.

- Obama cruised over Romney statewide by 5.2% in 2012.
- Trump nearly doubled that margin by trouncing Clinton by 9.5% in 2016.
- That gap matched Obama's 53.9%-44.4% 2008 drubbing of Republican John McCain

(Note: McCain largely skipped Iowa during the 2008 caucus cycle. He was short on campaign cash, plus he hadn't historically been a big fan of Iowa's liquid gold: ethanol. So the terrain wasn't especially good for him when the general election came later that year.)

Speaking of drubbing, how about the differences between Trump's and Clinton's performances in four Iowa counties? Yowza!

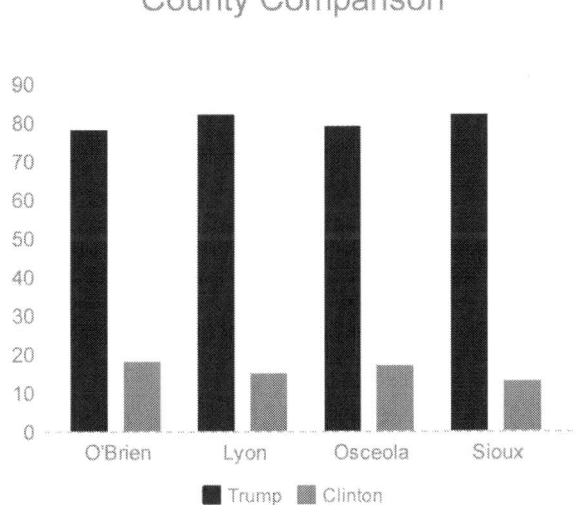

(Data source: Iowa Secretary of State)

How? How did it all happen? Pollard, that dedicated Clinton volunteer, summed up the Trump domination in her state this way: "Well, he says what he means."

Pollard didn't mean that as a compliment.

CHAPTER 4

POLITICALLY INCORRECT

"It's been horrible. It's been depressing. Unbelievable," Cindy Pollard on what life has been like after Donald Trump defeated Hillary Clinton and became president.

Cindy Pollard (far right), her wife Gayla Snook (far left) and Hillary Clinton (center).

Photo courtesy of Cindy Pollard

C indy Pollard found out the hard way that neighbors in Jasper County--and much of Iowa apparently--didn't give a rip about political correctness. They liked what Donald Trump said and how he said it.

"We have to get much tougher. We have to get much smarter. And we have to get much less politically correct. We're so politically correct that we're afraid to do anything."

President Donald Trump, November 1, 2017

In other words, "&!ck political correctness!"

President Trump, candidate Trump, citizen Trump. All three have not been politically correct. And supporters are thankful for that.

politically correct [puh-lit-ik-lee kuh-rekt]

Adjective

Marked by or adhering to a typically progressive orthodoxy on issues involving especially ethnicity, gender, sexual orientation, or ecology: The actor's comment about unattractive women was not politically correct. The CEO feels that people who care about being politically correct are overly sensitive. Abbreviations: PC, P.C.

(Source: dictionary.com)

There is clearly a segment of our population that thinks that political correctness--the effort to make sure a person doesn't offend anyone with his/her words and thoughts--has gone too far.

Some think that we too often are just tip-toeing on eggshells so we don't crack the fragile egos of those around us. We don't let our children play sports that keep score. Participation ribbons for everyone instead! We can't say "Merry Christmas." Only "Happy Holidays" is permitted.

Spank your kids?
Reaction: "You are a monster!"

Raise your voice to a subordinate at work?
Reaction: "You are a bully boss!"

Compliment a co-worker's outfit?
Reaction: "Stop harassing me!"

Stop undocumented immigrants from coming into the U.S.?
Reaction: "You are a racist!"

Obviously, we have some people, including politicians, who have pushed the boundaries of this anti-political correctness to a disturbing level. And we will get to that a bit later. But during the Republican presidential primary, Trump tapped into a segment of our communities that believe political correctness went too far and that it was time to be real, no matter how difficult that is for some people to hear.

Here is part of what Iowa City author Joseph Dobrian wrote about political correctness for the Iowa City Press-Citizen newspaper on November 7, 2017:

"Political correctness, on the other hand, is a weapon. It's a childish—yet deeply malevolent— game of offense-seeking, in which words mean whatever you want them to mean, and feelings trump facts.

Political correctness is a weapon of terror. America's youths are taught that they may not state certain facts...that their opinions might be punishable...that even their questions might be punishable by self-righteous professors and ruthless grievance-grifters. Because of political correctness, people live in fear of losing their very livelihood if they say the wrong thing and who knows when right might suddenly become wrong?

Political correctness is not about politeness. It's about power."

Power. For fans of Ben Carson, they believe he not only showed true power by working to save lives with his hands as a surgeon, but also by NOT being politically correct with his words.

Carson, a famed neurosurgeon at Johns Hopkins University in Baltimore, became an internationally-recognized name. His efforts to separate two German brothers, who were born connected by the back of their heads, fascinated the medical community. Even Hollywood noticed. Oscar-winning actor Cuba Gooding, Junior, portrayed Carson in the 2009 movie, *"Gifted Hands: the Ben Carson Story."*

But Carson's true entrance into politics came four years later on February 7, 2013, at the National Prayer Breakfast in Washington, D.C. His speech ripped the healthcare system and national debt and urged people to refocus on celebrating education excellence and not just athletics. However, he spent much of his time lamenting the rise of political correctness in society.

Here are some of those comments:

"Now, it's not my intention to offend anyone. I have discovered, however, in recent years that it's very difficult to speak to a large group of people these days and not offend someone. And people walk around with their feelings on their shoulders, waiting for you to say something...'Ah, did you hear that?' And they can't hear anything else you say. The 'P.C. (Politically Correct) Police' are out in force at all times.

I remember once I was talking to a group about the difference between a human brain and a dog's brain. And a man got offended. He said, 'You can't talk about dogs like that!' But...people just focus in on that, completely miss the point of what you're saying. And we've reached the point where people are afraid to actually talk about what they want to say because somebody might be offended. People are afraid to say 'Merry Christmas' at Christmas time. Doesn't matter whether the person you're talking to is...is Jewish or, you know, whether they're any religion. That's a salutation, a greeting of goodwill. We've got to get over this sensitivity, you know. And it...keeps people from saying what they really believe.

...What we need to do in this 'P.C. world' is forget about unanimity of speech and unanimity of thought. And we need to concentrate on being respectful to those people with whom we disagree. And that's when, I think, we begin to make real progress.

And one last thing about political correctness, which I think is a horrible thing, by the way. I'm very, very compassionate, and I'm not ever out to offend anyone. But P.C. is dangerous. Because, you see, this country...one of the founding principles was freedom of thought and freedom of expression. And it muffles people. It puts a muzzle on them, and at the same time, keeps people from discussing important issues while the fabric of this society is being changed. And we cannot fall for that trick. And what we need to do is start talking about things, talking about things that are important, things that were important in the development of our nation."

The Taylors of Waukee weren't there to hear Carson in person that day. But what they heard about Carson's words were so much of what they wanted and waited to hear from a presidential candidate (Carson didn't officially enter the presidential race until more than two years later). They had been craving something different.

I don't want to give the wrong impression about Rob and Dr. Christie Taylor, though. They supported their Republican Party's presidential nominees: George W. Bush, John McCain, Mitt Romney. Both have chaired the Dallas County Republican Party. And Rob served as a Republican state representative for three terms.

But for them, there had been something lacking from some of their party's previous nominees: "it."

They aren't trashing the military heroism of McCain, a man who somehow defied death when he was repeatedly tortured by enemy soldiers while being held captive during the Vietnam War. And they aren't putting down Romney's commitment to public service as a former Massachusetts governor, Mormon missionary, President/CEO of the Salt Lake City organizing committee for the 2002 Winter Olympics and U.S. Senator in Utah.

No, they weren't criticizing any of that. But, in their eyes, neither man brought that "it" to politics. Carson could.

They saw "it" back in 2013 when they listened to Carson speak at the American Medical Association's gathering at the Grand National Resort in National Harbor (near Baltimore), Maryland. The AMA had honored Carson for comments he made at the National Prayer Breakfast earlier in the year, where he pushed for individual health savings accounts that Americans could pass along to future generations. Carson had made the case that we would be more judicious with our health care dollars if we (and our heirs) had a vested interest in saving as much money as we could by focusing on prevention and realistic spending on medical care rather than relying on expensive emergency room visits and treatments that may or may not provide better outcomes for the patients.

Dr. Christie Taylor, an internist at the Iowa Clinic in West Des Moines, was the one attending the event as the medical professional in the family. Her lawmaker husband was the "plus one" on their R.S.V.P.

When Dr. Taylor, the internist, heard Dr. Carson, the neurosurgeon, she, of course, felt the medical connection. "He appealed to us as doctors," Taylor said, "Health care, Medicare, is going broke. Be part of the solution, or they will solve it for you. He's saying that if you don't do anything, don't turn around and b*tch about it. Although, he would never say, 'b*tch about it,' but he's saying, 'get involved.'"

For Dr. Taylor, though, that day was about so much more than medicine. She also felt a spiritual and political connection, too. Almost like a calling. "He gives this great speech," she recalled Carson saying that day, "You're a physician but you're members of the community. You need to remember that you're part of a community. Whether that's helping with the Boy Scouts, Little League, whatever, pick something. If you're not involved, you're letting your God-given skills being wasted."

Connection made. On many levels. And not just with the doctor in the Taylor family.

"Rob was there, too. When it was over, we just looked at each other…" Dr. Taylor said.

"Wow!" Representative Taylor interjected.

The two interrupted each other frequently during our hour-long conversation, by the way. But not in an argumentative way. Just like a couple who has been together for a few decades and clearly shared similar, deep passions for this political novice, Carson.

"We had said that we weren't getting involved in the presidential cycle. But we were like, 'Oh, boy!'" Dr. Taylor said, "If he (Carson) were ever to…(run for office), we said we have to get involved."

So they did. Twice. First, they helped lead the "Draft Ben Carson for President" movement. They officially joined that movement in September of 2014, almost a year after hearing Carson for the first time at that Maryland event.

They hadn't spent a single second with Carson at this point. Not even on the telephone. Yet, they were blown away by his words, mannerisms, spirituality, commitment to community and call to action. That's how enamored with the thought of a President (Dr.) Ben Carson they were.

"He had a servant's heart…" Dr. Taylor started.

Her husband then jumped in, "And he understood medicine and Christ...he's so driven and intelligent."

It would be months later before they actually met Carson. Then, they were all in. They officially became Carson's Iowa campaign Co-Chairs for his caucus effort in his run for president.

"He is everything you see. He's transparent," Representative Taylor told me, "Transparent in thought and in action."

And that meant Carson was not politically correct.

Indeed, he was not.

"You know, Obamacare is really, I think, the worst thing that has happened in this nation since slavery."

Carson's remarks at the Values Voter Summit, October 11, 2013

"There is no doubt that this senseless violence is breathtaking. But I never saw a body with bullet holes that was more devastating than taking the right to arm ourselves away. Serious people seek serious solutions."

On Carson's Facebook page, October 5, 2015

"I would not advocate that we put a Muslim in charge of this nation. I absolutely would not agree with that."

Carson's answer on NBC's *Meet the Press*, September 20, 2015

Offensive? Yes, for some. Calling Obamacare the worst since slavery comment didn't do Carson any favors with many.

But the Taylors believed Carson's extremely laid-back speaking style made his words less jarring for people. Perhaps.

However, there is the idea of being *too* laid back. After I aired my first one-on-one interview with Carson on TV that I did with him from inside his Des Moines hotel room, I had several people ask me, "Was he stoned?"

No, but maybe he was too laid back in some people's minds.

The Taylors acknowledged that it worked against Carson in those spectacles that were the nationally-televised debates. Although when a Republican field has 17 candidates, maybe there just isn't a simple, obvious format to best serve voters.

Here is what I know, though. Having the 10 candidates who had the highest numbers in the national polls on the stage for the main event and then having the other seven lesser-polling candidates on the stage earlier in what was referred to as a "happy hour," "undercard" or "kids table"...that was not the best format for voters. All we saw were candidates trying to jump in with whatever canned, pre-rehearsed attack they could work in following the moderators' questions.

The format rewarded aggressive candidates who could talk over the rest and interrupt whenever possible. Carson wasn't that person.

"He didn't jump in," Dr. Taylor lamented, "He was patient and responded."

Patience wasn't a good look.

Representative Taylor lost his patience. "I (later) said to Ben, 'I don't care if it's real or whatever,'" he recalled telling Carson, "But you have to slam your hand on the podium. Aggressive...It needs to be animated!"

"Dammit, Ben!" Dr. Taylor added as she remembered what Carson supporters yelled during a watch party for that debate, "Jump in!"

That was the fine line, a line that Carson couldn't quite master. The electorate was fed up with the politically correct crowd. Carson gave them an alternative they craved. But he couldn't deliver that with the zing that some demanded.

He also didn't deliver the brash, oftentimes rude, crude, vulgar twist that Trump did.

Carson failed to get the nomination. And the Taylors had a tough time suffering through the process of Trump verbally filleting the man they grew to admire so much. The debates were difficult enough. Trump's comments on the campaign stump were especially cutting.

In one long--95 minutes long--freewheeling, stunningly unbelievable, disconnected stream of outbursts, Trump questioned Carson's psychological fitness and essentially compared him to a child molester, who also contemplated bashing his mother's head in with a hammer.

Stunning.

"I don't want a person that's got a pathological disease," Trump told a crowd in Fort Dodge on November 12, 2015, "I don't want it. Now, I'm not saying he's got it. *He* said it."

He (Carson) did say that.

Carson had written this in his 1990 book, *Gifted Hands*:

"I had what I can only label a pathological temper—a disease—and this sickness controlled me, making me totally irrational. . . . Totally without thinking, when my anger was aroused, I grabbed the nearest brick, rock, or stick to bash someone."

In his book, Carson told stories of contemplating hitting his own mother with a hammer and of stabbing a friend with a knife. Violent, disturbing stories, no doubt. Carson said God helped him to overcome.

Trump wasn't so sure. And he let loose in a way I have never seen any other presidential candidate. Here's how he ripped to shreds Carson, the man who had been pushing him in the national polls at the time:

"Now, if you're pathological, there's no cure for that, folks. OK? There's no cure for that."

"That's a big problem because you don't cure that. As an example: child molesting. You don't cure these people. You don't cure a child molester."

"There's only one cure...We don't want to talk about that cure."

"Well, there's two. There's death and the other thing (castration?)"

Here's how Trump continued by coming after Carson for the story about possibly taking a hammer to his mother:

"Wow, that's tough! Man, did anybody in this audience ever go after your mother to hit her on the head with a hammer. Ok?...I didn't. I didn't."

But it was Carson's claims about assaulting his friend that made Trump the most animated that day and incredulous about whether Carson's knife blade could have really just gotten stuck in the friend's belt buckle as he wrote.

"But lo and behold! It hit the belt! It hit the belt! And the knife broke. Give me a break. Give me a break. Give me a break. The knife broke."

Trump took a few steps away from the podium and then grabbed his belt, yanking it up and down, showing the audience how ridiculous he thought Carson's claims about the knife incident were.

"It (the belt buckle) moves this way. It moves that way. How stupid are the people of Iowa? How stupid are the people of the country to believe this crap?"

Rob and Christie Taylor thought Trump's words were crap. They could handle a candidate not being politically correct. They could not stomach Trump's level of unsettling ugliness.

Carson's political incorrectness was one thing for them. But it was far different than Trump's level. Far different. The baffling thing to them, besides the fact that the country elected Trump as their president, was that President Trump ended up making Carson the U.S. Secretary of the Department of Housing and Urban Development. How does that make any sense if he thought Carson was such a terrible person? It didn't make sense to the Taylors. Trump's tough talk on the campaign trail was just a bunch of B.S., they thought.

"His (Trump's) campaign reflected who he was," Dr. Taylor said, "And he still is. What you see is what you got--similar to Carson--but obviously, Trump wasn't what we wanted."

"It soiled me," Representative Taylor interjected, "I was pissed. I was angry...that Trump was the nominee. He doesn't represent us."

Trump's words, in their view, were far too often inappropriate and mean-spirited. Carson's weren't, largely because they believed most everything Carson said and did were guided by his faith. The Taylors had numerous questions about what Trump's commitment to faith was. And they were often repulsed by Trump's moral and ethical behavior, so much so that both of these dedicated long-time Republican activists decided NOT to vote for Trump for president.

Representative Taylor said, "Many of us were appalled, were angry."

"It's a conscience matter," added Dr. Taylor, "Twenty years from now, I didn't want to have to tell my daughter or granddaughter that I voted for Trump. No way!"

They didn't cross over to the other side and vote for the Democrat, Hillary Clinton. They couldn't stand her either. But Representative Taylor voted for Evan McMullin--the former chief policy director for the U.S. House of Representatives Republican Conference and former CIA operations officer--who ran as an Independent candidate. And Dr. Taylor voted for Gary Johnson, the former New Mexico governor and Libertarian candidate for president.

They both figured--correctly--that Trump would win without their support.

The Taylors didn't support Trump in the caucuses, didn't support him in the general election and still don't support him.

They still support other Republican candidates in other races and still consider themselves to be Republicans. But they also can't wait to have the chance to vote for a different Republican in the 2020 election.

They both recognize, however, that Trump found a unique way to connect with people, and not just as a tough talker who wasn't afraid to fight political correctness. Trump also formed a bond with those who had become frustrated with traditional politicians, both Republicans and Democrats. And that's the part that Democrats may have underestimated the most.

Trump found a way to make people feel like he genuinely cared about their views, dreams and yearning to love their country. And he capitalized on it.

"There was a real movement in this country," Dr. Taylor said, "We didn't want more of the same. The thought for so many was, 'I just don't want another senator (to become president). They're all lying SOB's!'"

> Sorry, Senator Marco Rubio.
> Sorry, Senator Rand Paul.
> Sorry, Senator Ted Cruz.
> Sorry, Senator Rick Santorum.
> Sorry, Senator Lindsey Graham.
> Sorry, Senator Hillary Clinton.
> Sorry, Senator Bernie Sanders.

Sorry, traditional thinking. Americans had enough of it. They wanted something else: a non-traditional candidate.

After all, look what traditional thinking had brought them.

In the 1990s, voters gave former Arkansas Governor Bill Clinton and his fellow Democrats control of the White House and both the United States Senate and the United States House of Representatives. That lasted just two years. For the other six years of the Clinton two-term presidency, Americans were more comfortable with Republicans controlling Congress.

In the early 2000s, former Texas Governor George W. Bush and his Republican Party got one-party domination for four years. But then voters decided Democrats should handle the majority in Congress.

And later that decade, former U.S. Senator Barack Obama of Illinois and the Democrats controlled it all for just two years, before Republicans stormed back to eventually lead both chambers of Congress.

Two former governors and a former senator. Traditional choices.

Voters endured adultery and lies with Clinton.

"I did not have sexual relations with that woman, Miss Lewinsky."

President Clinton, January 26, 1998

Except that he *did* have sexual relations with that woman, Monica Lewinsky, his 24-year-old White House intern. The Republican-led House of Representatives impeached him for that lie. There have been numerous other accusations of improper sexual behavior by Clinton for several decades.

The Bush and Obama terms didn't bring that same level of seedy tales of an affair, lies and a reluctant confession that the Clinton years did.

But other issues that remained after their time in office may have planted their own negative seeds in voters' minds and raised levels of frustration--in one way or another--for a candidate like Trump to rise to power.

Here are several that come to mind.

The Never-Ending War Against Terrorism

The country has essentially been at war ever since the terrorist attacks on the World Trade Center and Pentagon in 2001. That's a long, long time for Americans to endure thousands of family members, neighbors, co-workers, church friends or their relatives who were directly impacted because someone left to go off to war. Many returned far different from the person who left. Others never made it home at all. So much fighting in Iraq and Afghanistan. So many lives lost. Even more lives impacted. It has been difficult to see real, lasting, discernable progress in those countries where the U.S. intervened.

The National Debt

The federal debt just keeps soaring, no matter which party is in control.

It surpassed $1 trillion (1982) and then $2 trillion (1986) under Republican President Ronald Reagan.

The debt topped $3 trillion (1990) and $4 trillion (1992) under Republican President George HW Bush.

Democrat Bill Clinton watched the debt-load top $5 trillion (1996) under his watch.

But then those levels really escalated. Quickly.

The federal debt raced past $6 trillion (2002), $7 trillion (2004), $8 trillion (2006), $9 trillion (2007) and $10 trillion (2008) under Republican President George W Bush.

Democrat Barack Obama led the White House when the debt crossed $11 trillion and $12 trillion (2009), $13 trillion and $14 trillion (2010), $15 trillion (2011), $16 trillion (2012), $17 trillion (2013), $18 trillion (2014) and $19 trillion (2015).

The $20 trillion debt threshold fell in 2017 after Republican President Donald Trump took office. In 2018, the figure topped $21 trillion and approached $22 trillion by year's end.

(Numbers courtesy: www.thebalance.com)

Democrats under Obama had the chance to change tax policy or some other measure to increase revenue for the federal government if they believed that was the way to eliminate debt. They chose not to do that.

Republicans under Bush 43 had the chance to slash government spending to reduce the debt if they thought that was the way to accomplish that. They chose not to do that.

Instead, the two major political parties' leaders put wars, entitlement program expansions, tax cuts and numerous other government expenditures or revenue reductions essentially on one big credit card.

Perhaps, their children or grandchildren or great-great-great grandchildren will step up to take care of that one day before the country's economy collapses under the weight of its own debt. Perhaps, they won't have a choice.

Income Inequality

Yes, this is a charged phrase to some. And not everyone seems upset with the growing gap between the very rich and everyone else. But if you aren't a member of the "one percent" at the top of the wealth scale, then you are probably aware that the very rich seem to keep enjoying the greatest share of new wealth, while most other income levels feel stagnant or fall further behind the cost of living.

What is "income inequality?"

"A measurement of the distribution of income that highlights the gap between individuals or households making most of the income in a given country and those making very little. From 1980 to 2010, income inequality in the U.S. increased. The top 20% of earners in the U.S. in 2010 earned almost 50% of the total income while the bottom 15% earned less than 4%."

(www.businessdictionary.com)

The rich can afford the lobbyists to best watch out for their interests. They can afford the best tax attorneys, accountants and overseas tax shelters. They are far more shielded from the technological improvements that can mean a robot can do the job a person used to do. They aren't as impacted as manufacturing jobs--once-integral careers for many in the middle class--have shifted to other lower cost countries. The rich most benefit from the stock market gains and can pay for the best health care, food, shelter, transportation and everything else that stresses out those whose paychecks don't seem to keep up with the changes of tomorrow.

Immigration reform

There are millions of people living illegally in the United States. Why? Well, it didn't happen overnight. Decades of failures from both Democratic and Republican presidents led to millions of people coming into communities, workforces, schools, churches and elsewhere. Their presence scares, confuses, challenges or inspires those here legally. It's complicated. It's emotional. It's divisive.

Seal up the borders and let undocumented immigrants stay here, as long as they haven't broken any additional laws? O.K., but what about those who come here illegally next week or next month or next year? Shouldn't they, too, be able to stay if those who are already here illegally get to stay?

Let everyone stay who makes it into this country? If so, why have border security at all? Why not just open the doors and let everyone in? But isn't that dangerous? How will we know who is here? How do we make sure they are not terrorists?

Deport everyone in this country illegally? They did break the law, after all. But how is that practical? How will law enforcement find them all? And what happens when parents are here illegally but their children are here legally? Raids will tear families apart. Is that humane?

There is no simple solution. And the longer politicians failed to find a fix, they just allowed the situation to become even more complicated and even more politically impossible for them to solve.

Scandal, war, debt, income disparity and illegal immigration all took their toll on voters. It isn't fair to say that Clinton, Bush or Obama's failures to solve these complex challenges are solely responsible for the emergence of Trump. After all, these three men did win enough support from Americans to earn two terms in office.

But if you add those lingering issues with a culture that became increasingly too political correct and leaders who tried too hard to be traditional, you might see how a segment of the electorate decided the time had arrived for someone like Trump.

CHAPTER 5

THE NON-TRADITIONAL CHOICE

 **Christopher Rants**
@C_Rants

Last thing my wife says to me before going to pick up Carly Fiorina- "Don't eat in the car!" Apparently I'm messy eater w crumbs everywhere

10:27 AM - 16 Aug 2015

4 Likes

Christopher Rants was once one of the most powerful leaders at the Iowa Statehouse as speaker of the house. For Carly Fiorina, he was a key strategist but also her chauffeur.

Snapshot from Twitter on August 16, 2015

C hristopher Rants knows what it's like to be a "traditional" politician. He spent two decades in the Iowa legislature, much of the time in leadership. By the way, I don't want to imply that Rants' time at the Iowa Statehouse was robotic or that "traditional" is necessarily a bad thing.

Christopher Rants Bio

1993-2011: State Representative
1999: House Majority Leader
2003-2006: Speaker of the House
2010: Candidate for governor
Republican
Consultant
Golf fanatic
Lives in Sioux City

Rants followed a traditional path as a leader. He worked his way up the leadership chain in the Iowa House and gained experience as majority leader, speaker and then ultimately decided that he should be governor.

He backed off that last decision when Terry Branstad decided that he wanted to return as governor. Branstad had already held the job from 1983-1999. So Rants was wise to know that he couldn't compete with Branstad's familiarity with Iowans (and theirs with him), a four-term governor's fundraising ability and likelihood of recapturing his old job.

Rants, though, offered plenty of experience of his own. Nearly 20 years as a representative, along with the access a leader gets to the constant stream of out-of-town presidential candidates who crave those leaders' counsel, campaign experience and public endorsements, left him with the realization that Iowans--and the country, for that matter--wanted someone not so traditional in the 2016 race.

"*She* would be a much different voice and look," Rants said of Carly Fiorina, a history-making CEO of Hewlett-Packard, who had become the first woman to head a Fortune Magazine top 20 company.

Rants is a white male. But he isn't blind to the fact that his party chooses white men to be the presidential nominee. So for him, Fiorina brought a handful of alternative traits--not just her gender--that the voters could find appealing.

- Executive experience without the baggage of a politician (although, she had previously unsuccessfully run for the U.S. Senate in California)
- International experience (corporate and philanthropic work took her to dozens of countries)
- An effective communicator

Add those up and Rants thought Fiorina would deliver the new look, new sounding, non-traditional leader the country sought.

Although I don't see how this tweet helped her.

Fiorina posted that message on Twitter as her alma mater, the Stanford Cardinal, was preparing to take on the Iowa Hawkeyes in the college football Rose Bowl game. Pandering at its best. Or worst.

Fiorina claimed it was just a joke that she pushed support for the college team that plays in Iowa, the first-in-the-nation caucus state, rather than the school where she graduated. Didn't that just make her a typical politician, who would say (or tweet) just about anything to win over someone's vote?

Here is how Fiorina explained it to CNN's Dana Bash on January 3, 2016, "Oh, for heaven's sake, Dana, for heaven's sake, can't a girl ever have a little bit of fun?" Fiorina asked.

"That was a tongue-in-cheek tweet, which the people of Iowa understand, because I was asked over and over again in Iowa, having attended a Hawkeye tailgate. I was asked. They knew that my heart was torn," she finished.

For heaven's sake, indeed.

So, not a problem of authenticity for Fiorina, she would argue, just a problem of a joke that not everyone appreciated.

Even if it would be a problem for a few people, Rants was convinced that Fiorina could handle it.

"I try to find the best problem solver," Rants said of his accolades of Fiorina, "I want the person who can come up with the best solution to the problems I don't even know exist."

He agreed to run her Iowa campaign. And serve as chauffeur of her campaign bus. And prep her for interviews. And help her craft her message. And carry her bags, drink or anything else she may need at any moment in Iowa.

You get the picture here? Rants had to do a little bit of everything. Or a LOT of everything for this low-budget campaign that never seemed to find the connection with Iowans or their wallets that Rants figured it could, despite what he figured would be Fiorina's unique ability to connect.

Sixteen male Republicans running for president in one race. One woman. Surely, that meant Fiorina could stand out. Surely, not enough, as it turned out.

"That's one of my downfalls," Rants said, "I go for the smartest person in the race as opposed to who is the most electable."

Rants backed former Massachusetts Governor Mitt Romney for president in the 2012 race, and Romney eventually became the party's nominee, of course, before losing to Democratic President Barack Obama.

Fiorina's campaign tried to be unique, stretching the boundaries of the walls between a candidate's efforts and the "Super PAC" that is set up to help that candidate.

That was where "Carly for President" met "Carly for America."

Sounds nearly identical, right?

Here is how it worked: Fiorina's campaign committee--Carly for President--would publicly announce her schedule. And then the Super PAC that supported her--Carly for America--would take care of most of the other details: organize the venue, invite supporters and arrange the chairs/stage/lighting/microphone/food and drinks/signs. Oh, and most importantly, pay most of the bills associated with the event. Those were things, previously, that campaigns would do. But not for this campaign.

"Super PACs are also known as Independent Expenditures Only Committees (IEOCs). These PACs can accept unlimited contributions and spend an unlimited amount supporting or opposing federal election candidates, but they cannot directly donate to federal candidates or parties."

(As defined per Ballotpedia)

Fiorina's campaign had to deal with those pesky federal guidelines that limited contributors to $2,700. But a SuperPAC doesn't have those restrictions. Contributors can donate whatever they want. So Fiorina largely left much of her efforts to become president to the SuperPAC that backed her.

"It was always a tough hill to overcome," Rants said, "We were one of the smallest campaigns with some of the least amount of resources. We were fighting from the get-go for attention from the media and the ability to get funds."

Relying on the SuperPAC, while it helped some with resources, made it difficult in other ways. "We stepped back and let other entities do some of the grassroots work, while we focused on campaign messaging. So you don't know exactly know what would happen," Rants said, "You go into a room and you wait to see...will there be anyone in that room? Any crowd? That makes it tough."

Another thing made it tough.

"Look at that face! Would anyone vote for that? Can you imagine that, the face of the next president? I mean, she's a woman. And I'm not supposed to say bad things, but really, folks, come on. Are we serious?"

Rolling Stone Magazine laid out those lines in a story published on September 9, 2015, after spending time with Donald Trump.

Sure looks like the future president of the United States was dogging Fiorina for her looks, doesn't it? He claimed later that he wasn't, of course. But for Rants, Fiorina's supporters and the candidate herself, it was an eye-opening, jaw-dropping look into Trump's opprobrium.

And it tapped into several things at once:

1. Trump would say just about anything (when voters were looking for a different kind of candidate).
2. Trump gave challengers a chance to hammer back at him (and Fiorina did during the Republican presidential debate at the Ronald Reagan Presidential Library in Simi Valley, California eight days after that *Rolling Stone* story. When asked about Trump's "Look at that face" slam, Fiorina responded during the

debate, "I think women all over this country heard very clearly what Mr. Trump said." Point made.)

3. Trump, though, with that comment about her appearance and the attention it brought, could have also tapped into the "woman problem" in Iowa and beyond (to that point, Iowa had never had elected a woman as governor or as president).

That third point is particularly complicated for Rants. He doesn't really want to believe that there remain Iowans who won't back a woman for higher office--regardless of her skills, abilities, background--just because she is a woman. He doesn't want to believe that. But he fears that still exists--not as much as it used to--but it still exists.

"People would never say anything directly," Rants said of caucus goer reluctance to back the only female in the Republican race. But some may have had those thoughts, even if they didn't vocalize them.

"People, when they go into caucus, they think not just who they like, but we also think, 'Can this person go the distance? Is this person electable?'" Rants said looking back at the feelings then, "I still think a certain sector wondered if she could win."

That left Rants frustrated with the amount of time, energy and passion he spent trying to get Fiorina into the White House. But it also left him disappointed.

Not only did he fail to push Fiorina to victory to fulfill his own goals, but he knew he also failed to finally send a Republican woman to victory in his state's caucuses. And he knew that would leave his two daughters disappointed. "I look at my own kids and think this is a kind of candidate they would support. They're not going to support a Donald Trump," Rants said.

But what about Rants? Could his party loyalty eventually trump his serious, serious misgivings about the man Republicans sent to the White House?

"Don't ask me about that. I would rather not talk about it," Rants said.

He would talk about a few concerns -- major concerns -- he has about the direction of his party.

2017 Republican federal tax cuts that could add more than a trillion dollars to the nation's debt

"I think Republicans are searching for what it means to be a Republican. I mean for years, we cared about deficits and now we threw that out the window."

Trump's morality (three marriages, dishonesty, plus allegations of infidelity, sexual harassment and an affair with a porn star)

"We would hold our candidates to a higher standard. We would laugh at the Democrats for all of their scandals (especially Bill Clinton). Now, we don't care about that. We're all amazed at Donald Trump's behavior and how he has been able to survive and I'm at a loss to explain it. It would have sunk anybody else. I'm worried what that standard is for future Republicans."

Tomorrow's Republicans

"We know we have to grow our party. We know our country celebrated immigrants. My grandparents were. We are party of a free trade. Are we still? The president has hijacked our party."

Rants, the Republican

"I've stayed true to my core beliefs. Let every president, anybody who has been the leader of the party...be it Obama, Bush, Clinton, Reagan...they all put their stamp on what their party means. I'm not entirely sure President Trump's philosophy, but it will shape our party for the future."

Rants is an academic in politics, well-read, well-versed and well-prepared to talk philosophically about policy, mindsets and voters' expectations.

Chris Larimer also offers a deeper perspective. Larimer is a political science professor at the University of Northern Iowa in Cedar Falls. UNI is the smallest of the state's three public universities and enrolls about 12,000 students on its campus that is located about 110 miles northeast of Des Moines.

Chris Larimer Bio

Assistant Professor Political Science, University of Northern Iowa since 2009
UNI graduate, 2001
Author of five books
Television commentator

Larimer has followed politics since he was a kid, when at the age of 12, he met President Bill Clinton and Vice President Al Gore at the Clay County Fair. That far northwest Iowa county's fair is one of the state's best-known, calls itself "The World's Greatest Fair" because of its tradition of great crowds and celebrated its 100th anniversary in 2018.

Larimer observed how the Clinton-Gore campaign worked the crowd back then, won over Iowans and became a two-term team in office. Later as an academic researcher, Larimer follows political behavior, get out the vote methods and voter decision-making.

Trump gives him plenty to research, study and try to figure out how this non-traditional politician got the job and now operates as the president of the United States.

"In terms of what is expected in Iowa and what successful candidates have done in Iowa, Donald Trump's campaign was unusual to say the least," Larimer noted, "Consider what has traditionally worked in the state: retail politics, frequent visits, small and accessible meetings, an attempt to relate to rural voters, particularly farmers and a clear courting of the religious right for GOP candidates."

From Larimer's observations, that traditional game plan wasn't Trump's strategy. "Trump's efforts on any one of those was minimal at best. He did not have a strong organization in the state relative to other campaigns, he rarely visited, and when he did, it was in the form of large rallies where face-to-face conversations with voters are nearly impossible. And some of his past statements and behavior likely raised suspicion among evangelical voters," he said.

That strategy didn't deliver a caucus night victory for Trump. But it wasn't like Trump didn't do well. "In the end," Larimer said, "He won more votes on caucus night than any previous candidate, only to finish second to Ted Cruz by a few thousand votes. Trump's 'tell it like it is' personality and celebrity status may have been enough to overcome the above-mentioned shortcomings."

Larimer said Trump successfully connected with Iowans as "an outsider who could bring change to the system."

And enough Iowans were looking for an outsider. Trump's notoriety helped connect with hard-to-connect-with Iowans, too. Larimer said, "Trump's celebrity status afforded him attention to voters who didn't like watching politics, were extremely frustrated with government and wanted someone to fix it without going into all the nuances that are required."

Nuances came from typical politicians. Specifics weren't generally part of Trump on the stump.

Not all Trump's supporters spend much time contemplating nuances, philosophy or what he means for the future of the Republican Party. Some of them couldn't care less. "President Trump calls it as it is," Ken Tipping told me.

Tipping, describes himself as a "conservative." He didn't use the word "Republican." Tipping is also a Trump supporter and has emailed me from time to time to rip the media and point out what he sees as media bias against Trump. A LOT of media bias, in his eyes.

"I love how he has gone against the 'fake news,'" Tipping told me as we exchanged another series of emails, "I have always called it a bunch of garbage!"

Trump uses the derogatory term "fake news" frequently, as he tries to get supporters to distrust media who don't report his words, actions or events exactly the way as he demands.

Tipping owns his own small wealth management company in West Des Moines. Trump was and is exactly what Tipping thinks his adopted state and country need.

Tipping wrote me this, "My parents immigrated from the UK to Canada. My father from England, my mother from Scotland. I was born in Canada. Became a US citizen 1992. That was the first year I was able to vote. Grew up in South Texas, Washington State, Iowa, lived in Canada, lived in the UK. Been to Europe several times, the far east, South America."

So he has seen a few places and experienced different cultures. Tipping never described himself as "worldly," but, no doubt, his time outside Iowa shaped a broader view of the way he views the political landscape.

"I have started from basically nothing," Tipping wrote me, "My parents didn't pay for my college. I didn't go back to school till I was 27. I went door to door as a kid washing cars to earn money, going through ditches to collect cans and bottles, and I have gone door to door to build my business from scratch as an investment broker. That has been for the past 20 years. I'm 54 years old."

Tipping told me that Trump wasn't perfect. Who is, right? But in his mind, Trump is the perfect fit for what the United States needs in an increasingly paralyzed Washington, D.C., changing economy and challenging world.

Time to fix the mess President Barack Obama left behind, Tipping believes. "Get rid of the racial divide that Obama inflicted on this great nation," Tipping emailed, "And I sincerely believe he did that. All of that Black Lives Matter, not supporting the police, not supporting our military, was because of Obama. So far I see him (Trump) standing up to true values in our country. I would like to add I went to high school in Texas that had 50 percent color, 50 percent white. We never had this much racial divide."

He added some lines about Hillary Clinton, too, because she may be the only Democrat that he and some of his fellow Trump supporters despise more than Obama.

Tipping emailed, "Hillary didn't have any type of message at all. I have liberal friends, black, Harvard grads, that thought that Hillary/Clintons are complete crooks. Which they are. One other point, they tried to make it look like Trump was sexist? And here Hillary stood by her husband who is an absolute cheater with women! Joke's on the press!"

Yes, another reminder as I pointed earlier, Tipping isn't a fan of the media. Another thing he seems to have in common with President Trump.

CHAPTER 6

TRUMP VS. THE MEDIA

Donald Trump and members of the media. It's complicated. Trump tries to demean most, especially CNN. He praises a few, especially Fox News. The combination makes cable television ratings and internet clicks soar.

Screenshot from Twitter

"The enemy of the American people!" That's quite a statement. Disturbing. Potentially dangerous.

But notice the "retweets" and "likes" on that post President Trump tweeted to his millions of followers. Clearly, many people agreed with his absurd claim.

Trump, like no other politician I can ever remember, mobilized a mass of people to join him while making the media the perceived enemy. Yes, the media are biased. So are you. So am I.

I try the best I can to be as politically unbiased as I can in my professional work. Do I always succeed? I'm sure that I don't.

There are politicians whom I have found to be easier to talk with than others. It doesn't have anything to do with their political beliefs. I think it comes down to personalities, shared experiences and interests. Politicians are no different to me than people in other professions, in this regard. It's just like people at church, work or the neighborhood. It's just easier to have a conversation with some people and more challenging with others.

When it comes to politicians, does our mutual ease in conversation impact my coverage of them? I would hope not. Although, I do think I have a better chance of accurately reporting candidates' positions and beliefs on issues and events if they give me access, time and insight. The more conversations that we have, the more I think that I can understand them. And hopefully that means my reporting regarding them is more complete. But be clear about this, I don't need to like a politician. And the politician doesn't need to like me. Journalism isn't about that. I have to be fair. I hope that I am.

I am biased in my opinion of the need for access, of course, because I think politicians should be open, honest and accessible both with journalists and the public (not necessarily in that order). And my job is far easier and more thorough if I can get that access.

But I know many people couldn't care less about my access. They couldn't care less about the access my colleagues and competitors get either. They care most about what is reported, how it is reported and in many cases, whether it reaffirms their beliefs.

As I said, I know the media are biased, some intentionally, some not. Cable news and opinion-driven talk radio rarely seem to play it straight. Although, they get paid to give opinions. So, they offer them.

And social media? That, to me, changed the political atmosphere the most. Social media can be an incredibly useful tool to share information quickly. I know there are consumers who rarely, if ever, see my work live on television but read/watch it on Facebook, Twitter, Instagram and LinkedIn. Social media can be important in the daily dialogue. I can get immediate feedback on stories and observations. It isn't like that on television.

Social media users have shared insights or details I never knew or that never entered my mind before. Invaluable. Those give me ideas for future stories and angles. And I think this helps provide more complete coverage.

But there is the other side: the trolls, haters, eternal contrarians and malcontents. And there are plenty of them. Some people out there truly can't seem to say anything nice about anyone who they don't believe shares 100 percent of their opinions and beliefs. Many of them can't say anything remotely close to something nice. They seem to exist on social media just to be mean-spirited. Sad.

They don't bother to click on a story link to see what's inside before they retweet, support, snark or criticize what they assume the story is. They are also the ones who immediately pounce on reporters--or anyone, for that matter--who point out something that runs counter to their beliefs.

If I write a story about how the federal debt keeps soaring--despite the fact that Republicans, who control Congress and the White House, promised to control spending--then some Republicans will say, "But what about Obama?" and "Why didn't you care when Obama imploded the debt?"

I did, actually. I wrote about it.

If I write a story about how more Americans are working and the unemployment rate keeps falling under recent Republican leadership, then some Democrats will write, "But what about Republicans' war on women?"

Are Republicans really "at war" with women because some believe abortion is immoral or that they don't fund women's health services adequately for Democrats? Why can't this simply be a personal and philosophical argument over positions?

Social media, talk radio, cable television, churches and social circles allow people, if they choose, to surround themselves with only the people who share what they want to hear and give the opinions that back up what they already feel. Classic confirmation bias.

Our country is undergoing a major resettling, as author Bill Bishop revealed in his 2009 book *The Big Sort: Why the Clustering of Like-Minded America is Tearing Us Apart*. People are choosing to live in neighborhoods that reflect their personal, political and spiritual beliefs. We are sorting ourselves to street-level precision with neighbors who think like we do.

Some people don't want to be challenged. They don't want to think about another view. And even if they are firmly grounded in their opinions, they don't want to even bother to listen to an alternative viewpoint. Even if it is only for the purpose of better understanding of others.

That is their choice, of course. This is the United States of America. Believe what you wish. I fear, though, that isolating yourself with only like-minded friends (whether they are real friends or just "friends" on Facebook) robs you of the chance to let your mind be exposed to an alternative view on something. Maybe you will actually learn something. Maybe you will even change your opinion. Or maybe it will just further strengthen the opinion you already had. But hearing an alternative point of view could allow you to at least better understand those who disagree with you.

One final point on this...I do think it can be difficult for people to distinguish different forms of media. The massive number of television, radio, newspaper, cable, internet, podcast, blogger, social media and magazine platforms can add up to an overwhelming number of voices, styles and political perspectives.

It can be especially difficult to remember which reporter or which media entity reported what. I hope that consumers know that I try to accurately report on people, events and issues that impact our local residents in an unbiased way. Whereas, talk show hosts, bloggers or other opinion media may intentionally incorporate their political beliefs in their coverage.

An MSNBC talk show host, for instance, may relay information far differently than a reporter who appears on NBC and MSNBC. Some people may choose not to see a difference. In their minds, a reporter appearing on MSNBC must be a liberal. Or a journalist appearing on Fox News must be a Republican. And some people just lump "the media" into one interchangeable group of untrustworthy, disreputable muckrakers. They are either unwilling or unable to discern differences in objectives and purpose in members of the media or their organizations.

Trump has been remarkable at uniting people to stand behind him while he discounts or denies those who don't see things as he does.

"Fake news!" he screams when the media report something that isn't flattering to him.

And, look, sometimes, I think he has been correct in that what has been initially reported is not accurate or is biased. Reporters shouldn't be out to get him just because he calls them the "enemy." They can't take his insults personally.

Also, the rush to be first with a scoop is a dangerous game of roulette for the media. Dishing out a scoop, no doubt, can mean an explosion of engagement on social media and accolades. Your followers "retweet" your headline with their followers on Twitter. They "share" your work with their friends on Facebook. Some of them will decide your work is worthy of a future connection, so they will sign on to social media to anxiously await your next exclusive.

The other side to this quest for first is all that is wrong with the media. Sloppy, rushed work that too often relies on anonymous sources (or just one source) with the sole goal of getting the information out first can be dangerous. It ruins the reporter's credibility if the information isn't accurate. And it can ruin someone else's life. The media must take this more seriously.

Be first? Sure, but it's better to be right. Getting something wrong in that thirst to be first just fuels the trolls. And it emboldens the distrustful to merely discount anything that they don't want to hear. The media have to get the story accurate. That is the only option. Always. And when we don't, take action. Take responsibility. Apologize. Get it right.

Journalists--those who aim to remain neutral in their pursuit of the truth--already face an uphill climb with some in the public, so they don't need the additional burden of "scoops" that turn out to be incorrect.

Here is a sample of a message I received to show what I mean from people who claim that they see bias in my reporting:

"Your news is not news, but one-sided propaganda... Sadly your news is suffering from delusions of their own importance. If it involves the President he is depicted as bad. It is like watching on the late night talk shows. Everyone of them takes their nightly shot at the President and his staff. Funny thing it did not happen with the last President...It used to be whatever is wrong is Bush's fault and now we have moved on to Trump's fault."

--Aloysius Kling

My response: "Not true, Aloysius. I wrote plenty of stories that included criticism from people about President Obama's time in office. The stories covered the rising cost of health insurance, federal debt and the never-ending wars, just to name a few."

"Dave Price needs to quit and go work for Fox News."

--Patti Collins

My response: "Patti, you should go talk to Aloysius sometime."

"Seems like you are following the trend of WHO Radio and becoming staunchly conservative Republican. Your political commentary seems slanted toward Trump, as are the comments. I expect fair unbiased reporting."

--Larry H.

My response: "Larry, I agree that WHO Radio (the dominant talk radio outlet in Des Moines for years) features pro-Republican talk shows, especially the syndicated programming it carries like Rush Limbaugh and Sean Hannity. And I agree that I need to be unbiased in my reporting to the best of my abilities. I disagree that my coverage was slanted toward Trump during 2016 or afterwards."

"I have been a fan of your news channel for years but since the election of Trump you all seem to criticize him. We should stick by our president no matter what. Stop praising Obama. It's time for change... Show the good that Trump has done once in a while."

--Dennis P.

My response: "Dennis, I'm not quite sure what 'stick by our president' means in terms of the media's role in our society. I'm sure the president appreciates your support and

loyalty. My role, though, is not to be a cheerleader for a politician, even if that politician is the president of the United States. I do agree, however, that the media need an accurate account of what's happening. Improving economic number deserve the media's attention, for example, not just the latest controversial claim that the president made."

The bulk of the strongest complaints I receive, both through email and social media, accuse me of being anti-president, pro-Democrat, a purveyor of the "fake news" President Trump denounces or just too liberal.

So these are typical:

"Journalism has gone down the tubes lately because its display of unfairness. Doctors are dedicated to saving lives. Journalists should be dedicated to being fair!!
--MJ V.

My response: "MJ, the perception of unfairness has hurt the media's reputation. I agree journalists should be dedicated to being fair. Good journalists do their best to do that."

"F*ck that man, the media is all over Trump about everything and nothing about Clinton."
--Joe

My response: "Joe, I think Hillary Clinton and her emails would disagree that there was nothing about her unwise decision to have someone set up a secretive, homemade computer server to handle her emails. There was a LOT of media coverage about it. A LOT."

"The problem is that (and it is well established) the media is hugely left which results in 'group think' and you all think you're right and the right is nuts. The last election should have woken some people up. I give up. I'm 70 and have lived a good life. I fear for my kids and grandkids...and even you, Dave."
--Steven H.

My response: "Steven, I do agree that 'groupthink' hurts the media industry. Journalists should not just accept something as the 'story of the day' or a trend because we see someone saying that on cable television or social media. I also agree that the last presidential election should be a wake-up call for journalists, politicians and our citizens. We in the collective media missed out on how unhappy a sizeable chunk of our population was with politics and the media. We all need to find ways to better connect with people, no matter where they live, how much money they make and what their personal politics may be. We have to intentionally venture outside of our immediate circle, whether that's in Des Moines or D.C. Smaller towns deserve our attention, too, as well as the people who depend on them."

The criticism in the emails and social media comments are far more frequent and much more biting since Trump entered politics in 2015. And they have persisted. I don't think I can say that he is responsible for all of this, but he has undoubtedly helped fuel it.

There are several factors at play. Consumers have far more sources--some legitimate, some not--for their information. Social media helped to polarize our politics like never before. So has the way politicians draw district boundaries (dare I say gerrymander?), so that few Congressional districts are truly competitive in the traditional two major political party sense. Instead, the battle is more likely the primary contest (if there is a contested campaign at all), rather than the general election.

Democratic candidates often must make sure a challenger doesn't attack from the left and Republicans have to protect themselves from the right. It doesn't matter as much what voters from the other party think or the formerly much sought-after Independents.

Compromise is a dirty word for many, both the politicians and their rabid followers. Belittle, trash talk and defeat the opposition. Those matter more. That seems to come before the commitment to improve our country for our neighbors and the future generations.

And there is Trump...his language, coarseness and repeated attacks on the media.

Trump is a master of turning a phrase on Twitter. I do think because of the harshness of his repeated attacks on the media, some reporters are too quick to try to nail him for saying something false or inappropriate. Personal feelings, hurt or bias have no place in objective reporting.

Donald J. Trump ✔
@realDonaldTrump

`Following` ⌄

The media is so dishonest. If I make a statement, they twist it and turn it to make it sound bad or foolish.They think the public is stupid!

1:42 PM - 10 Jul 2016

13,325 Retweets 41,143 Likes

💬 7.4K   🔁 13K   ♡ 41K   ✉

Can Trump's threats and anti-media chants be scary? Of course they can. As reporters, I think we sometimes don't want to show fear or show that we can be intimidated. We are supposed to pursue the truth. Cuss us out and threaten us? No, that won't dissuade us from searching for the facts. Slam a door in our face? Fill up our email inbox? Troll us on social media? We reporters still can't let that deter our purpose for holding decision makers accountable, uncovering injustices, shedding light on policies, ideas and issues that impact our community, giving voice to the voiceless, sharing stories of triumph, inspiration and sadness. We must push onward, despite the obstacles that come before us, whether those attacks come from Trump or any other leader.

When reporters are covering Trump during a rally of hundreds or thousands of people and he encourages followers to turn toward the camera and vent their rage, when the crowd yells at, taunts, spits on and physically threatens the media, yes, that can be frightening. It is ridiculously scary. And, yes, it is completely, utterly unnecessary and dangerous.

I pray no one gets hurt because of the violence he could incite.

But Trump also uses his verbal attacks as a defense mechanism when the media catch him spreading something that isn't correct--whether the president believes it is or not--or when the president has contradicted something that he has said or done previously.

Trump frequently makes claims that are not true. Sometimes he says them. Other times he tweets them. *The Washington Post* called 2018 for Trump "A year of unprecedented deception."

(Source: Glenn Kessler, December 30, 2018)

The newspaper's "Fact Checker database" counted an astounding 15 erroneous claims a day by the president over the course of the year. And the analysis found that Trump's frequency of falsehoods in 2018 were three times greater than 2017. For whatever reason, Trump became far more misleading in his second year in office.

The media pointed out the untruths and Trump would fire back. It's a constant source of friction.

Trump's mastery can be how he is able to express his attack on the media, attempt to defend himself and then wrap it all up in a bow by ending with, "They think the public is stupid!"

That is how he keeps supporters on his side. He is standing up for them against that bad, ol' media.

Add up all of these factors--Trump's media-bashing, where and how consumers get their information and the country's polarized politics--and we live in a powder keg where a 10 second clip on television, viral moment on social media or explosive Twitter rant can light the fuse for an explosion that divides us even more.

This is what much of politics has become right now. And Trump has a forest full of matchsticks at the ready that he can use to ignite an inferno whenever and however he chooses.

Burn, baby, burn.

Donald J. Trump ●
@realDonaldTrump

Following ⌄

Network news has become so partisan, distorted and fake that licenses must be challenged and, if appropriate, revoked. Not fair to public!

7:09 PM - 11 Oct 2017

19,597 Retweets 85,732 Likes

♡ 49K ♺ 20K ♡ 86K ✉

Network news is not state-run media. The president, no matter who he is and no matter how he deems the coverage against him, does not have absolute power to dictate the content of the public's media. Threatening to revoke a media organization's license, regardless of whether that tweeted threat was real or just a ploy of distraction, is beyond serious. It also goes too far. Way too far.

Granted, ratings for those evening newscasts aren't what they once were in this increasingly splintered media world where consumers have numerous alternative sources, especially those that provide opinion-slanted coverage or offer "stories" from people with zero journalistic skills or integrity.

Regardless, Trump's rants against the media have had an impact.

"Public trust in the media is at an all-time low."

That headline blared from the *2017 Gallup/Knight Foundation Survey on Trust, Media and Democracy* of more than 19,000 American adults that was released in January 2018.

Not good. Not good for anyone. People in that survey acknowledge that more sources of information make it more difficult than ever before to be well-informed, because it is more difficult than ever to determine the authenticity of that information.

Others have added to the distrust of the media, as well. Brent Bozell's work at the Media Research Center pointed out what he saw as liberal bias in the mainstream media for years. Rush Limbaugh and Sean Hannity use their talk shows to mobilize followers against the "traditional, mainstream" media. Breitbart.com and conspiracy theorist Alex Jones use their platforms to spread what they claim is news. And even Newt Gingrich, the former United States Speaker of the House and presidential candidate, who had been a prominent guest on network news shows for years has now turned into a full-throated critic of the press. It is rich with irony as he and the media's other biggest critics would have a far more limited platform if the press didn't provide it.

This all impacts how Americans see, read, consume and feel about what is reported. That Gallup/Knight Foundation Survey also showed what to me has become an astounding partisan divide in people's views of the media.

54% of Democrats view media favorably
68% of Republicans view media unfavorably

There is also this about those who think there is a "great deal" of political bias in news coverage. Notice how much that view has changed over the past three decades:

25% of Americans sensed a great deal of political bias in 1989
45% of Americans sensed a great deal of political bias in 2017

A deeper look at those numbers when you consider political party reflects a major difference:

26% of Democrats sensed a great deal of political bias in 2017
67% of Republicans sensed a great deal of political bias in 2017

Perhaps, those numbers help explain the lopsided nature of the email and social media complaints I get about my work.
Here are two other numbers that stood out to me from that survey:

73% of Americans say the spread of inaccurate information through the internet is a major problem with modern-day news coverage.
50% of those surveyed felt confident that Americans can make their way through bias to determine what truly are the facts.

Major challenges, right?
One other number underscored, again, the partisan divide on the media.

40% of Republicans say news stories that cast a politician or political group negatively should always be considered fake news. Always.

Trump led this charge. The media now have to restore their reputation. But they have to earn it.

You also may wonder what do Trump's words mean long-term? Does he mean them? Or does he just use them at that very moment to make a point? And do the words of his critics mean anything?

Case in point--what Trump has said about other Republicans and what they said about him.

Trump on 2016 Republican primary opponent Ben Carson and Carson's ability to lead:

"It's not his thing. He doesn't have the temperament for it. I think Ben just doesn't have the experience."

Donald Trump, November 3, 2015

(As I pointed out earlier, President Trump later made Carson the United States Secretary of Housing and Urban Development.)

2016 Republican President candidate Rick Perry on Trump:

"Let no one be mistaken, Donald Trump's candidacy is a cancer on conservatism and it must be clearly diagnosed, excised and discarded. It cannot be pacified or ignored, for it will destroy a set of principles that has lifted more people out of poverty than any force in the history of the civilized world and that is the cause of conservatism."

Rick Perry, July 22, 2015

(President Trump later chose Perry as the United States Secretary of Energy.)

2016 Republican Presidential candidate Ted Cruz on Trump:

"This man is a pathological liar. He doesn't know the difference between truth and lies. He lies practically every word that comes out of his mouth."

Ted Cruz, May 3, 2016

Trump on Cruz:

"It is no surprise he has resorted to his usual tactics of over-the-top rhetoric that nobody believes. Over the last week, I have watched Lyin' Ted become more and more unhinged as he is unable to react under the pressure and stress of losing..."

Donald Trump, May 3, 2016

(President Trump later endorsed Ted Cruz in his 2018 U.S. Senate re-election.)

Trump, of course, didn't just use his most vicious lines against his own party. He had plenty for his 2016 general election foe, Democrat Hillary Clinton.

"Crooked Hillary"
--Donald Trump, numerous times.

"Lock her up!"
--Donald Trump, numerous times.

(President-Elect Trump later told a rally in Michigan on December 10, 2016, "That plays great before the election. Now, we don't care, right?")

The meaning of Trump's words can apparently be temporary.

CHAPTER 7

THE TRUMP IMAGE

"I'm proud to be a deplorable!" -- Yvonne Brandt
"They better wake up!"-- Connie Whitaker

Two longtime friends laughed off Hillary Clinton's "basket full of deplorables" cutdown of Donald Trump's followers and also warned that fellow Iowans need to see Trump as their best hope for the future.

Trump campaign rally in Clive, Iowa on September 13, 2016.

Photo by Dave Price

"I think he was trying to create the 'Donald Trump image.'"

Those words came from Yvonne Brandt. She was one of 1,600 people in the crowd to listen to Trump speak at a rally in the Des Moines suburb of Clive on September 13, 2016. Brandt, of Norwalk, came to the event with one of her closest friends, Connie Whitaker, of Grimes.

Neither woman sounded much like Trump, at least not during our 10 minute conversation. Their words were far more measured than Trump's generally are, but still passionate.

They both considered themselves to be political Independents, who had grown frustrated with Republicans for failing them for too many years.

"It's America's last hope," Whitaker told me about the election of Trump.

That sounded pretty dramatic. Really, America's *last* hope?

"He's the only one who can change what's going on in this country. We're headed in the wrong direction," Whitaker responded. "They (voters) better wake up!"

Trump tried to wake them up that day (not that he has ever stopped trying to wake everyone up since he became president).

"I am running to be a president for all Americans...Democrat, Republican, Independent, everyone. Whether you vote for me, or whether you vote for someone else, I will be your greatest champion," Trump told them that day.

Instant connection for the dissatisfied like Brandt and Whitaker, who long felt like disaffected politicians of the past refused to serve their best interests.

These two friends also showed me that the national media narrative, again, may not have always been accurate about Trump supporters. Let's be honest, so many of us in the media didn't completely understand this uprising that put Trump in office and that continues to support him. Many of his supporters weren't the familiar faces we would see in a typical Republican gathering. Trump's supporters often avoid those traditional events.

Instead, they had vented about the state of politics while they sat at coffee shops, around dinner tables or at work. They may have ranted on social media, just like those who had been politically engaged. But others just fumed in silence as they felt largely disconnected to elected officials.

Because of all of this, the media didn't do a good enough job of keeping tabs on them or their desires.

Trump fared well in rural Iowa, where some of these previously disengaged people live. But he also connected with Iowans, like Brandt and Whitaker, who represented the middle class, suburban types. They were nearing retirement, in these women's cases, and aren't worried about their own financial well-being. But they were concerned for their grandchildren's generation and the future direction of the country.

I mentioned earlier a few of the major issues politicians failed to fix--immigration laws/border security, the national debt, war and income inequality. But there are so many other changes, many major, that Iowa has undergone in the past few decades. Some Iowans are still trying to process them.

Marriage--It is no longer just "traditional." Since 2009, couples of the same sex can legally marry in Iowa. Younger people overwhelmingly support this equality. Older people aren't as fully convinced.

There has been a remarkable switch overall nationally in people's views on marriage. Just look what has happened this decade, according to a Pew Research Center study. In 2010, Americans opposed marriage equality: 48 percent were against same-sex marriage while 42 percent supported it. But notice the seismic shift in 2017: 62 percent supported it, while just 32 percent opposed. Broken down by age, you can see that all but one group agreed with the new, legal definition of marriage:

Millennials (those between the ages of 18 and 36) favored it: 74 percent to 23 percent.

Generation Xers (those between 37 and 52) supported it: 65 percent to 29 percent.

Baby Boomers (those between 53 and 71) approved it: 56 percent to 39 percent.

Silent Generation members (those between 72 and 89) were the only group against it: 41 percent backed same-sex marriage, while 49 percent opposed it.

White evangelicals were one prominent group that still stood against same-sex marriage: 35 supported it, 59 percent opposed.

(Pew Research Center, conducted June 8-18, 2017, among 2,504 adults)

Not-So-White--Iowa's demographics are changing. Iowa is still overwhelmingly white but not as much as it once was.

The state's population registered 93 percent white in 2010. By 2016, that had shrunk to 91 percent white. Again, not a huge change, but it is noticeable as the state is becoming more diverse. The Hispanic population is six times greater now than it was three decades ago. That growth is fueled by an expanding presence in cities like Denison, Storm Lake, Perry, Marshalltown and Carroll.

The changes have meant a learning curve for some white residents as the growing minority population brings new traditions, customs, languages and heritage into town.

(Source: U.S. Census Bureau)

Off the Farm--Iowa's countryside is shifting. Over the past decade, the state lost about 6,000 farms. That represents a continuation of what has been happening for far longer. If you go back to 1950, the change is much more dramatic. There were 206,000 farms in the state in 1950. By 2016, that had shrunk to 86,900, a 58% contraction.

The size of the farms substantially increased, thanks to technology, machinery and farmers leaving the fields for good as economic pressures and corporate farms replaced them.

Agriculture still makes up a sizable part of the state's economy and producers still lead the way in corn, beans, hogs and eggs. But the overall makeup, size and family members needed on the farm look much different than a few generations ago.

(Source: U.S.D.A. annual farm census)

Rural Iowa--The decline in farmers is just one factor leading to the shrinking of much of Iowa. One of the most stunning figures to me about the state of Iowa is its population. Most counties are losing residents. Many are now far smaller than they were a century ago. And the residents are graying, too. Without younger people providing a stable tax base, the towns struggle with providing the services that older residents need.

Good luck finding children in towns like Durango, Buck Grove, Beaconsfield, Carbon and Clayton, unless they are visiting. All of those communities saw their populations dwindle to fewer than 50 and not one of them had a child living there in late 2017 when the *Des Moines Register* checked. Not one.

(Source: Kyle Munson, Des Moines Register, "Childless Iowa," December 27, 2017)

That made a town like Wiota look like a baby boom town in southwestern Iowa's Cass County. Wiota's 100 residents included one boy and one girl. Nearby Marne--which doesn't even have a third of the 400 people it did in 1900--is now so desperate for young families, it offered to give you land--for free--if you build a house. Have to try something, anything to buck the trend, town leaders believe.

The situation is widespread. Of Iowa's 99 counties, only 28 have increased in population this decade.

So for Lyon, Dickinson, Sioux, Plymouth, Bremer, Woodbury, Black Hawk, Buchanan, Dubuque, Boone, Story, Linn, Dallas, Polk, Jasper, Johnson, Cedar, Scott, Pottawattamie, Madison, Warren, Washington, Muscatine, Mills, Clarke, Jefferson, Wayne and Davis Counties, consider yourselves the exception.

But for the futures of the other 71 counties, that means fewer schools, longer bus rides for kids, strained resources to meet residents' educational, health, recreational and governmental service needs, plus fewer job opportunities and added commute times for workers.

Most of the state faces serious concerns of decline. Rural Iowa is in crisis and has been for a century.

(Statistics courtesy: Iowa Data Center)

(Not) Made in Iowa--Disappearing manufacturing jobs add to the woes. I mentioned earlier in this book how Maytag took the last of the 4,000 jobs away from Newton in 2007.

In 2011, Electrolux--which once had an Iowa workforce near 2,000--decided that it would rather make washers and dryers in Mexico, instead of Webster City and Jefferson.

A decade before that, southeast Iowa got decimated with pink slip after pink slip. No more commercial trailer production lines at Wabash National in Fort Madison. No more pens made at Sheaffer Pen in that town, either.

Alloy production for the steel and automobile industries ceased at Keokuk Ferro-Sil. Bus manufacturing halted at Blue Bird Midwest in Mount Pleasant. West Burlington watched the locomotive repairs end for Burlington Northern Santa Fe. And automobile battery-making was no longer part of Exide in Burlington.

Those shutdowns erased nearly 2,000 manufacturing jobs.

They were just a fraction, though, of the nearly 100,000 positions in that sector that left Iowa's 300,000 manufacturing workforce that the state had in 2000.

(Numbers courtesy: The Hawk Eye in Burlington, April 26, 2018)

Add all of those up and Iowa has experienced substantial changes in its demographics, workforce, lifestyle and anxiety. And those represent only the changes that have already happened. What happens when driverless vehicles replace the people who make a living driving taxis, semis, school buses and other delivery vehicles? Or what about when companies don't need to pay cashiers because all of the purchases you make in a store just debit from your account through your smartphone? Think about the robots replacing assembly line workers.

And too many parts of the state still deal with subpar broadband, further limiting opportunities. So even if rural residents want to take part in the new economy, they may not have access to the sufficient fast-speed connection that they need.

A generation of workers (likely two or three) already is thinking about all of these changes. And worrying. How will they make a living? How will their kids and grandkids make a living? Who will buy the house when grandma and grandpa have to move?

Researchers are paying close attention to those unanswered questions.

"This 'Make America Great Again'" (Trump's theme) united all of these different dissatisfied sects," said Dr. Wayne Steger, a political science professor at DePaul University.

Steger has more than just a passing interest in what has happened to the west of his Chicago office.

"If you build it, he will come."

Remember that line? Actor Kevin Costner's character, an Iowa farmer named Ray Kinsella in the 1989 movie "Field of Dreams" (filmed in the northeast Iowa town of Dyersville), heard a mysterious voice from his fictional cornfield whispering that line. That voice urged him to get rid of his crop and build a baseball field instead. The idea was that well-known professional baseball players from yesteryear could emerge and once again demonstrate their skills and love for the game. He built it. The players came.

"If you build it, he will come."

Fast forward to 2016. Many factors had formed the foundation slowly over decades for a populist to win over those living near Iowa's sacred corn fields. Trump didn't need any mysterious voice to lead his message to Steger's hometown of Dyersville and numerous other smaller towns.

"If you build it, he will come."

Trump was ready to play ball. "There's an economic and cultural transformation," Steger said of what he has studied in the rural parts of Iowa and other similar states, "The last time we had a populist wave was the industrial revolution."

A key difference, though: the cotton gins and steam engines of the late 18th Century and early 19th Century that dramatically increased production also substantially raised wages. The automation of the late 20th Century and early 21st Century replaced workers, eliminated jobs and limited wages.

So the economics of those periods weren't exactly the same. But the yearning for populism is the constant, it would seem.

"Rural areas aren't coming back," Steger lamented.

Enter populism, the newest version.

Wayne Steger Bio

Dyersville native
BA, History & Political Science, Iowa State University
PhD, Political Science, University of Iowa
Instructor, Iowa State University
Asst. Professor, Marquette University
Professor of Political Science, DePaul University since 1996
(former department chair)

To be clear, Steger wasn't saying rural areas can't ever improve. He hasn't given up on his small town background. But Steger is a researcher for the past three decades, after all. So he has to put aside sentimentality and emotions. Steger has to think about the facts. That means focusing on that economic and cultural transformation he cited.

First, that economic change.

"Really because of automation," Steger has concluded, "Don't need as many workers. Just don't have those diversified family farms like they used to."

Those smaller, family farms learned they couldn't compete with corporate farms that, aided by massive investments in automation, could outproduce their efforts at less cost (after that initial influx of cash to buy the new technology). So those family farms that survived often chose to specialize in one area...dairy, corn, beans, whatever...in the hopes to up their production in their own--limited--way.

Many found out that they just couldn't do it. They sold out or went under, as those statistics I cited earlier reflect (nearly 60% of Iowa farms vanished since 1950).

Steger underscored it like this, "The bottom line is far fewer people in rural areas making a living out of it...don't have near the amount of people working in crop services...so rural America has really been impacted adversely."

Fewer farmers mean a crushing ripple effect in the region. Fewer customers left to support the local car dealer. Fewer people who need to buy gas, meals and clothes or find services at the community bank, tax preparer's office or repair shop.

Churches, schools and government services don't get the financial contributions they once did. One by one, most everything in the area contracts or closes altogether.

What remains for the older people who have spent their entire lives there while many others leave for better opportunities?

"A great deal of discontent," Steger said.

Then, there is the less obvious side of this transformational shift: cultural.

"It's related to the economics." Steger reminded me, "...a lot's been focused on immigration but I think that's secondary. High paying jobs are in technology and finances, which most people don't realize is a much higher sector of American employment. None of that is locating in these small towns."

With that in mind, here is where the cultural changes develop.

"Tech firms aren't, for the most part, locating in Sioux City," Steger said (and he wasn't picking on northwest Iowa's largest city of 83,000, which is larger than every other city in the state except for Des Moines, Cedar Rapids and Davenport.)

"They (tech firms) are locating on the coasts and the large urban areas," Steger explained, "The new economy jobs aren't where the old rural jobs were."

And rural students want their share of those new economy jobs. So they go off to universities, which don't tend to be in those smaller towns. And once they go to those larger college towns (Des Moines, Ames, Iowa City, Cedar Falls--not all huge towns but larger than most other Iowan towns), they get accustomed to the amenities like larger dating pools, new social circles, more available entertainment options, sports, music, restaurants, etc.

It is a new experience. "They are being exposed to more cosmopolitan views...more accepting of diversity, gender, lifestyles...not like their families back home," Steger said.

And, yes, he realizes that isn't true for every student or every family. But it is for enough of them to make a difference.

"Traditional values" versus "cosmopolitan values" as Steger describes it. "So we are getting a huge rural-urban divide," Steger said.

What the college students experience in their college towns is frequently not what they experience when they go back home to visit family. Some of the students find they more closely align with what they found at college, so they choose to live in a similar place after studies conclude. Others just follow wherever a new job takes them. In either case, it adds to the shrinking rural landscape and takes away from those small towns' futures.

Steger mentioned immigration earlier and downplayed its significance, to a degree, in Trump's rural appeal. But he does acknowledge that immigration plays a role for those living in rural communities. "Immigration... does matter. You look at where Trump did really well," Steger said, "It's areas that are really white (Most of Iowa is really white but rural areas are typically whiter than urban areas).

Vermont Senator Bernie Sanders, the Democratic Socialist presidential candidate in 2016, did well with whites, too, Steger points out. But those were the "progressive whites," he said. Trump dominated with the "religious whites."

And many of the latter populate rural Iowa. Some of their communities--most of them losing population, especially with whites--experienced what little growth they have thanks to immigrants, largely Hispanic and Latino.

But some of those white residents aren't sure what to make of it. Some--to be sure--have made it clear that they don't want brown-skinned people moving into town. "White national/white pride people," Steger would classify them.

Those people simply want their towns to stay white. Racists. Not sure what else you could call them, whether they acknowledge their racist feelings or not.

Others aren't racists. They are just unaware of other cultures. They don't understand their new neighbors' language, clothes, music or day-to-day lives.

Still others see jobs disappearing and immigrants taking some of the positions that remain. Those rural Iowans get territorial, possessive and fearful that the next job opening will go to the newcomer, not to themselves, friend or family member, especially when the immigrant will be willing (or forced by necessity) to work for less money.

So when Trump talks to those rural Iowans with promises of "building a (border) wall" or stopping "those animals" (members of the especially violent and inhumane MS-13 gang that frequently have Central American roots...terrorizing, torturing and murdering innocent people), he finds an audience eager to listen.

They are especially willing to hear, too, when Trump adds to criticisms that other Republicans were saying about Democrats. "Republicans have painted the Democrats as latte-sipping liberals, more interested in supporting Muslims than Americans," Steger said, "That stereotype has resonated."

Especially in rural Iowa. Trump knows his audience. And he knows how to play to them.

And Steger knows that Trump's ability to connect with the politically disconnected gives the professor plenty to research and discuss in the classroom. He said, "In a highly-polarized world, he was better at doing that than anyone."

That connection kept Yvonne Brandt and Connie Whitaker listening back in that crowd in Clive.

Trump offered plenty for those two friends and something for most everyone else in his sales pitch to Iowans on that day. "The White House will become the 'People's House,'" he told them, "We will tackle and fix the problems that have gone unsolved for years."

Trump followed that with a list of pledges that read like a Christmas wish list for the starry-eyed in the room, like idealistic youngsters the night before St. Nick comes down the chimney.

"We are going to fix our crumbling infrastructure, renegotiate our disastrous trade deals, free children from failing government schools, eliminate government waste, and create a fair, simple and efficient tax code that adds millions of new jobs. Prosperity will rise, poverty will recede and wages will finally begin to grow. And they will grow rapidly. This is a campaign about big ideas designed to help everyday people," Trump laid out.

Wow. Iowans would be able to drive down better roads, in better cars because they would make more money, work more because other countries will buy more U.S. goods, send their kids to better schools and they would pay less in taxes because the government was more efficient and less regulated and freed up because there would be fewer poor people. And it would happen fast. Thanks, Santa Trump!

But there was something else that Trump delivered that day and numerous days that followed that proved to be more important to his loyalists: he would have their back.

"The way that he cozies up to white supremacists, makes racist attacks, calls women 'pigs,' mocks people with disabilities. You can't make this up. He wants to round up and deport 16 million people, calls our military a disaster. And every day he says something else which I find so personally offensive, but also dangerous."

Hillary Clinton, September 9, 2016, New York City

If only Hillary Clinton would have just stopped there. She could have made her point to voters that Trump's words offend various groups of people and embolden those with hatred. If only...

"You could put half of Trump's supporters into what I call the basket of deplorables. Right? The racist, sexist, homophobic, xenophobic, Islamophobic...you name it. And, unfortunately, there are people like that. And he has lifted them up," she said.

Uh oh. "The basket of deplorables." Clinton already had a sizeable chunk of the population that was fed up with all those years of the Clintons' drama--Bill's infidelity and eventual impeachment for lying about his affair with a White House intern, the questionable business dealings, Hillary's 2008 presidential campaign that critics felt was wrought with arrogance and a sense of entitlement for the throne--just to name several.

But, "the basket of deplorables" gave people one more reason not to like her or support her (never mind the fact that Trump made name-calling and ridiculing a daily occurrence). Clinton's cutdown gave Trump a simple line to repeat for the cameras to show voters what Clinton truly thought of them. She thought that she was better than they were, was his implication.

"While my opponent slanders you as deplorable and irredeemable, I call you hard working American patriots who love your country and want a better future for all of our people," Trump told that Clive crowd.

Brandt and Whitaker laughed off Clinton's cutdown but it also gave them one more serious reminder that Washington, D.C. doesn't need another longtime politician--who may or may not really care about their needs--especially another politician named Clinton.

"I laughed," Whitaker chuckled when she thought about what Clinton had called Trump's followers. After all, if half of Trump's supporters were among that "basket of deplorables," then either she or Brandt must be deplorable, per Clinton's declaration.

"I'm proud to be a deplorable!" Brandt beamed, "I'm glad that I'm a deplorable."

121

Come on, I implored, these two seemingly well-spoken, modest, dare I say "Iowa Nice" women weren't offended that someone called them deplorable?

"Not at all," Brandt said, "That's *her* (Clinton). She doesn't know when to stop."

Neither woman denied that Trump routinely mocked others and used language that made them uncomfortable. But they both expected Trump to take his rhetoric down a notch...or two...or three...as he got comfortable in office.

That didn't happen.

Gayle Goble, of Des Moines, is just fine with that. Goble didn't stand in the crowd with Brandt and Whitaker in Clive that day. But she joined them in their frustration with the Republican Party and more specifically, the actions--or lack of actions--by its leaders.

She was upset, quite upset and that is saying something based on her past.

Goble had served her party in a variety of ways: Jack Kemp's presidential campaign in 1988, Lamar Alexander's presidential campaign in 1996, the Republican Party of Iowa, legislative secretary for State Representative Barry Brauns of Muscatine, staffer for U.S. Senator Chuck Grassley and Senior Journal Editor for the Iowa House of Representatives. That alone represents four decades of dedication to Republicans.

But over time, Goble's doubts grew more frequent and her dissatisfaction steadily rose over the direction of the party to which she had devoted so much of her life.

"Each year I became more and more frustrated with watching the Republican Party campaign one way and leading in the opposite direction," Goble emailed me. "They continue to spend over one third of the Iowa budget on a failing education system that has purposely dumbed down the country.

I've been around long enough to see the reason for killing unborn babies from a way to stop child abuse (by killing?), to population control, and now, sold as a right to kill based on choice or inconvenience for any reason, during all 9 months. We've also seen the campaign cash raised from the killing and selling off of baby parts. The golden goose for the Democrat Party."

The failure to change the mission of public education and stop abortions were just a few of her grievances. Her Christian faith helped align her more closely with Texas Senator Ted Cruz in the 2016 Iowa Caucuses. And she acknowledges that she didn't know what to make of a President Trump, after having envisioned a President Cruz would be a better fit.

"I wasn't sure what Trump would actually do when elected, but the more he spoke, the more I liked him," Goble emailed. "I especially like his straightforward, tell it like it is, way of communicating."

Trump in front of a microphone is far different than those state lawmakers she watched for more than a decade in the Iowa Statehouse. "After having listened to countless hours of representatives droning on and on about their intentions in the House and then seeing the results, I have little time for double-speak and pretty words that are used to invoke emotion but have no real bearing on the problem that needs fixing," Goble emailed.

"I've always suspected that the lobby and major donors have been running the politics in Iowa for years. The issues are decided and the money divided, tax credits awarded, before every session starts. Trump tells us what he plans to do and then DOES IT! That's what makes him unique. I love the tweets!! He is so far ahead of the Democrats and loves to mess with you people in the press, whom have gone out of your way to continually cast him in a negative light. Pointing out nit-picky things and ignoring his accomplishments," she wrote.

Goble, like Trump, seems to despise much of the mainstream media, the Democrats, some top law enforcement in the federal government and establishment Republicans.

She wrote, "The Russian collusion scam isn't working as hoped by both the media, the Democrats and the treasonous FBI (Former Director James Comey), CIA (former Director John Brennan) and National Security (Former Director James Clapper), not to mention the Bush league RINOs ("Republicans In Name Only"--the pejorative term conservatives use to imply that some Republicans aren't conservative enough).

Goble nailed what helped fuel Trump's rise--a rise that seemingly baffled so many politicos, prognosticators and media (especially those who rarely venture out of their bubble, outside of an occasional day or two where they parachute into Iowa and make oversimplified, generalizations of their quick take on the electorate).

She wrote, "I believe the anger of the American people over how our country has been run by both Democrats and Republicans wasn't realized and was downright ignored for years. Trump won because the American people are tired of being ignored by the elite and want action. We want our money back as we see how much of it is wasted and used for political purposes rather than for the good of the people. We've dangerously opened our borders and seen corruption in the highest places for years with nothing being done. Trump is cleaning the swamp and I sure appreciate that."

Goble's comments borrowed one of the phrases that Trump used as a candidate: "Drain the swamp."

I have never quite understood what Trump considered the swamp or how he was draining it. But it was a line that resonated with supporters. Whatever it meant.

Goble's words echoed what other Trump supporters told me. Trump's rise to power was a wakeup call--or at least should be a wakeup call--for politicians and the media, about the importance of listening to people.

Now, will Goble feel the same way as the dreaded media tally up how Trump has spent their money...the countless millions spent on his security as he spent most every weekend of the first year of his presidency traveling to one of his properties in Florida or elsewhere? Will loyalists discount it as just "fake news?" Or is this just the cost of doing business for a non-politician who does things his way? That what else he accomplishes is far more significant?

Goble, Whitaker and Brandt all seem willing to trust that Trump will indeed bring tremendous improvement to the country, regardless of how he does it.

CHAPTER 8

TOUGH LOVE

"Utterly amoral."

Iowa Caucus 2016 winner Ted Cruz on what he thought of Donald Trump, on May 3, 2016.

Photo by Dave Price

G ayle Goble leans on her Christian upbringing when politicians stretch her patience and faith in humanity. So does Bob Vander Plaats, one of Iowa's most well-known social conservative leaders. Donald Trump tests him. Frequently.

"Wow!"

Vander Plaats used that word several times during our conversation as he looked back on Trump's first two years in office. It just seemed like the best word to sum up what he was thinking in a variety of ways.

Bob Vander Plaats Bio

Former teacher, coach, high school principal
President of Opportunities Unlimited
President of MVP Leadership, Inc.
Candidate for governor: 2002, 2006, 2010
Nominee for lieutenant governor: 2006
2015-2016: National Co-Chair, Ted Cruz for President
President/CEO, The Family Leader

Vander Plaats wasn't publicly a **#NeverTrump** (the social media hashtag designation for Republicans who would support almost any other Republican in the world rather than Trump) person during the 2016 election.

And in 2018, Vander Plaats still didn't think of himself as anti-Trump. Admittedly, he didn't want Trump to become president, at least not nearly as much as he wanted Texas Senator Ted Cruz to win the job. Cruz much better represented his view on abortion, marriage, faith and government, Vander Plaats surmised. And Vander Plaats put in a good bit of work to try and get Cruz to the White House.

Leading up to the 2016 campaign, Vander Plaats held numerous meetings with Christian conservative activists, pastors and political leaders in Des Moines, New York, Denver and elsewhere. Electing Trump as the next president was never the game plan.

"We go through our (Iowa) Caucus. We are all divided," Vander Plaats said of the activists' actions in the past, "Then we end up with John McCain (the 2008 Republican presidential nominee) or Mitt Romney (the 2012 Republican presidential nominee)...and we lose."

Vander Plaats didn't want to lose with another Republican nominee who refused to champion Christian conservative values. He wanted a Republican who would push hard for progress. And, of course, he wanted a Republican who would become president.

He wanted Cruz, as did many of the others. They just had to figure it out first. "We weighed candidates from the message to the messenger to the money to the company they were keeping...the campaign managers, the people who had influence on them," Vander Plaats talked of their brainstorming gatherings, "We had transparent, unvarnished conversations."

"He (Cruz) basically threaded the needle of all the things that were important. Plus, he had the resources," Vander Plaats said after adding it all up.

Vander Plaats backed former Arkansas Governor Mike Huckabee in 2008. Huckabee won the Iowa Caucuses. He backed former Pennsylvania Rick Santorum in 2012. Santorum won the Iowa Caucuses. Notice a theme here? Vander Plaats knows how to pick an Iowa Caucus winner.

The situation got tricky, though, in 2016 because both Huckabee and Santorum ran for president. Both would need to do well in the Caucuses, if they had any shot at being a serious contender for the nomination.

The political reality was that each one--since each had won a previous Caucus--would need to win the Caucus in 2016, too. Anything else but victory would be a disappointment. Sky high expectations. Vander Plaats had his doubts and even if he didn't, he would have had to choose one over the other. That would be difficult. Very difficult.

As it turned out, Vander Plaats didn't have to have the uncomfortable conversation telling Santorum, "Hey, sorry Rick, I'm going with Mike this time" or, "I like you, Mike, but Rick is my choice this time."

No, this time he would pass on both after witnessing both of those candidates in their winning Iowa Caucus campaigns of the past then later fall short in the primary process.

"Huckabee or Santorum could win Iowa (in 2016)," Vander Plaats figured in a best case scenario for either man...best case, "But we weren't sure beyond."

And the "beyond" was what mattered to Vander Plaats and the rest of his group of Christian conservative leaders. They wanted to find one of their own who could not just win Iowa but also win the White House.

Cruz could do both, they figured. So they decided to go all out for Cruz. Drama ensued. When the polls showed that the 2016 Caucuses would come down to a battle between Cruz and Trump, tensions rose. Cruz and Trump bickered back and forth during campaign rallies and on social media. It got ugly.

Trump mockingly nicknamed Cruz "Lyin' Ted," offered a conspiracy theory that Cruz's father, Rafael, was involved in the assassination of President John F. Kennedy and also retweeted an unflattering meme of Cruz's wife, Heidi.

"Serial philanderer." "Pathological liar." "Utterly amoral." Those were some of the choice words Cruz had in response for Trump. And specifically in response to Trump's attacks on his wife, Cruz responded, "Donald, you're a sniveling coward. Leave Heidi the hell alone!"

Vander Plaats, because of his loyalty to Cruz, found himself in the crosshairs. Trump accused him of a being a freeloader and mooch, accusing Vander Plaats of asking to stay at Trump properties for free. Vander Plaats fired back that it was Trump who insisted that Vander Plaats and his family stay in the Trump hotels, that they should not pay and that Trump was essentially trying to buy his endorsement with the free lodging.

It wasn't pretty.

Cruz ended up narrowly winning the Iowa Caucuses. Trump finished second. The rivalry continued until Cruz ultimately conceded the race four months later and dropped out.

Vander Plaats' concerns didn't end there, just because the Republican race had finished. Trump had given him too much reason for concern in the months that led up to that point.

Vander Plaats had considered Trump to be a "mixed bag" when it came to some of those issues that Vander Plaats promoted. He found Trump inconsistent over the years on abortion and marriage, just to name a few.

And it wasn't just discomfort that Vander Plaats had with Trump on crucial issues, it was also about Trump's behavior that Vander Plaats had witnessed leading up to the nomination.

He couldn't block out what he experienced watching Trump on stage at his organization's Family Leadership Summit on the Iowa State University campus in Ames in July, 2015. (The organization sold 2,900 tickets for the event, by the way, again demonstrating how the 10 presidential candidates who attended viewed Vander Plaats' importance in Iowa Republican politics.)

That day also overflowed Vander Plaats' mixed bag of long-term concerns about Trump's core beliefs. Trump's words were to blame.

Here was Trump on Arizona Senator John McCain, the former presidential candidate and prisoner of war in Vietnam, whose captors savagely tortured him for months, nearly killed him and left him with permanent injuries:

"He's a war hero because he was captured. I like people that weren't captured, OK?"

Ugh.

Vander Plaats was among those who were outraged as Trump's comments drew audible gasps from people in the crowd and an even sharper firestorm of criticism from other candidates, military supporters and commentators across the country.

This added to it.

Here is how Trump answered on whether he seeks God's forgiveness for his sins and mistakes:

"I am not sure I have. I just go on and try to do a better job from there. I don't think so. I think if I do something wrong, I think, I just try and make it right. I don't bring God into that picture. I don't."

UGH! That response shocked Vander Plaats and other Christian conservatives in the audience. Vander Plaats' dismay only increased when Trump added that he does take part in communion at church, though, and explained it this way:

"When I drink my little wine...which is about the only wine I drink...and have my little cracker, I guess that is a form of asking for forgiveness. And I do that as often as possible because I feel cleansed. I think in terms of 'let's go on and let's make it right.'"

Ugh isn't a strong enough word now as Vander Plaats sat in disbelief as Trump's words sunk in. Vander Plaats recalled thinking those words would sink Trump.

"Self-inflicted," Vander Plaats said, "We thought he was done."

Of course, it turned out that Trump wasn't done...far from it. And Trump wasn't done testing Vander Plaats' patience...far from that, too.

But Vander Plaats--while he couldn't forget about all of those incendiary, insensitive remarks--knew that he had to make peace with what happened. He really didn't want Hillary Clinton to become president.

So, what could he do? He would be Trump's friend, he determined, but be a realistic friend. "I told him that I'm not going to endorse him (following the 2016 Iowa Caucuses, when it later became evident that Trump would be the Republican presidential nominee)," Vander Plaats said he told the future president in a private meeting in Trump's office in New York.

It is difficult to determine what kind of value Vander Plaats' endorsement would have had. Perhaps it could have calmed concerns that Iowa Evangelicals had about Trump's character. Or perhaps it wouldn't have really swayed many opinions.

Most of those reluctant to support Trump over moral unease may not have gone to the extreme of voting for Clinton. They might have been more likely to just not vote in the presidential election. I have no empirical data to back that up. That's just a guess.

Regardless, Vander Plaats said he told Trump that he wouldn't publicly support the future president. But Vander Plaats did have something else to offer.

"I promised that I am going to shoot straight with you," Vander Plaats said he mentioned to Trump in that conversation.

Vander Plaats has become politically astute over the years. He never found success as a candidate. Three times he ran for governor and three times he failed to get the Republican Party's nomination. Vander Plaats later passed on opportunities to run for the U.S. Senate or House.

Instead, he has made The Family Leader relevant. Vander Plaats has learned what issues are important to his social conservative followers, and he knows which national leader may best espouse those issues.

He knows how to make The Family Leader front and center in the caucus conversation: host events; talk with candidates; speak with the media about those events and candidates. The Family Leader is the state's most prominent faith-first, politically conservative, activist organization that has become a must stop for any serious Republican presidential candidate who wants to compete in Iowa. And its awareness goes well beyond the political circles in Iowa. Social conservative circles pay attention, regardless of their borders. And they notice how the organization has morphed over the years.

As the gay rights movement grew in the mid-2000s, Vander Plaats initially became one of the most prominent, vocal opponents of it. He tried to champion the efforts to block same-sex marriage during his gubernatorial campaigns in 2006 and 2010. "Let them vote!" he and his supporters would chant during rallies outside the Iowa Statehouse as they tried to encourage the legislature to allow Iowans to have the chance to vote on a constitutional amendment to guarantee marriage could only be between a man and a woman.

Those efforts failed.

Vander Plaats did, however, later successfully orchestrate a judicial purge like Iowa had never seen before. In 2010, a year after the Iowa Supreme Court legalized same-sex marriage, Vander Plaats (aided by money and support from the National Organization for Marriage) channeled social conservative outrage and ousted three of the state supreme court justices--Chief Justice Marsha Ternus, Michael Streit and David Baker--in what is traditionally an unremarkable retention vote.

All justices needed to get were more "yes" votes than "no" votes and they could serve another eight-year term on the state's highest court. It is normally quite routine. Justices don't raise money. They don't campaign. They just get retained. Not this time.

The efforts Vander Plaats helped lead blindsided same-sex marriage supporters and the court's backers. A hastily-organized and poorly-funded campaign to save the justices' jobs failed. The country took notice.

The movement elevated Vander Plaats as a crusader for "traditional marriage" and those with a more stringent, conservative biblical view of politics and life.

Trump was well aware of Vander Plaats' standing. Vander Plaats was well aware, though, too, of how complicated this "friendship" with Trump would be.

Sometimes, it got REALLY complicated, like when *The Washington Post* posted on October 7, 2016, a decade-old "Access Hollywood" video of Trump seemingly bragging to host Billy Bush (off camera and apparently not realizing that their microphones were still on) about his ability--because of his fame and fortune--to do whatever he wanted with women.

Trump: "Grab 'em by the pu**y. You can do anything."

Trump's video response late that night didn't calm Vander Plaats. Trump somehow managed to apologize, downplay the severity of the tape, rip the Clintons and promise to be a better man all in that 91-second video.
Here is the verbatim of that video:

"I've never said I'm a perfect person, nor pretended to be someone that I'm not. I've said and done things I regret, and the words released today on this more than a decade-old video are one of them.
Anyone who knows me knows these words don't reflect who I am. I said it. I was wrong. And I apologize. I've traveled the country talking about change for America, but my travels have also changed me. I've spent time with grieving mothers who've lost their children, laid-off workers whose jobs have gone to other countries, and people from all walks of life who just want a better future. I have gotten to know the great people of our country and I've been humbled by the faith they've placed in me. I pledge to be a better man tomorrow and will never, ever let you down.
Let's be honest. We're living in the real world. This is nothing more than a distraction from the important issues we're facing today. We are losing our jobs. We're less safe than we were eight years ago. And Washington is totally broken.
Hillary Clinton and her kind have run our country into the ground. I've said some foolish things, but there's a big difference between the words and actions of other people. Bill Clinton has actually abused women and Hillary has bullied, attacked, shamed and intimidated his victims.
We will discuss this more in the coming days. See you at the debate on Sunday."
Enough. That was it for Vander Plaats. Time to get out. And Vander Plaats said he told Trump that. No more.
"I told him to get out of the race. Pay attention to Melania (Trump's wife)," Vander Plaats said that he relayed to Trump, "Make sure that she's okay. This is about beating Hillary."
And then Vander Plaats said he added this, "Have Pence do it." (Replace Trump as the Republican presidential candidate, that is.)

This was only about three weeks before the election. And the suggestion to end his candidacy apparently wasn't what Trump wanted to hear from Vander Plaats.

"Obviously, that didn't go over well," Vander Plaats said, without elaborating.

Trump stayed in. Vander Plaats tried to stay positive in the hopes that Trump would get better. Trump himself may not have felt it important enough to seek forgiveness from God (as he confessed at that Family Leadership Summit in Ames). But Vander Plaats knew the importance of forgiveness. So he decided to forgive Trump, even if Trump didn't ask him for forgiveness either.

Forgive Trump. Don't endorse Trump's behavior, though. That was Vander Plaats' decision.

But back to that series of "Wow!" where Vander Plaats and I began our conversation…they were complicated and dependent on the particular situation.

"Wow!" Vander Plaats said of the positive actions that have happened since Trump became president.

Trump's conservative nominee to fill the vacancy, Neil Gorsuch.

The seat had been vacant for a record 422 days after U.S. Supreme Court Justice Antonin Scalia died unexpectedly on February 13, 2016. The previous record was 389 days, the period between Abe Fortas' resignation on May 14, 1969 and Harry Blackmun's first day on the job of June 9, 1970.

(*Source: Alana Abramson, Time Magazine, April 7, 2017*)

Iowa Senator Chuck Grassley, the chairman of the Judiciary Committee at the time, insisted the seat remain unfilled until Trump became president, so that Democratic President Barack Obama couldn't put someone of his own choosing and potentially influence the direction of the court for decades. (That decision infuriated Democrats who pointed out how Grassley had made the process even more political than it already was).

Appointed numerous other conservative judges to federal courts across the country and at a faster rate than most presidents.

Aided by Senate Grassley's judiciary committee. And, remember, those are lifetime appointments, so that could be a lasting part of the Trump legacy.

Trump tax cuts that slashed rates for businesses and reduced them for nearly every individual tax bracket.

Barring some super-charged economic growth, the tax cuts will likely cause the federal debt to escalate to an even more unfathomable amount. That aside, millions of Americans could see higher take home pay although some will pay higher taxes depending on their situation. The stock market loved it, initially. The Dow soared 25 percent in 2017.

Although, investors soured on Trump's chaotic leadership, trade war with China and other countries, inflation worries, rising interest rates and workforce shortages in 2018. The Dow dropped 5.6 percent, the biggest drop in a decade, despite those massive tax cuts.

Moving the U.S. Embassy in Israel from Tel Aviv to Jerusalem.

Other U.S. presidents have floated that option for decades. All previously failed to move forward, as the decision proved problematic. The Middle East is always unstable in the seemingly eternal quest to determine whether the Jews or Palestinians should get their rightful claim to the Holy Land. The concept of moving the embassy further inflamed tensions. But Trump sided with Israel and made the move.

Reinstituting the "gag rule" globally, which bans federal funds from going to international family planning efforts that provide abortion services.

And this is from a president who had professed numerous views over the past few decades about whether he supports or opposes abortion.

Add those all up and Trump deserved a "Wow!" from Vander Plaats. "That was huge," he added.

"There are a lot of things that we were hoping (President) George W. Bush would have done," Vander Plaats said, "When Trump was elected, we were thinking just thinking of getting *some* of these things."

Instead, they got them *all*. Hence, the "Wow!"

But, then there is what Vander Plaats referred to as "the other Wow!"

"Did you really tweet that?" Vander Plaats found himself on too many occasions silently asking Trump after yet another presidential, controversial outburst on Twitter.

"Retweeting" a video that makes it appear that Trump is punching a character whose head has been replaced with a CNN logo.

His loyalists loved it. Journalists and other critics condemned it, charging that Trump could incite violence against the media or at least put the thought of committing such an act into people's minds.

The original video came from the days Trump, years ago, used to appear on events like "WrestleMania." That was long before CNN became one of the president's favorite punching bags by decrying the organization as "fake news" and an opposition to his efforts. Of course, the wrestling appearances Trump would appear in from time to time were, without a doubt, fake. Admittedly, my Dad, brother and I used to watch it every Sunday morning from St. Louis when we were growing up and thought it was real. At least my brother and I thought it was real.

"Little Rocket Man"

That was President Trump's derogatory nickname for North Korea's diminutive dictator Kim Jong Un, after that country launched a series of ballistic missiles to try to show the world that it could cause harm to others outside its borders.

Donald J. Trump ✔
@realDonaldTrump

Following ⌄

Just heard Foreign Minister of North Korea speak at U.N. If he echoes thoughts of Little Rocket Man, they won't be around much longer!

10:08 PM - 23 Sep 2017

34,962 Retweets 129,381 Likes

♡ 48K   ↻ 35K   ♡ 129K

"Total hoax"

Trump repeatedly, on social media and to reporters, ripped former F.B.I. Director Robert Mueller's work as special prosecutor for the U.S. Department of Justice into Russia's interference with the 2016 U.S. election.

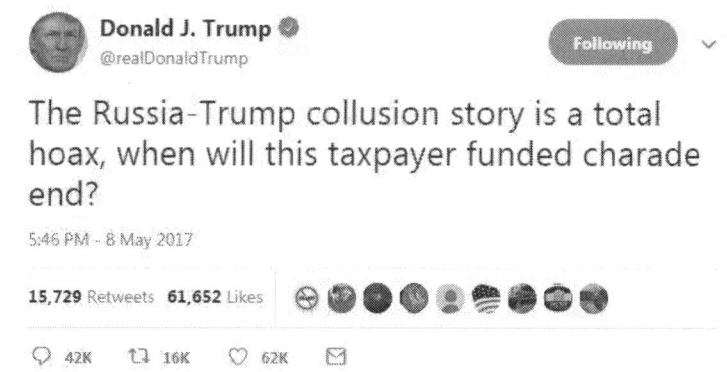

Vander Plaats doesn't know what to make of the Russian collusion investigation. Did Trump's campaign (or Trump personally?) work with the Russians to defeat Clinton in the 2016 presidential election? Trump numerous times denied he was part of any collusion with Russia.

"There's certain instability. There's smoke," Vander Plaats is left wondering, though, "Is there fire?"

The uncertainty with the collusion cloud hanging over the country, along with a daily dose of presidential pandemonium with Trump's leadership style had everyone searching for calm, Vander Plaats said. "The country's on edge. I would not characterize it whether you're a Republican, Democrat, conservative," Vander Plaats told me, "I don't think anybody's saying that we have nothing to worry about. People, by their very nature, are just on edge."

On edge, perhaps. But some had clearly not lost faith in the president. And those included to other faith-first, Iowa Republican voices: Steve Scheffler and Tamara Scott.

Scheffler and Scott are Iowa's National Republican Committee members. They are Iowa's two activists who represent the state in party functions and, perhaps, most importantly, make sure the state's caucuses remain the first in the presidential selection process as they meet with party officials from other states.

Both are socially conservative Republicans of deep religious spirituality. Both have remained loyal to Trump. Their loyalty seems to remain constant and also confounds some who question how these two can continue to support Trump...a leader who is on his third marriage, has faced allegations of adultery, accusations of affairs with a porn star and others, plus charges that he is a serial liar.

To be clear, though, these two never have claimed Trump is a perfect person. Who is, right? But their faith in Trump reflects their public patriotism for their country, their party and their belief that Trump, despite his flaws will push the country past empty political promises and instead toward true political promise.

Scheffler and Scott have full faith in the president.

"How blessed we are and what a God send (sic) Donald Trump was elected!" Scheffler posted on his Facebook page on June 8, 2018.

"Without a doubt in my mind, with his election, God is giving us as a nation one more opportunity to get our act together!" Scheffler continued, "Christians need to step up to the plate and sacrifice in giving sweat, blood and tears in our quest to defend religious and personal freedoms!"

Scheffler's line reminded me of what those two best friends, Yvonne Brandt and Connie Whitaker, had told me during that rally in Clive before the 2016 election about this being "America's last hope."

"Last hope." "One more opportunity." That's how fatalistic some of Trump's followers saw what had been happening in this country. Gays and lesbians marrying. Abortions continuing. More unmarried women having babies. Christianity no longer the centerpiece of people's priorities. America's leadership in the world questioned.

Major, deep concerns with the direction of the country and its people.

Here is how Scott explains to me what she hears in her conversations with fellow social conservatives on their view of what is happening in the country:

> **"What do you think about the media?**
>   *They grumble.*
> **What do you think about Congress?**
>   *They groan.*
> **What do you think about this president?**

They cheer."

Scott talks with people often...at group luncheons, county party dinners, her internet/radio talk show and through her work as state director for the Concerned Women for America (an organization that supports abortion alternatives, marriage between a man and a woman, Israel and opposes obscenity, prostitution, pornography and sex trafficking).

She knows Trump's poll numbers could be higher but remains convinced that his followers stick with the president. "We all like to have great poll numbers," Scott concedes but doesn't seem worried that Trump's performance has only allowed him to maintain most of the support that got him elected and not built upon it as he works toward a potential second term.

"We always need to be on guard and ready," she says, urging followers to continue to be prepared for criticisms from Democrats, #NeverTrump Republicans and the dreaded "mainstream media," which she frequently castigates for failing to sufficiently relay the true concerns and beliefs of her fellow social conservatives.

She maintains that those forces will work to further erode Trump's support and try to block him from accomplishing the necessary change the country needs.

That loyalty aside, that doesn't mean that Scott approves of everything Trump does and the way he does and says things. But her criticism of Trump's aggressive, personal demeanor comes with a caveat.

That caveat is that she doesn't know what it is like for Trump to be Trump.

"I've not played in Donald Trump's arena," she told me, "I've not been on that level of...the art of the deal."

And because of that, both of her criticisms that followed each came with a..."but..."

"Obviously, we always want to be civil and respectful," Scott said, "*But* it's a nasty world out there."

Be civil, BUT the world isn't civil.

And she followed with this, "Is it how I would tell my children to behave? Maybe not."

Now, the "but..."

"*But*, you know, look at Winston Churchill (Britain's former prime minister). He was bold. He was brash. And sometimes, he was ill-behaved," Scott said with a smile.

Is Trump the statesman that Churchill was during World War II? No, not in the same way. However, Churchill was fighting for his nation's survival. Trump, in his own way, was arguing with his rhetoric that he was, too.

Scott also adds, though, that Trump is still a work in progress and she remains optimistic that he can improve. "I think we are going to reform the man," Scott said, "I think he has grown and we are going to see good things out of him."

Vander Plaats, the most critical of these three Iowa social conservatives, also shares optimism that Trump's best days in office remain ahead.

"Trump, like all of us, is still on a religious journey...he just may have further to go," Vander Plaats figures.

However, Vander Plaats recognizes that Trump may feel a sense of obligation to those supporters of the Christian faith, including those Iowans who had initial and serious reservations about him earlier. "He (Trump) fully recognized the movement of the Christian conservatives and he saw them as good, decent people," Vander Plaats believes, "He can look back at it (the support of those Christian conservatives for his presidential campaign) and say that if it weren't for that movement...for the church, 'I may not have won.'"

Vander Plaats concluded, "I think he is paying back for that."

CHAPTER 9

ALL IN THE FAMILY

"Yes."

One very powerful word from Iowa Governor Terry Branstad when he told me that he wanted Iowa caucusgoers to stop Texas Senator Ted Cruz and support Donald Trump.

Prairie Meadows Casino in Altoona, Iowa on January 19, 2016.

Photo by Dave Price

B ob Vander Plaats hopes that Donald Trump is on some kind of religious transformation, albeit ever so slowly. Terry Branstad--the man who beat Vander Plaats in the 2010 Republican primary for governor--already underwent a *political* transformation and ended up in Beijing because of it.

Terry Branstad Bio

1969-1971: Served in the U.S. Army in the Vietnam War
1973-1979: State Representative
1978-1983: Lt. Governor of Iowa
1983-1999: Governor of Iowa
2003-2009: President of Des Moines University
2011-2017: Governor of Iowa
2017: Sworn in as U.S. Ambassador to China

Branstad is a political icon in the state. He served two different stints as governor, holds the record as the nation's longest-serving governor ever (22 years) and has spent a half century in public service.

Nearly all of that time in public service involves politics, aside from his time in the Army. I should probably count his time as president of Des Moines University as "politics," as well, since most people who have worked in academia will say politics can play a big part of the day-to-day.

That aside, Branstad is intensely loyal to his Republican Party but he is even more dedicated to his native state of Iowa.

While he was still Iowa's governor in 2015, Branstad--ever the Iowa cheerleader for his birth state which hosts the nation's first-in-the-nation caucuses--scoffed at the notion of Trump becoming president.

"I don't think it's likely that he will be the nominee in the end. Polls at this point in time tend to reflect name recognition. And, obviously, he is a TV personality who has a lot of recognition."

Governor Terry Branstad, July 28, 2015

Branstad chuckled when he looked back at that initial skepticism, "Yeah!"

I sat down with him on December 21, 2016, more than a month after Iowans overwhelmingly decided that Trump should be their next president. Branstad's hesitation in 2015 to take Trump's campaign more seriously had a lot to do with the travel schedule. Trump simply wasn't visiting Iowa like Branstad always recommends (demands) that candidates do. Branstad, one of the most prominent Iowa politicians in the modern age, simply wasn't buying this reality TV star-turned presidential candidate.

Branstad never really expected Trump to run in the first place. Branstad closely follows politics, both in his native state and across the country. He knew Trump had talked in previous cycles of running and then never followed through. So when Branstad first heard about the possibility of Trump running in 2016, he mostly dismissed it.

Another factor was that Trump certainly wasn't talking like successful candidates Branstad had watched come through Iowa--George W. Bush and Ronald Reagan--just to name a few.

With Trump it was way too much controversy, way too few specifics on what Trump would actually accomplish and how he would accomplish them.

Perhaps, it was also easier for Branstad to dismiss, too, because Trump didn't offer the resume that typically attracted Branstad's early interest. "I'm partial to governors," Branstad offered.

Governors had to balance a budget, make far-reaching decisions and work with the legislature, just to name a few.

Branstad had demonstrated his affinity for governors in a very strong and public way just as he was getting started in politics. He supported a governor over a president.

Ronald Reagan, the actor-turned-politician, had been the Republican governor of California. Branstad, when he was a state representative, backed Reagan in the 1976 Iowa Caucuses, instead of the Republican President Gerald Ford. Ford hadn't previously served as a governor but had been a 12-term Michigan Congressman.

Branstad sensed that Reagan could bring a charismatic leader to the White House, who wouldn't be connected to scandal like Ford. Ford had ascended to the presidency after Richard Nixon resigned in disgrace following one of the country's darkest and deepest political scandals, Watergate.

Ford narrowly beat Reagan in the primary but then got defeated by Democrat Jimmy Carter, a former Georgia governor, in the presidential election that November.

That election further cemented Branstad's belief that serving first as a governor best prepared a politician for the White House.

Years later, after Branstad was on his way to becoming the longest-serving governor in the history of the country, he looked at the 2016 landscape and figured a governor would be the party's best chance to take the White House back from the Democrats after the two terms of Barack Obama, a former U.S. Senator.

Branstad knew that there would be plenty of Republican presidential candidates in 2016 with previous experience as governor.

Jeb Bush: Florida
Chris Christie: New Jersey
Mike Huckabee: Arkansas
Bobby Jindal: Louisiana
John Kasich: Ohio
George Pataki: New York
Rick Perry: Texas
Scott Walker: Wisconsin

It was quite a list. And while Branstad was partial to those governors' professional backgrounds, he was also partial to a few of them personally. "I like Huckabee," Branstad volunteered of the former Arkansas governor, who had impressed him so much during his winning 2008 Iowa Caucus campaign.

Then there was Christie, the New Jersey governor. I had suspected Branstad of having a professional "man crush" on the outspoken East Coast moderate. (Branstad, of course, would never phrase his admiration that way). But Christie had worked in the past to curry favor with Branstad, and Branstad seemed fond of Christie's blunt style. There was some loyalty here, too.

Branstad had been running for re-election in 2014 and Christie was the chairman of the Republican Governors Association, the partisan association which can provide a high-profile position of leadership for those aspiring to higher office one day (Romney, Perry and Jindal also served as chairs in the past). Branstad, by the way, had also led that group from 1996-1997. So did Branstad's predecessor in office, Governor Robert Ray, from 1977-1978. Becoming RGA chair doesn't always guarantee a future run for president. But it's a strong addition to the professional resume nonetheless.

"Christie called me in the Fall of 2014," Branstad said, "Asked if he could do anything for me."

Christie helped direct some of RGA's financial resources to Iowa, particularly to the northeast part of the state where the area's incumbent Democratic Congressman Bruce Braley was instead running for the open U.S. Senate seat of Iowa's longtime liberal leader Tom Harkin. Republican State Senator Joni Ernst, previously barely known outside of her rural, southwest Iowa town of Red Oak, was giving Braley all he could handle in that race.

Ernst, an Iowa Army National Guard war veteran, who as a lieutenant colonel led troops in Kuwait and Iraq, was shocking Democrats with her easy but confident demeanor. Branstad sensed a good year. He figured he could trounce little-funded, Des Moines State Senator Jack Hatch in the race for governor, Ernst could beat Braley and give Republicans that seat and Rod Blum, a Cedar Rapids businessman, could beat former Speaker of the House Pat Murphy of Dubuque and allow Republicans to pick up a seat in Braley's Congressional District.

Show him the money. That was Branstad's request of Christie. He got it. And—just as Branstad had told him—Republicans won all three of those contests. "He came, and we won it," Branstad said with a smile.

Scott Walker, considered by some in the party to be a rising Republican star as Wisconsin's governor, had also impressed Branstad at that 2015 Freedom Summit hosted by Congressman Steve King in Des Moines.

Walker, not known for an exciting speaking style or soaring rhetoric, had surprised some conservative activists at that event when he shared an impassioned story about haters who had threatened to "gut my wife (Tonette) like a deer" when Walker was sparring with union supporters as he worked to dramatically cut back their contract bargaining rights.

"Really did well," Branstad said of Walker's performance during that speech.

Then there was Florida's governor, who came from the family Branstad had admired for decades: the Bushes. But Branstad's political instincts and inside knowledge of Iowa's activist landscape told him that Iowans weren't in the mood for a third President Bush. "A lot of people (consultants, pundits) thought it was going to be Jeb," Branstad said of the early thinking of the

2016 race. But he knew better. "So much Bush fatigue," Branstad said as he recalled his thinking that this third Bush had no path to the White House like the previous two.

But as much as Branstad paid attention to the governors running in 2016, he was starting to get increasingly concerned with a U.S. Senator from Texas: Ted Cruz.

Vander Plaats (Branstad's former rival when they battled for the Republican gubernatorial nomination in 2010) had seen something in the potential of Cruz as the nation's next president. So did Branstad. Although rather than the social conservative warrior that Vander Plaats envisioned Cruz would be, Branstad saw a threat.

And after watching, listening and observing Cruz for months during the intense Iowa Caucus campaign, Branstad—who routinely pledges to remain publicly neutral during the Caucus cycle and instead essentially campaigns for ALL of the candidates by saying they should "come early and often" to his beloved state—stunned people all over the country with an answer he gave me at a news conference in Altoona, a town of 18,000 people 10 miles northeast of Des Moines.

Leading up to that moment, Branstad had determined two things.

1. Only two Republicans, Branstad surmised, had a legitimate chance of winning the 2016 Iowa Caucuses: Trump and Cruz.
2. Cruz would be bad for Iowa if he became president. So Cruz must be stopped. And Branstad would personally get involved to make that happen.

Stunning. No more Mr. Neutral Governor. While Trump's tactics may not have been anything like Branstad would have laid out, they were far less dangerous, in Branstad's evaluation, than Cruz's positions on Iowa's most valuable liquid: ethanol.

Iowa produces more ethanol than any other state. The Iowa Renewable Fuels Association pegged that production at 4,200,000,000 gallons per year in 2017. That is more than a quarter of the entire yearly production in the United States and it shows that Iowa's overall annual output has increased ten-fold over the past two decades as ethanol has gone more mainstream.

Branstad probably recites those figures in his sleep. Cruz would prefer to drift off to sleep counting oil barrels instead, Branstad figured. And in case Branstad missed anything that Cruz was saying (or not saying) about renewable fuels, all he had to do was talk to his son.

Eric, Branstad's oldest son, led America's Renewable Future, a pro-ethanol organization that hounded Cruz at his Iowa campaign stops.

It essentially went like this: "Senator, you don't like the Renewable Fuel Standard that mandates a certain amount of the nation's fuel supply contain renewables? Well, then you will have to deal with these fervent fuel followers."

And follow they did. The group's members tailed Cruz to keep the pressure on him. They wanted him to know how important ethanol was to the agricultural community in Iowa. "They know," Eric Branstad said of presidential candidates' awareness of Iowans' reliance on renewable fuels, "but they don't *know*."

Both Branstads determined that no matter how much Eric's group followed Cruz and questioned him, there was no way they would win him over. It was a lost cause. Cruz would be far more loyal to Texas crude than Iowa corn.

"He was the one candidate who was unabashedly against ethanol," Terry Branstad told me of his thinking in no uncertain terms, "I just thought it was important to drive home the message that if you believe in renewables, he (Cruz) would be a disaster."

Terry Branstad also decided that there was no point hiding his disdain for Cruz.

"Eric was trailing him with that van asking him questions about ethanol already, so I was guilty by association already!" Terry Branstad snickered.

The Branstads knew that Cruz had plenty going well for him at the time, though:

- Leading in the Iowa polls
- Strong organization in the state
- Support of Evangelicals (vital for a winning Republican Caucus campaign
- Poised to win the Iowa Caucuses

"It would be bad for Iowa, but it would also be bad for the party, too," Governor Branstad told me, "Since I didn't think that he could win (the general election)."

Governor Branstad decided that it was time to take action.

And, again, I have to point out how out of character Terry Branstad's actions would be. He usually, almost painstakingly, keeps his thoughts to himself about individual candidates in the Iowa Caucuses.

"Come one, come all!" from Terry Branstad, instead became, "Go back to Texas, Ted." (I'm paraphrasing here).

January 19, 2016...13 days before Terry Branstad's beloved Iowa Caucuses...he delivered his uncharacteristic, pre-Caucus Cruz wallop.

Terry Branstad had just finished speaking to a room full of alternative energy supporters at the Iowa Renewable Fuels Summit in Altoona.

He walked down the hall to a side room and walked up to the microphone set up before a handful of reporters waiting. Governor Branstad started talking about the importance of supporting candidates who back the Renewable Fuels Standard, protecting the thousands of Iowa jobs and numerous communities that depend on the additional revenue that flows in because of biofuels and stopping critics who don't believe in the importance of renewable fuels.

It was a strongly laid out argument. But it seemed to me that there was more he wanted to say...like there was an exclamation point he wanted to add to that.

"We're proud of the Iowa Caucuses being first and we need to keep it that way and this will be a great way to send a strong message," Governor Branstad said.

"This will be a great way to send a strong message"--that was the part that stuck out to me. Hmmm, "*send a strong message*"...it sounded to me like that was a call to action from the Iowa governor to those who want to protect the renewable fuels industry...and a warning to a certain Texas Senator.

So I asked, "So you want him (Cruz) defeated?"

"Yes."

That was the only word Terry Branstad said in his initial response to me.

Wowza! That was the exclamation point that he wanted to put on his warning to Iowans if they chose to support Cruz's bid for the White House.

After his one-word response, the room was silent for a few moments. Heads turned immediately.

Terry Branstad then added, "I believe it would be a big mistake for Iowa to support him. I think it would be very damaging to our state."

No more Governor Neutral. Terry Branstad was flat out telling Iowans that they should caucus against Cruz. What he didn't directly say at the time was also that Iowans should caucus instead for Trump. More on that a little later, though.

Terry Branstad would tell me later that he really hadn't planned the moment to fire off a warning about Cruz. But my question apparently offered the ammunition. And he went for the kill shot.

And people noticed.

That included his Lieutenant Governor Kim Reynolds. "I was in the back of the room (when Branstad made his comment)," Reynolds said, "I didn't really know who to look at first!"

"I didn't know it was coming," Reynolds told me later, "But it was no secret that the Governor was so passionate about renewable fuel. I don't think it was his intention to say anything. I just think...he was just so frustrated."

Eric Branstad hadn't heard about the bombshell that day until I walked back down the hall in Altoona to him afterwards. "It's news to me!" he told me.

The news travelled fast through social media. "My phone was blowing up!" Eric Branstad said and those in the renewables industry weren't sure what to make of what his father had just said. "They were trying to figure out if it was a good thing or a bad thing," Eric Branstad said, "They just didn't know."

Eric Branstad told me that he didn't know his father was going to say what he did that day. "Off the cuff," he told me of his father's remarks. "I'm glad it happened. It raised everything to a new level. I always wanted it to be *THE* conversation," Eric Branstad told me.

THE conversation to him was about renewable fuels. *THE* conversation in politics was Governor Branstad's efforts to make sure Cruz didn't win the Caucuses.

Congressman Steve King, the Republican Fourth District conservative, was later miffed at *THE* conversation because, for King, Cruz was *THE* best choice for president and he wasn't thrilled that Terry Branstad had broken his traditional pledge of neutrality.

"It think it was out of character for the Governor to make such a bold statement," King said the day after Governor Branstad's call to action against Cruz.

King maintained that the Branstads had Cruz all wrong, that he wasn't the anti-ethanol villain that they imagined. King argued that Cruz merely doesn't like fuel mandates--ethanol, petroleum or otherwise. "I wish he'd (Terry Branstad) been listening to someone other than his son when he was getting his information on Ted Cruz's position," King retorted.

The Congressman then took a shot at the Iowa governor for getting involved in the politics of the Caucuses and said that involvement could hurt the Caucuses in the future. "If we lose it (the first-in-the-nation status of the Caucuses), we'll look back at this time," King said, "As the day the process started when the Governor attacked Ted Cruz and didn't stick to the truth."

Although, truth was a sticky matter for King and some other Cruz supporters later on Caucus night. Supporters spread false rumors that Ben Carson was dropping out of the race, just as Iowans were gathering at their precinct sites to decide their favorite Republican presidential choice. Did it make a big difference? Maybe not a big difference. But anecdotally from stories that activists shared with me, some Iowans decided not to caucus for Carson that night, since they felt their support would be wasted.

Senator Chuck Grassley, the Republican who entered politics 60 years ago, didn't take issue with the anti-Cruz comments from Terry Branstad--a man he has known for some four decades--for trying to stand up for renewable fuels, even if it meant Branstad broke his traditional pledge of neutrality before the Caucuses. "Over 40 years, we've developed a good reputation (with the Caucuses), regardless of what's said," Grassley figured.

Grassley stayed neutral before the Caucuses, as he typically does.

Looking back, Governor Branstad's last-minute attempt to stop Cruz was a culmination of not just his fears about Cruz but also his realization about the political possibility of Trump.

For much of 2015, Governor Branstad wasn't convinced that Trump was serious about being a serious political leader. But as the months wore on, he watched Republican candidate after candidate flounder with missteps, backfired attempts to take down Trump and a lack of overall ability to grow any kind of sufficient support. Trump was starting to grow on him and Terry Branstad saw Trump's potential to mobilize the politically dissatisfied. That potential intrigued Branstad, who really wanted to see his party retake the White House after eight years of Democrat Barack Obama.

But Trump brought pause to that potential, at times, in Terry Branstad's mind. Trump's decision to skip a nationally-televised debate from Des Moines with the other candidates four days before the Caucuses and instead hold his own rally to support veterans across town had Branstad just shaking his head, especially since that debate was aired nationally on Fox News, a friendly outlet for the Republican candidates.

Branstad said of Trump's decisions like that one: "Defy conventional wisdom."

And that decision, Branstad figured, might cost Trump a Caucus night win, something even Trump himself later conceded might have been the case. As it turned out, Trump's Caucus night total was actually higher than any previous Republican. It just wasn't good enough in 2016. Cruz beat him by more than 6,000 votes.

2016 Republican Iowa Caucus Results

Ted Cruz	51,666 (27.64%)
Donald Trump	45,427 (24.3%)
Marco Rubio	43,165 (23.12%)
Ben Carson	17,395 (9.3%)
Rand Paul	8,481 (4.54%)
Jeb Bush	5,238 (2.8%)
Carly Fiorina	3,485 (1.86%)
John Kasich	3,474 (1.86%)
Mike Huckabee	3,345 (1.79%)
Chris Christie	3,284 (1.76%)
Rick Santorum	1,783 (0.95%)
Others	117 (0.06%)
Jim Gilmore	12 (0.01%)

Total: 186,932

(Source: Republican Party of Iowa)

Something else that happened with Trump's second-place finish was a leadership change. A big one.

Chuck Laudner, the former executive director of the Republican Party of Iowa--the man who once thought about sitting out of the 2016 race until Trump hired him to lead his Iowa

Caucus efforts--became the recipient of the line Trump made famous on his NBC reality show, "The Apprentice."

"You're fired."

Trump doesn't like to lose. Politically-speaking, he may not have "lost" in Iowa with a second-place finish, at least not according to the conventional wisdom of the political pundits. Second place meant that his candidacy would move forward to the next contest in New Hampshire in good shape.

But to Trump, second place was apparently the equivalent of a loss.

"Eric Branstad, you're hired."

Terry Branstad, the proud papa, beamed while he told me the story about his son's job with the Trump campaign. "It really was an unusual year," he said of Trump's unexpected emergence as a legitimate Republican presidential candidate.

"Trump to me was 'Reaganesque."

Eric Branstad on his affinity for Donald Trump and the reason he and his father worked to get him elected president.

Photo by Dave Price

Terry Branstad said that Trump explained to him that second in Iowa just wasn't good enough. "Laudner didn't deliver the Caucuses," Branstad said.

He recalled Trump then telling him, "'Laudner's not working for me in the general election.'"

That was it. Laudner was out. Eric Branstad was in to replace him. A few months later, I ran into Laudner at a Trump rally in Clive and again later that July at the Republican National Convention in Cleveland. He declined to talk about what had happened. I presume that a non-disclosure agreement had something to do with it.

What a turn of events for Laudner. Trump gave him reason to get involved in the 2016 Caucus campaign. And it turned out that Laudner was right about Trump. He accurately predicted that Trump would be a different kind of candidate who could attract, not just the typical Republican caucus crowd, but rather, expand that following. Laudner just didn't get to see it through to the end.

Eric Branstad did and recognized that same potential in Trump. "The reason that I never played in the 2012 Caucus and also 2008...in my mind, we had candidates who were not attracting new blood. It was the same people at every event...have to beg them all to come," Eric Branstad explained it to me.

"Trump to me was 'Reaganesque.' Trump to me was (former President Ronald) Reagan to Dad," Eric Branstad said. "This was actually someone who gives you an answer, not a polled, prewritten, studied answer," he elucidated.

Eric Branstad's efforts to build loyalty from the presidential candidates for Iowa's renewable fuels had taught him that about Trump. And in the process, the two became loyal to each other, too.

Eric Branstad said that he first met with Trump on April 8, 2015, before Trump had declared his candidacy. Trump didn't officially announce his campaign until two months later.

"People weren't even taking it seriously," Eric Branstad said of the early insider chatter about a possible Trump candidacy.

By that point, Eric Branstad had been working for America's Renewable Future for about three months, trying to get and keep the candidates' attention on the industry. He didn't know what to expect from Trump, a real estate man, not a Midwest guy.

"I was worried that it would be a two minute meeting...photo-op (where a politician shows up, shakes a few hands, looks interested in front of the media cameras and then leaves)," Eric Branstad recounted, "It turned out that it was an *hour-long* meeting."

Eric Branstad admits that before the meeting, he "Googled" Trump to see the latest news on him. He read that Trump, the day before, had opened his new tennis center at the Trump National Golf Club in Sterling, Virginia. And the top-ranked female tennis player in the world, Serena Williams, showed up, too. Williams and Trump even hit some balls to each other on the court.

Eric Branstad is an accomplished tennis player himself. So the internet news about what Trump had done the before gave him a conversation starter to serve up. And he aced it.

The two talked about the new tennis center and Eric Branstad told Trump that he would have to check it out sometime. That is when he said Trump asked who his favorite tennis player was. "I said (John) McEnroe (one of the greatest men's tennis players ever, who also had one of the most legendary tempers on the court) and Trump said, 'John is one of my friends,'" Branstad recounted.

The two volleyed tennis talk back and forth before the topic turned back to fuel. "I'm teaching him about renewables...the history...value-added agriculture...how to follow the kernel of corn from the farm to a plant.... and how it comes out as food and fuel...and all kinds of products...just from that one kernel," Eric Branstad laid out in detail.

And to Branstad's surprise, Trump responded, "How do I invest?"

Invest? Not only was Trump buying into the value of the renewable fuels industry in Iowa, but it seemed like he may actually want to literally buy into the industry. Eric Branstad said, "I'm thinking this is a win!"

Trump wasn't just faking conversation here, pretending like he cared just to try to win over Governor Branstad's son and the thousands of renewable energy supporters in the state, Eric Branstad was thinking. No, Trump was actually asking detailed questions.

"He wasn't just drifting off," Eric Branstad said of their meeting, "He was asking, 'Well, if China does *this*...if the market does *this*.'"

"He was asking questions like an investor, a businessman," Eric Branstad said.

Other presidential candidates later showed some kind of support to the renewable fuels industry during subsequent conversations with Eric Branstad but Trump's conversation stood out to him.

"(Florida Senator Marco) Rubio, (former Florida Governor Jeb) Bush...their answers were 10 minutes long...like...'I believe in market access, a level playing field,'" Eric Branstad recalled, "At the end of the day, it's complete bullsh*t. I mean they know what the RFS is, but they're trying to have their cake and eat it, too, with both oil and renewables."

"But not Trump," Eric Branstad said, "He answered directly."

Trump would be loyal to the industry, Eric Branstad decided, and Branstad would be loyal to Trump. He just couldn't let it be known to people before the Caucuses, since he still held his renewable fuels' job. So Branstad kept his fondness to himself, instead of having others accuse him of trying to influence his fellow renewable supporters after what they had considered a non-partisan educational campaign to win over both the Republican and Democratic candidates.

As it turned out, both Branstads--father and son--came out in support of Trump on caucus night. Eric did it publicly before the secret ballot vote that happens in the Republican version of the caucus (Democrats break into preference groups for individuals, which means other people in the room know which candidate you support. Republicans can keep their choice private in that secret ballot but they have the option of speaking in front of their precinct group and declaring their allegiance).

Eric Branstad stood up at his caucus precinct site at Merrill Middle School in Des Moines and spoke in support of Trump. He said his wife, Adrienne, actually talked on behalf of New Jersey Governor Chris Christie.

Terry Branstad offered his support for Trump only in that secret ballot vote, Eric said.

Quite a remarkable metamorphosis for the father, this Iowa political sage, the one who admittedly preferred governors as his presidential candidate of choice and who had earlier dismissed the thought of a President Trump. But there he was, first breaking his traditional pledge of neutrality by urging Iowans to defeat Cruz days earlier, and then on caucus night underscoring that effort by voting for Trump.

Those two Branstad votes for Trump, though, still left the candidate too many short in the state on caucus night. That's why Eric Branstad's phone rang afterwards. It was a New York number.

"Corey Lewandowski (Trump's campaign manager) on the phone, says, 'Hey, Eric, Mr. Trump would like you to come to New

York. Would you like to run the (Iowa) campaign for the general election?" Eric Branstad told me.

"I started crying," Eric Branstad admitted, "I just didn't see it coming."

But once the tears disappeared, he also had to admit that he wasn't sure what was happening, even after he later flew to New York and was waiting for his meeting with Trump. Was it a meeting? Was it an interview?

"I was nervous," Eric Branstad said, "I was REALLY nervous. I had no idea. Was I one of three candidates? Five candidates? I just didn't know."

But he said that Lewandowski walked over and told him that he was going to be Trump's state director in Iowa. It would be official. "I was so relieved," Eric Branstad said.

Had Lewandowski not stopped by first, he may have witnessed an unfortunate incident. "I could have peed my pants!" Eric Branstad told me as he burst into laughter, recalling how anxious he was that day.

Following the "interview," he returned to Iowa and laid out the game plan to win in November. Free, trusted advice was never far away. "It's nice to have Dad," he said, "So I can talk all of these strategies and about where to take the candidates, etc."

"They gave me my dream budget," Eric Branstad said of the campaign's emphasis on winning Iowa," Although, he concedes that once Trump's popularity soared over the next few months and resources were needed elsewhere, "I never actually got my dream budget!"

Eric Branstad didn't share dollar figures with me. He did offer a big smile as he told the story, though, so he didn't seem too distraught that all of the dollars he had wanted never arrived.

Both son and father experienced firsthand what Trump ignited in the state. Neither anticipated it.

"Thousands of calls for turnout," Eric Branstad said as he looked back at work he had done on behalf of other campaigns over the years to get people to show up, "Calling your friends, giving your first born!"

It was so different for Trump. Eric Branstad said that one of Trump's campaign events in Davenport, a city on the far eastern edge of Iowa along the Mississippi River with a population of about 105,000, made both Branstads grasp what Trump was doing.

It was Trump's first stop in Iowa following the Republican National Convention in July of 2016, exactly a week after he officially accepted the nomination. The historic Adler Theatre, one of downtown Davenport's centerpieces that has stood since 1931 and is on the National Register of Historic Places, was about to add to its history.

"I remember that about 48 hours before the event, it went online that the event was coming," Eric Branstad proudly told, "But by 10 p.m. that night, we were double-sold out for a 3,000 capacity event!"

On the afternoon of the event, he hurried over to check it out. "I got there three hours early and the lines were lined up around the block. The energy, it was unreal!" Eric Branstad exclaimed.

Eric Branstad said his father and Senator Joni Ernst were to serve as the "warm up" for Trump at the event. Ernst took the stage first. Governor Branstad was up next. "Dad hadn't seen the crowd yet. He went out to a rock concert!" Eric Branstad said, "Not the typical Republican events that he's been used to his entire life."

"When he came off the stage, he told me, 'I felt like a Beatle in the 1960s!'" Eric Branstad recalled his father saying to him.

After the event, the Branstads got to fly on Trump's plane to the next event in Cedar Rapids. A reward for their loyalty.

Eric Branstad told me there was a time before the caucuses that his father was actually leaning toward supporting Florida Senator Marco Rubio, which seemed surprising given Governor Branstad's preference for gubernatorial experience in presidential candidates. And Eric Branstad said Rubio was actually the Republican candidate he most feared in the caucus process. Rubio was a non-traditional candidate for Republicans, not a white senior citizen, but rather a youthful Cuban-American, bilingual and from a blue collar family. His was a good story for a country whose demographics were rapidly shifting.

In the end, both Branstads questioned the operation Rubio put together in Iowa, along with his infrequent appearances. "Instead of dumping it (campaign resources) into TV (ads) at the end...if he would have spent that a year earlier on staff...he could have done so much better," Eric Branstad said, "You gotta work it."

Tim Hagle, the University of Iowa political science professor, sensed at one point that the Branstads had good reason to fear Rubio. Hagle is the faculty advisor for the campus College

Republicans. He shared a story about Rubio's following with students.

"When the University of Iowa College Republicans had their first meeting of the Fall 2015 semester, they took a vote to see who they favored in the Republican nomination race. Of 50 or so who attended the meeting, the winner by far was (Wisconsin Governor) Scott Walker. At that time, Trump didn't get a single vote. When Walker dropped out, the CRs (College Republicans) were a bit adrift in terms of their preferences. A few went with (Carly) Fiorina, some with Cruz, but eventually the bulk of them started supporting and volunteering for Rubio," Hagle said.

Hagle felt that Rubio had built enough enthusiasm with some Iowans that he could have actually won the caucuses. "Had there been another week or two, Rubio might have passed Trump and maybe even Cruz," Hagle explained.

As it was, Rubio still managed a strong third place finish.

The Branstads managed much better. Eric Branstad led Trump's campaign to a lopsided victory over Democrat Hillary Clinton in the general election.

President Trump rewarded him with a job as senior White House advisor to the U.S. Department of Commerce Secretary Wilbur Ross.

And the president also did something no Democrat had ever been able to do: get Terry Branstad out of office. Branstad became the U.S. Ambassador to China.

Loyalty.

A few laughs came along with it. Governor Branstad and his wife, Chris, flew to New York to meet with the president-elect about the ambassador position. Trump asked Chris if she wanted the move to China. After she told him that she did, Trump said, "Let's call Eric."

Seems simple, right? Two parents could call their son with the good news. There was a problem. The Branstads, for security reasons, weren't allowed to bring their cell phones into the meeting with Trump. And like many of us, I suspect, they were used to just calling Eric with his number that was programmed into their phone. But, again, they didn't have their phones. They also couldn't remember Eric's cell phone number.

So the big news had to wait.

CHAPTER 10

GENUINE

"There's a lot of background noise," Hillary Clinton told me as she downplayed the scandal about her use of email while U.S. Secretary of State.

Simpson College in Indianola, Iowa on January 21, 2016.

Photo courtesy of WHO-TV

Even before President Donald Trump gave Terry and Eric Branstad their new jobs, both men had already determined that he was the best Republican for the country's top job.

"At the end of the day, I think we both...having gotten to know the president and how much he does care and his focus on the American people...that did it," Eric Branstad said.

Ambassador Branstad said they had worked for months to let Iowans understand that getting behind Trump was okay. "We needed to make it known that it's acceptable to support Trump," he said.

And they did it because they believed Iowans would feel like Trump was behind them. "The way he connected with people at the rallies," Ambassador Branstad said, "Trump has a sixth sense. He has an ability to connect with working people...a billionaire from New York! Connects with Midwest people in the heartland like no one else can."

At that point, those people had no way of really knowing whether Trump would deliver or whether he was just a brilliant marketer who said what the crowd wanted to hear.

Why was Trump able to connect so well? Ask the Branstads, Gayle Goble, Yvonne Brandt, Connie Whitaker, Ken Tipping and many other supporters. It's because followers consider Trump to be "genuine."

What you see is what you get with him. Genuine. Democrats, and other Trump critics, would sharply disagree with that assessment. Their take on whether he is genuine is this: It's hard to be genuine when spreading half-truths, exaggerations and lies.

Interestingly, "genuine" also came up frequently when I talked to activists about the three main Democratic presidential candidates from 2016. So let's take a step back for a bit here before we see how Democrats try to move forward.

"What are YOOUU DOOINNGG here?" a voice from behind called out to me. That voice was one I immediately recognized but the playfulness in it was not. It was former U.S. Secretary of State Hillary Clinton.

Clinton had walked into the room normally reserved to display some type of art (if I recall correctly) at Simpson College, a small, private Methodist-affiliated institution of about 1,200 students in Indianola, 20 miles southeast of Des Moines.

She wasn't *really* asking why I was there. Her campaign set up the interview, after all, to follow her speech there that day, just 12 days before the Iowa Caucuses on February 1, 2016. And

Clinton was fighting a much more difficult primary battle than anyone expected with Vermont Senator Bernie Sanders.

Clinton's playfully rhetorical question was really because of this: it was January 21, and 16 hours after my wife, Emily, gave birth to our daughter, Lyla Marie.

I told Clinton that day that my wife insisted I still come and do the interview. And as Emily reminded me, we don't get to talk to Clinton very often. True.

I will say that Clinton's 2016 campaign gave us more access to her than the 2008 campaign. We reporters are arrogant in that we demand access. But all self-serving grandiosity aside, we are the public's conduit to these people who want to lead our country. So...yes, these people should talk to us. And it seemed to me like the campaign dealt with that need better in Clinton 2.0.

"You surely have pictures, right?" Clinton said to me after she walked into the Simpson College room.

Surely, I did, of course. I mean what proud Dad, especially in these modern times, doesn't have a smartphone full of pictures of his newborn daughter? I proudly showed her Lyla. Clinton was very complimentary. And how couldn't she be? I mean, have you seen how cute my daughter is?

Now, I don't pretend that I really know Clinton. In covering her as a reporter, on and off, for the past decade, she frequently seemed to me to be pretty guarded and very careful, both on and off camera. One conversation about my daughter doesn't change that impression.

And full disclosure: I was talking to her in my very sleep-deprived and euphoric state after witnessing that miracle of childbirth less than a day before.

Having said that, I do feel like Clinton shows a different side when she talks about children. Why she didn't do more of that during the campaign, I will never understand.

Nancy Emanuel noticed Clinton's fondness for children, too. Emanuel opened up her Ottumwa house for a Clinton gathering on July 7, 2015.

"You really get to see how genuine she is," Emanuel told me.

Nancy, a retired nurse, and her husband Dennis, an attorney, hosted a house party two months before then. That party filled with just Clinton fans. The second gathering also had the candidate.

There weren't enough seats this time, though, as some guests had to peer into the event from the back deck. That was likely by design. Campaigns love pictures/video of event sites overflowing with adoring supporters.

This July day was a reunion for Emanuel. In 1996, she and some friends met Clinton—who was midway through her tenure as the nation's First Lady--following a speech at Simpson College. Two decades later, Clinton arrived at Emanuel's house to win the chance to return to the White House.

"An honor to have the next president of the United States in our living room," Emanuel said to the people gathered.

The Emanuels' home was just the type of backdrop Clinton would want: it held the guests the campaign hand-picked and the intimate warmth the Emanuels emanated. And a bonus: the candidate didn't have to talk to the media.

More on that, in a bit.

First, the inside story of the day from Emanuel.

"I was surprised to be asked," Emanuel later told me. "Well, in some ways I was and other ways, I wasn't."

Emanuel loved Clinton and was convinced that Clinton would become the next president of the United States. She just didn't think *she* would ever be afforded this privilege to play host. However, she had to keep it a secret.

As it turned out, at least she didn't have to keep the secret for long. On a Thursday night, Emanuel had been sipping a glass of wine with her husband on their back deck. It's quite a view as their property backs up into thick, green, luscious woods. The campaign called to request the house party with Clinton. But the party would be that next Tuesday! Not much time. Not even five full days. "I didn't expect it to be so quickly!" she recalled.

The campaign told them not to tell anyone. The woman who Emanuel had dreamed for years would eventually become president and she couldn't tell anyone?

Fine. But Emanuel had her own request for the campaign: you take care of the invites, not us. "That way we didn't worry about not being able to invite everyone we wanted and then we'd have to deal with no more room," Emanuel explained, "and they could also make sure the people they really wanted to be there would be there."

There was one complication to all of this: the Emanuels had already scheduled a holiday party that weekend. They were a patriotic family, after all.

"We had already planned a Fourth of July weekend party for about 30 people," Emanuel said.

That made the Emanuel home "party central" for about 72 hours. They couldn't vent to friends about the stress of it all, though, because they were determined to keep the second party a secret, as the Clinton campaign requested.

Despite that determination, the Emanuels found out that the secret got out. But at least it wasn't their fault. "A few guests came up to us (at the 4th of July gathering) and told us, 'Hey, we got invited to a house party at your house!'" Emanuel recounted.

Not much she could do but smile. She did her best to hold that smile as the next 48 hours brought her family fascination, chaos and a lot of pre-house party guests. She took us through the schedule:

The Hillary Clinton House Party

Saturday
  Clinton's advance team arrived.
Sunday
  Two Secret Service agents showed up with questions. "Who are your neighbors?" the agents wanted to know. In other words, any reason to worry about any of them? The agents talked with neighbors and warned them the cul-de-sac would have to be shut down Tuesday. They also checked out the airport where Clinton's plane would be landing Tuesday. "Any pets?" No pets, so no worries there that the agents' dogs would come across other animals looking to cause drama and needing some four-legged lovin' (can't have the service dogs getting distracted, after all!).
Monday
  Staff checked out the house. Made plans for where to temporarily pen the media on Tuesday in the Emanuels' garage. But Nancy was thoughtful enough that day to fill it with freshly baked sweets for us to indulge ourselves.
Tuesday morning
  The Emanuels had to clear their vehicles out of the garage and driveway and park down the street. The trained security dogs did a final sniff-through of the home and then joined agents checking out the woods behind the house.

Tuesday afternoon
> *Emanuel double-checked to make sure Secretary Clinton didn't need anything special. "I had made bars and cookies, but they said 'no thanks.'" The campaign did have a couple of asks, though. Fresh lemon would be great for Clinton's warm tea and they wanted the air conditioner cranked up. No sweat wanted when the place later filled up. "No problem on either," Emanuel let them know.*

Tuesday evening
> *The Emanuels hosted 80 friends, a few dozen media, a few dozen more agents and campaign staffers and one woman destined to become the next president of the United States. Or so the Emanuels figured.*

Clinton strolled into the Emanuels' living room, throwing her arms up as if she were blown away by the ovation. The event seemed to go well. Clinton stressed the need for universal preschool (after reminding the supporters she was a grandmother, something she did often on the campaign trail in Iowa). She praised President Obama. "I don't think he gets the credit he deserves," repeating a line she frequently used.

Praising Obama was not a bad idea in Iowa in front of a bunch of Democrats. After all, Obama shocked Clinton by winning the 2008 Iowa Democratic Caucuses and also won Iowa in the general election that year and again in 2012.

Clinton also called for improving the healthcare system, ending the dreaded "dark money" that groups use to fund political efforts without being forced to detail the sources of that money. It might take a constitutional amendment to do that, she added.

Clinton did make a wise move at the house party that Democratic activists loved. She ripped Branstad. Iowa Democrats complained that the longtime Republican governor had become more partisan after returning to office in 2011, following more than a decade in the private sector. Their case in point: Branstad unilaterally decided to close two of the state's mental health institutions by vetoing lawmakers' funding for them. Can't keep them open without money, obviously. The governor maintained the facilities were outdated, inefficient and substandard and he determined that Iowans' mental health needs could be better served in other private facilities.

Democratic lawmakers and the state's largest employee union went ballistic. They sued and said Branstad overstepped his legal authority. But the state supreme court later sided with the governor.

Clinton wisely tapped into the leftover Democratic anger from that decision during her remarks at the Emanuels' gathering. It showed that she was paying attention to Iowa. "From what I'm hearing in Iowa, you are losing facilities and programs," Clinton said. "And people are ending up in nursing homes and jails."

"Boooo!" the assembled crowd around her responded in unison. Well played, Madam Secretary, well played.

The campaign staff kicked the media out for the last part of the event. Clinton was supposed to have some "private time" with the supporters, away from our prying microphones and cameras.

Emanuel filled me in later on some of the private conversation she had with Clinton, though. "Nancy, *love* those colors in that bathroom," she remembered Clinton saying to her. "Just like anyone would say...so real, so personable," Emanuel gushed.

She also was touched by Clinton noticing a family picture on the wall. It showed the Emanuels' three sons. All had moved away from Ottumwa. "Do you have grandkids?" Clinton asked her. "I said 'yes!'"

"Oh, wonderful!" Clinton exclaimed.

Some grandmother bonding time.

"Extremely gracious," Emanuel said, "Just like we were visiting and having lunch someplace. Seemed very interested, not just because she thought it was a good thing to do, but seemed really interested. She (Clinton) said, 'I just can't tell you how much I appreciate you opening your home on short notice.'"

Emanuel seemed a little less than thrilled that she had to open ALL of her home that day. After the event had ended and the campaign moved the media away from the house, Clinton walked into the Emanuels' garage. That's where they had her go as the guests left the house. Clinton also had work to do. A few dozen of her books and other items sat in piles and awaited her autograph. She worked her way through them in a few minutes' time. Emanuel couldn't believe she had to do it THERE. "In our garage!" Emanuel laughed.

For the record, the garage was immaculate. We should all be so lucky.

Several times during our conversations, Emanuel mentioned the word "genuine" to describe Clinton.

Bonnie Campbell used it more than several times. "She's a genuinely nice, thoughtful and kind person," Campbell told me of her relationship with Clinton, "Somehow that gets lost in an election."

Campbell has known the Clintons for decades. She worked for President Bill Clinton as his head of the Violence Against Women office, a division he created within the U.S. Department of Justice. She backed Hillary's 2008 and 2016 runs for president, in part because of what she saw from and in her.

"When I was in the Clinton administration, she was very interested in my subject area: violence against women," Campbell said.

"When we passed the first federal law concerning violence against women, she took it to her international human rights work," Campbell said. "It literally changed the world for many, many women. It's just a continuation of the work she's done her entire life."

Those actions, for Campbell, proved who Hillary Clinton was. "I saw the kindness of her," she said, "I saw the passion."

But there was another time Campbell felt that passion even more. Bonnie and her late husband, Edward, both spent time as chairs of the Iowa Democratic Party. The two shared a few other distinctions, too: they both ran for governor and also both worked for Iowa Senators Harold Hughes and John Culver.

Ed died in 2010 after battling lung cancer. Campbell recalled how Clinton offered support in a more private, but deeply intimate way. "When Edward was sick, very sick and dying...every so often, Hillary would call and say, 'You can do this...you have a village to help,'" Campbell told me.

It Takes a Village was the name of a children's book Clinton authored in 1996.

Campbell thinks Clinton's critics have a bad read on the person she really is.

Supporters of Clinton's rival, Bernie Sanders, got a good read on the candidate he really was one day in Fort Dodge.

"He only took questions!" the voice shouted incredulously into the phone as a young man stood next to another outside the Iowa Central Community College campus. Fort Dodge is a north central Iowa town of 25,000 that is about two hours south of the Minnesota border.

I wasn't quite sure at the time, but the young men were staffers for Sanders' Iowa presidential campaign.

Sanders had just finished a rally on campus and television photojournalist Travis Jungling and I had been lingering outside afterwards on a mild summer day in July 2015. We sat on a bench and brainstormed our "teases" that would run later on TV to entice people to watch that evening's newscasts.

Between takes of shooting our videos (yes, unfortunately, "takes" is too often appropriate, since we TV folks don't always get it right the first time), we heard the commotion up the sidewalk from us.

From our distance away, we couldn't make out everything from the conversation. But it sounded like at least one of the staffers was getting animated as he relayed Sanders' performance at the rally to the other party on the other end of the phone.

"He didn't even do his speech!" the man exclaimed.

It was more than a year later before I met one of those young men and learned what had happened that day. "He (Sanders) gives a pretty similar speech every time, right?" Evan Burger told me, not as a criticism of Sanders, but rather the acknowledgement that almost ALL presidential candidates give essentially the same stump speech--or at least much of the main parts of it--at their events.

Burger served as Sanders' State Advance Director before the caucuses. He had never worked on a political campaign before. But his parents had immersed him into Democratic politics by taking him to caucuses when he was a child, giving him a quarter-century internship before Sanders' arrival in Iowa.

Burger was in charge of getting everything set before Sanders showed up at an event, reserving a location, making sure a crowd would show up, lighting, microphones, a podium, whatever the event needed.

"We build them as a town hall," Burger remembered of that event in Fort Dodge, "He would speak for the majority of it and then get into 'Q & A.'"

Not all of those candidates like the "Q & A" (questions and answers) format. They might get a zinger from an audience member who is looking for a moment of embarrassment, anger, or foolishness for the candidate that can later explode on social media. Candidates might also just simply get a question to which they don't know the answer (can't imagine too many politicians like having that happen in public, right?) Or...and let's be honest here...not all candidates seem to enjoy talking to people in unscripted atmospheres.

I still recall former New York City Mayor Rudy Giuliani--who was running a lackluster 2008 Iowa Caucus campaign during his Republican presidential run-- taking off after some brief remarks inside an overflowing deli in downtown Indianola.

The sweaty bunch of people packed inside were steaming mad that "Hizzoner" couldn't be bothered to stick around for some questions. I never got to ask Giuliani whether he liked talking to people. Maybe he did, just not on that day?

Speaking of New Yorkers...let's also not forget that infamous incident (don't know if it happened more than once) when Clinton's first presidential campaign got nailed for planting questions with the audience at a campaign event in Newton in 2007.

A Grinnell College student had told us later that the campaign requested that she ask Clinton a certain question about global warming at this energy-themed event. Magically enough, Clinton happened to call on that student at the event.

Maybe that type of campaign trickery happens more often than we know. But one thing that I know is that Clinton couldn't have liked the attention the incident brought.

Now, let's get back to Evan Burger and the Sanders campaign. He expected that Sanders would give his traditional speech that day in Fort Dodge. But so much for that expectation. "Instead, he (Sanders) got up there. It was a good crowd. These were everyday people," Burger said, almost interrupting his initial thought, "He puts his notes aside and said, 'Let's take some questions.'"

"Staff was like...'Uh, okay, this is how we'll do this. Okay,'" Burger recalled of the day.

"What is going on here?" That was the question Burger remembered another staffer texting to Sanders' national campaign headquarters in Burlington (Vermont, not Iowa).

"I wasn't freaking out," Burger said.

People in the audience asked about health care, stagnant wages and why big money and big business have too much influence on, well, just about everything. No one question nor no one answer provided an extraordinary moment on its own.

But afterwards, I was thinking there was something different about this. Something unique.

Burger noticed it, too. "It was a conversation. He was into it," Burger said, "And the crowd was into it. He read the room and decided, 'I'm going to take questions.'"

That wasn't the only time.

A similar event played out at Ellsworth Community College in Iowa Falls. It was just eight days before the caucuses. "A woman had stood up and was crying," Burger said of the emotional scene. "She had health problems and she was now destitute. It was an amazing exchange."

That woman was Carrie Aldrich of rural Alden, about 15 minutes west of the campus. Her tears were real that day, she would tell me more than a year later, and so was the pain behind those tears.

"I didn't even plan on saying anything," Aldrich told me. "I was just so moved by other people's stories."

Sanders apparently was moved by Aldrich and that wasn't something we saw frequently. Sanders isn't usually the warm and fuzzy type on the campaign trail. I remember several times during his town hall events when Iowans told him of their financial and physical struggles. One man at William Penn University in Oskaloosa stood up to rail on the problems of the healthcare system and insurance companies and said that he was dying from cancer. Another woman opened up about her long odds fighting breast cancer.

I'm not trying to say Sanders was cold to them. But he didn't really have much of a visible reaction. Maybe in that big auditorium setting, he didn't really hear what they said? Maybe he was just "all business" those days and didn't let the emotional stories get to him? After all, he heard so many of these similar woes.

His reaction, though, was obvious after hearing Aldrich's situation. She suffered from post-traumatic stress disorder, a serious nerve condition, constant pain and required 11 different medications to treat them. She couldn't afford her mortgage, couldn't find full-time work that her body and mind could handle and couldn't get the federal government to award her disability payment.

Aldrich stood up in front of 200 people at the rally and let it all out: the health problems, the struggles to support herself with minimum wage jobs, having to rely on her elderly parents to pay her mortgage, the financial, physical and emotional stress. All of it.

Pain flowed with her words. So did the tears. Maybe it was that she had already heard so many other people's struggles before her. Maybe it was because she was opening up about such personal feelings to the public person she admired most. Whatever it was, it was raw and real. So was Sanders.

"It was the warmest hug ever," Aldrich said of the embrace Sanders gave her that day with her face still flushed and moist from her emotional outpouring.

"It was like getting a hug by your dad," Aldrich said.

At that time she was 46, divorced with a grown daughter, full of hurt and burdened by debt. But Sanders, this man she had only previously seen at a rally once before and not been able to meet before this day, was the stranger who brought familial comfort. "It wasn't for the cameras," she said, "It was real."

She said Sanders told her he knew it wasn't easy to "pour her guts out on national TV" but people needed to know that it was a struggle out there. "He understood my plight and so many other people living like this," Aldrich said.

"I've shaken other candidates' hands," she said, "And it's all just, 'I won't remember you tomorrow...or in 10 minutes.' But Bernie was legitimate."

The emotional connection aside, Aldrich was equally impressed with the attention she received from Sanders afterwards, too.

She had given Sanders a letter that detailed her struggles. Aldrich said a few days later, she received an email from Sanders to follow up on her letter and their heart-wrenching conversation "He thanked me for being there (at his rally) and for writing," Aldrich said, "and thanked me for being honest."

Another impressive thing to Aldrich: in that letter she told Sanders about her difficulties getting the federal government to agree to award her the benefits she felt that she deserved for her mental and physical challenges. She said Sanders' staff connected her with staff of Iowa Republican Senator Chuck Grassley. A Democrat working to connect her with a Republican. Politics had nothing to do with this, Aldrich learned. Sanders was just being practical. He represented Vermont. Grassley represented Iowa and hopefully he could get the assistance a resident in his state needed.

"I'll never forget it," said Aldrich.

Burger didn't recall seeing tears from anyone in the crowd--like what happened with Aldrich--from his first real event with Sanders in Ames. But he did see what Sanders was all about.

"He shows up and says, 'Where's my podium?'" Burger recounted. "I thought, uh, I didn't think of that," Burger told Sanders on that December day in 2014, months before Sanders joined the race as a candidate.

Nearly 250 people had jammed into a church basement to hear Sanders. The campaign--well, there wasn't even a campaign at this point--hadn't done its logistical work. So Burger improvised.

"We ended up using a milk crate!" Burger said.

Yes, a milk crate for a podium so Sanders could rise above the crowd. Ever see Clinton stand on a milk crate? Doubtful.

I didn't see former Maryland Governor Martin O'Malley stand on a milk crate either. But Tom Henderson grew fond of him for other reasons. "Good guy," Henderson said of his first impressions of O'Malley.

"Just seemed like he could be president," he added.

During his nearly 20 years as Polk County Democratic Party Chair (including during the 2016 cycle), Henderson--a trial lawyer in his day job--had seen dozen of candidates. That typically gives him a chance to get up close to those trudging through the state.

Henderson endorsed John Kerry for president in 2004 but stayed out of the race in 2008. In 2016 he wanted back in.

"I thought as a party leader," Henderson explained, "We needed to get behind someone without a lot of baggage ...I felt (Hillary) Clinton was going to have a problem with trustworthiness. I just thought we were going to have trouble with her as the nominee."

For the record, he didn't just have issues with Clinton. Henderson wasn't so sure about Sanders either. "He wasn't even a Democrat and I had never even met him. I just didn't think he would be a serious candidate," Henderson said of Sanders' chances in the Democratic primary.

Henderson was not only impressed with O'Malley's personal traits, but also his resume.

- Local politics? Yes, O'Malley knows that thanks to his time as former city councilman and mayor of Baltimore.
- State politics? You bet. He was a two-term governor of Maryland.

- National politics? He can do that, too. O'Malley used to be chairman of the Democratic Governors Association.

That's three for three in Henderson's mind. To Henderson it didn't matter that few Iowans would recognize O'Malley if he walked past.

"He listened to me," Henderson said of his times with O'Malley and felt like the governor truly listened to him...didn't just make small talk until someone higher up on the political food chain walked into the room.

So Henderson signed on as an Iowa adviser for O'Malley, no matter how long this long-shot campaign would be. "You can't live life that way...just going with sure winners," Henderson said of his thinking back then.

No fancy title or fat paycheck, just his honest advice when O'Malley wanted it.

Henderson was loyal to O'Malley, no matter what the polls showed. O'Malley had already proven *his* loyalty, Henderson figured.

In 2014, O'Malley sent staff from his political action committee to help Iowa Democratic campaigns. In 2015, he did one better. He sent himself. O'Malley was the only presidential candidate to come to Henderson's Spring and Fall fundraising dinners for the Polk County Democrats. The best Clinton and Sanders would do was send a surrogate.

Henderson wasn't bitter. But he did remember. "He worked for it," Henderson said of O'Malley's Democratic devotion.

O'Malley's loyalty impressed Jake Oeth, too. Oeth, you might say, was actually part of that demonstrated loyalty to Iowa. Oeth, an Ogden native, first joined O'Malley's efforts as the Iowa representative on his political action committee, Generation Forward. Echoing Henderson's comments, Oeth said of O'Malley, "Good guy."

Oeth recalled the beneficiaries of the help O'Malley's PAC sent with staff and money in 2014:

- 2nd District Congressman Dave Loebsack's re-election
- Des Moines State Senator Jack Hatch's campaign for governor
- Political consultant Brad Anderson's bid for secretary of state
- A handful of state senate campaigns

The year didn't end up being a memorable one for Iowa Democrats. Let's be honest: no election had been particularly strong for Democrats since Obama in 2008.

But while O'Malley's people and money didn't help bring many victories (Loebsack did get re-elected), the future presidential candidate at least became more familiar to political insiders.

Oeth had previously worked in Washington, D.C. for a state political icon: Iowa Senator Tom Harkin, the creator of the landmark Americans With Disabilities Act.

Oeth came back to Iowa and helped the Democrat in 2014 hoping to replace the retiring Harkin, northeastern Iowa Congressman Bruce Braley. Braley had served four terms in the U.S. House. But his U.S. Senate campaign turned out to be a dud. He lost to a little-known Republican State Senator, Joni Ernst, who seemed to come out of nowhere in the small town of Red Oak (population 5,700) in the southwestern part of the state.

Ernst won easily by nearly nine points. In a purple state like Iowa where political power swings back and forth between the two major political parties like a sugar-starved five-year-old at a candy store, nine points is a decisive victory.

Braley had gone into the contest a heavy favorite.

Oeth knew O'Malley would not be any pundit's pick as the favorite to win in 2016, not with Clinton far and away the front runner. But Oeth did have the legend of Rick Santorum going for him. If a little-known, sparsely-funded presidential candidate like Santorum, the former Republican U.S. Senator from Pennsylvania, could win with persistence and perseverance, then maybe O'Malley could, too.

O'Malley was willing to do the work, Oeth knew. "Eight a.m. to ten at night," he said of his boss' work ethic, "Did it with great energy and passion and kept staff and supporters going."

Oeth also saw hope in Clinton. Not Clinton 2016, but rather in Clinton 2008. Clinton finished in third place in those caucuses, despite entering the race as a heavy favorite. Barack Obama, a U.S. Senator in Illinois at the time, and John Edwards, a former North Carolina Senator finished first and second respectively in the 2008 caucus.

By the numbers, Clinton earned about 29 percent of the votes on caucus night 2008. But to Oeth, that meant 71 percent wanted someone else. He saw an opening for 2016, no matter how small it was. "We knew beating Clinton was going to be tough," Oeth conceded, "I mean, she's one of the most-known names in political history."

True. Very true. "But there was a path," Oeth concluded.

Both Oeth and Henderson brought up Gary Hart in our conversations, but for different reasons. Back in the 1970s and 80s, Hart was an up-and-coming star in Democratic politics as a U.S. Senator from Colorado, although he wasn't well known yet when he ran for president in 1984. Yet, he managed to finish second in the caucuses, despite being far less familiar than the caucus winner Walter Mondale, Jimmy Carter's former vice president.

Of course, Carter also had been a little-known Georgia governor who traveled hard through Iowa before surprising the political world when he won the caucuses in 1976.

You see a pattern here? Come to Iowa often, even if most people have no idea who you are. Keep coming. Keep campaigning. You just might surprise somebody.

Hart had done that. O'Malley knew that. O'Malley worked on Hart's first presidential campaign in 1984. And O'Malley's duties back then took him to Iowa. Phone banking, leading volunteers, even some guitar-playing. O'Malley fancied himself a musician, outside of his time in politics. Although he had a knack for combining the two.

Fortunately, for O'Malley, he didn't work on Hart's second presidential campaign through Iowa. In that campaign, Hart faced allegations of adultery and foolishly dared reporters to prove it. Oops. They did. And the media nailed Hart gallivanting around with his alleged mistress, Donna Rice, on one of the most infamously-named boats ever: the "Monkey Business."

O'Malley should be thankful he only took part in that first Hart presidential run. O'Malley got some Iowa experience out of it, just not the "experience" Hart may have received on the campaign trail.

Clinton, Sanders, O'Malley. They were three Democratic caucus candidates for president. Supporters found all of them genuine, even if the contenders were genuinely different.

CHAPTER 11

GENUINE PROBLEM

"I would like to think that if I were on the ticket, we could have won Iowa. We could have won Wisconsin, Pennsylvania and Michigan," Former Iowa Governor Tom Vilsack told me. Vilsack thought he would have made a better pick for vice president than Virginia Senator Tim Kaine. But they ate pork chops together at the Iowa State Fair in Des Moines anyway on August 17, 2016.

Photo by Dave Price

The genuine problem for Democrats in Iowa was that 2016 was too disappointingly similar to 2012 and 2014.
Democrats in office were disappearing faster than ice cream in my 8-year-old son's bowl. It's fast. Believe me.

In 2010, Democrats had it all: majorities in the state legislature in both chambers, plus the governor's mansion. They held three of the five Congressional districts. And they featured U.S. Senator Tom Harkin, who was on his way to holding his seat for 30 years (after serving in the U.S. House for another decade before that).

After 2010, things changed. Harkin retired, other factors emerged and the political makeup transformed.

- The state labored in its recovery from the national recession, which officially ended in 2009 nationally but lingered longer in Iowa.
- Democratic Governor Chet Culver ordered 10 percent across-the-board budget cuts in 2009 that proved unpopular the following year as they took hold.
- Obamacare struggled with its launch in 2013 and delivering its promises.
- The population was getting older.
- Most counties declined in population.
- Rural Iowa--which comprises most of the state--became more Republican.

Republicans were taking over.

- Terry Branstad, a former longtime Republican governor, beat Culver to give the party the governor's mansion again in 2011.
- Republican Joni Ernst, a former state senator from Red Oak, replaced Harkin in 2015. That meant that both of the state's U.S. Senators were Republicans.
- Republicans took over four of the five Congressional seats in 2015.
- The legislature transformed from a Democratic majority to a Republican majority.
- By 2017, Republicans had statewide dominance. They controlled the governor's mansion, held 59 of the 100 seats in the house and 29 of the 50 seats in the senate.

- Finding any Democratic office-holder who didn't live in larger, more urban areas like Des Moines, Waterloo, Cedar Rapids or Iowa City became especially difficult.

Add those up and 2018 wasn't much like Tom Vilsack had envisioned it would be for his party or himself personally. Vilsack-- a popular former two-term Iowa Democratic governor and later President Barack Obama's two-term U.S. Secretary of Agriculture- -spent the year as the President/CEO of the U.S. Dairy Export Council. It's a great job. He makes a lot of money, gets to travel around the globe on behalf of the interests of the dairy industry and relies on his diverse background from serving at various levels of government. He is a valuable commodity.

Tom Vilsack Bio

Attorney
Mt. Pleasant city council
Mayor of Mt. Pleasant
State Senator
Governor of Iowa
Presidential candidate in 2008
U.S. Secretary of Agriculture
President/CEO of the U.S. Dairy Export Council

Because of that resume, Vilsack's name opens doors. He just figured his resume would be different. Vilsack thought he would be Hillary Clinton's running mate and ultimately her partner in the White House. He really thought that.

His trusted longtime aide, Matt Paul, assumed that, too. "I thought it was his," Paul told me.

Paul also figured that when he had received the call to work for the Clinton campaign in 2016, it would be to reunite with Vilsack again and become his chief of staff. Instead, the campaign offered him the position to work with Virginia's U.S. Senator Tim Kaine. Clinton chose Kaine instead of her longtime ally, Vilsack.

So, for Vilsack, just like in 2004, he got passed up. Back then, the party's nominee, Massachusetts Senator John Kerry, chose North Carolina Senator John Edwards over Vilsack and former U.S. Speaker of the House Dick Gephardt for the number two spot on the ticket. Edwards was a rising star at the time in the

Democratic Party. That was before he earned damaging headlines for $400 haircuts and his affair while his wife was dying of cancer.

Vilsack would have brought neither of those scourges to a campaign. But still, to get passed over twice by Kerry and Clinton? That's not easy.

"Villie, you're it!" Vilsack's close friend, Doug Campbell, had told him in 2004.

Campbell had found out from caterers at the Kerry's house in Massachusetts that there was signage for "Kerry-Vilsack." To Campbell, that meant that Vilsack was about to be named the running mate. Why else would the campaign have invested the time and money? Campbell's intel made sense to Vilsack. Although, unbeknownst to both of them, the Kerry team also had signage made up with "Kerry-Edwards" and "Kerry-Gephardt."

Disappointment.

Then, 12 years later, more disappointment with Clinton. Although, this time, Vilsack would confess, he had a gut feeling deep down that the decision may not go his way.

"I only had two or three hours of sleep the night before," Vilsack said as he looked back at his interview to be Clinton's running mate.

Vilsack had been traveling. So he and his wife, Christie, had to get up at 2 a.m. so they could get to the airport for the flight to Chappaqua, New York, where the Clintons had a home.

Just the Clintons and the Vilsacks in a room for the interview. No one else, Vilsack said. "Bill asked, 'What are you going to do for West Virginia?'" Vilsack recalled.

Vilsack was feeling good. He said he had recently talked with that state's governor about the struggles in the area. Armed with that insight, Vilsack proposed to the Clintons to cut off the tops of coal mountains (the coal industry was struggling) and plant agricultural products there instead.

Vilsack figured it would be a friendlier industry for the environment, it could give the area a new purpose and it could bring some much-need jobs to a region beset with poverty. Hillary Clinton didn't seem impressed.

"The body language of hers," Vilsack said, "...the way she was looking at me. Just seemed like she already made up her mind."

He said that Hillary Clinton followed up with a question about why Vilsack would want the job of vice president. "I told her to work for the country," Vilsack said that she then responded to him, "Why not chief of staff?"

Hmm, he thought. Sure, being vice president of the United States would be quite an honor. But Clinton's chief of staff? That was intriguing, too, and something that he told me that he would have actually accepted if she offered. "You (as a chief of staff) are the second most powerful person in the country," Vilsack explained to me, "You are the gatekeeper. You are the go between."

Clinton offered the vice president's job to Kaine. She offered Vilsack nothing.

Her mistake in Vilsack's mind. Vilsack--a man humbled as a boy who spent part of his early life in an orphanage away from an abusive, alcoholic upbringing--sounded confident to me that he could have made a difference for Clinton on her campaign ticket.

Vilsack could have gone to the "lower to middle market areas" as he called them. Let Clinton handle the campaigning in the big cities. He could talk about the potential of new forms of agriculture, products with high export potential and the ongoing success of the Obama administration. "Let's focus on the 270 map, not the 320," He added in a dig at the Clinton campaign strategy that (over)confidently mapped out a plan to secure a robust 320 of the 538 possible electoral votes for the nomination, instead of the 270 needed to clinch.

"I think I would have had a slightly different approach than Tim Kaine," Vilsack continued, "He thought of Arizona and Florida."

Kaine, the conventional wisdom was, would better appeal to the growing Hispanic demographic. Kaine spoke Spanish. Vilsack did not. But Vilsack felt, with his story of overcoming a difficult childhood and roots in the Rust Belt and Midwest (he grew up in Pennsylvania) that he, perhaps, could have made the winning difference for Clinton.

"I would like to think that if I were on the ticket, we could have won Iowa. We could have won Wisconsin, Pennsylvania and Michigan," Vilsack said, "But we'll never know."

Paul didn't share the confidence that his former boss had. "As popular as Tom is," Paul said, "She (Clinton) lost the state (Iowa) by 10 points. I think that's a lot to expect out of one person. I think he could have helped in Wisconsin, Pennsylvania…maybe Florida."

Paul wasn't trying to put down any potential strengths of Vilsack. He just felt like Clinton was in such a bad place in too many states that her running mate--no matter who that person was--wouldn't have really mattered much. "To say one person could have made a difference," Paul said, "...is not realistic."

Paul did feel that Kaine brought value to the ticket. And the campaign tried to use that in the last few months before the November 2016 election. "She (Clinton) was needed elsewhere. That's why Kaine kept coming."

As it turned out, Clinton was needed in a lot of places. Or maybe someone besides Clinton was needed. Regardless, in Iowa, instead of Clinton visits (Hillary, Bill or Chelsea) or preferred surrogates (Obamas or Biden), Iowa did get a lot of Kaine.

"He brought Virginia," Paul said, "He brought a connection with the Hispanic community. He brought a connection with the Senate. He made a strong case in his own way to faith-value and social-value Democrats."

But Kaine also demonstrated the limitations of what anyone could do for Clinton. I remember an event with Kaine at Iowa State University in Ames: September 19, 2016. It was one of those events that campaigns do to show that younger voters are with them, that there's excitement, youth and energy.

Those were supposed to be the optics. And Kaine tried to do his part to connect with the college crowd (although many of the 200 or so people there were not college students). "Some people look at the millennial generation and they find reasons to gripe about them," Kaine said as he walked around the stage with his microphone. "I look at the millennial generation. And I see diversity and I see tolerance...welcoming, embracing of diversity."

Millennials may have appreciated the praise, but they weren't appreciating the campaign like Clinton needed. Enough enthusiasm didn't join them during that rally that day. Before the event started, I had overheard staffers talking to some of the early arrivals in the crowd. "Can you reach out to your friends?" "Do you know anyone else who would want to come?"

The crowd wasn't what organizers had hoped. *Send out the S.O.S. Get people here!* Incidentally, I heard similar pleas from organizers when Vermont Senator Bernie Sanders--the Socialist Independent Clinton narrowly beat earlier in the Caucuses-- headlined a Clinton campaign rally for the college crowd at Drake University on October 5, 2016.

Sanders, too, had tried to do his part on stage to form the connection (some in the crowd were his former supporters) for Clinton that Clinton herself had failed to do. "When you look at the candidates issue by issue," Sanders said to the 300 or so in the audience, "You will find that Secretary Clinton has the progressive agenda, which will improve the life for the middle class."

It didn't have the same sales pitch as when Sanders laid out his own case as a candidate months before. But, that might be unfair. It's probably far more genuine for him to campaign for himself, rather than for the Democrats' nominee, a party he only joined so that he could run for president.

The energy wasn't there with Sanders at Drake in Des Moines, just like it hadn't been for Kaine at Iowa State in Ames three weeks earlier. No matter how hard staffers, Clinton or Kaine tried, they just couldn't duplicate what Obama had unleashed in the state in 2008 and 2012. They just couldn't build that energy.

"Hillary is a great tactician and would be a great president," Vilsack said. And echoing what others have told me about that 2016 race, he added, "She is always unfairly compared to her husband."

The husband had that energy. He got elected president twice. The tactician lost twice.

Charles "Chaz" Allen has never described himself as a "tactician" to me. He is also not one to trumpet his own abilities. He has been a Democrat, though, who found success in ways many in his party have not.

Allen is the former mayor of blue-collar Newton who represented the region as a Democratic state senator. He suggests that too many of his colleagues forgot how to talk to Iowans about what truly mattered in their lives. "You go into Kellogg and Baxter and Monroe (all are towns in Jasper County), you can't talk to them like you're in Des Moines (Polk County, the state's largest)," Allen said, "It's different there."

Different in populations, geography and overall makeup.

Population (According to the 2017 U.S. Census Bureau):

Kellogg: 594
Baxter: 1,129
Monroe: 1,869
Newton: 15,254
Jasper County: 36,842

Des Moines: 217,521

Des Moines is Iowa's largest city by far. It dwarfs those towns Allen mentioned--Kellogg, Baxter and Monroe. But it isn't just the population difference in the communities.

It's so much more than that to Allen: hard work, jobs, guns, trucks. God, too. Those are some of the main things about which people care in Jasper County.

What about equal rights when it comes to marriage, jobs, schools, religion and life? Allen does believe in those principles, too, and he thinks many of his Democratic neighbors do also. There's just a way to talk about those things in relation to every other thing--sometimes the most prominent thing--going on in their lives. "You just have to talk about it differently," Allen advises. "Your issue is jobs or corn prices...how do we keep good houses, how do we keep our schools open, how can we keep or get a grocery store, how do we get a health care plan."

That's how Democrats should talk to their neighbors, Allen believes. And he wants to underscore that doesn't mean that Democrats can't ever talk about guns, abortion or same-sex marriage. But, perhaps, those just shouldn't be the most prominent or most frequent topics, at least not in his neck of the woods. Not if Democrats want to make an immediate connection or re-connection with Iowans.

Allen knows that some people may misunderstand what he is saying in all of this. He doesn't want Democrats to give up talking about bedrock, core beliefs that so many activists have. Allen isn't a rube. He knows that discrimination, lack of fairness and opportunity exist in Jasper County and everywhere else. But in rural, white Iowa where he lives, Allen says jobs, health care, schools and housing likely rank higher on the priority list.

In his mind, one issue overrides most everything else in his community. "It's the economy, stupid," he said, borrowing the theme of the famous phrase of Bill Clinton's campaign strategist James Carville in their winning 1992 presidential campaign.

"Hillary just couldn't connect," Allen said of Clinton, his party's 2016 presidential nominee, on the important issues.

"It's rural, white Iowa," Allen stated.

I already outlined the decline of rural Iowa. That's why jobs that have left, paychecks that remain have stagnated, and concerns about what tomorrow's employment scene will look like dominate the thoughts, prayers and fears of most everyone Allen knows.

Clinton failed to connect with Allen and his neighbors on more than just the issues, though. Allen didn't appreciate getting pressured to endorse her before the caucus. Former New Jersey Governor Jon Corzine flew to Iowa to introduce Clinton at her campaign event at Des Moines Area Community College before the caucuses, Allen said.

Up to that point, Allen had never involved himself in presidential politics. As mayor of Newton, he governed as an Independent. In fact, he never even took part in a caucus. But he said the Clinton campaign was determined to get him to go public for her in 2016. "Corzine is pressuring me to sign a pledge card for Hillary," Allen said of what would have been a public show of support from him for Clinton in the Democratic primary process, "Pressuring me so hard. And I was thinking, 'Who cares what the mayor of Newton thinks?'"

Allen was also wondering why couldn't the campaign have been more like Barack Obama's was. "Obama was the coolest," Allen said.

Here is how he recalled a conversation he had with Obama in 2007:

Obama, "Can I get your support?"

Allen, "I can't yet. I'm trying to meet everyone."

Obama, "Well, when you're ready…"

That is how it should be handled, in Allen's estimation. Don't pressure. Show respect. Patience would help, too, when asking for an endorsement. This wasn't a coronation and a time for everyone to get in line behind the chosen one, as Clinton's critics would contend of her campaign. So don't treat it that way.

"Hillary was viewed as the elitist," said Michael Kiernan, a former state chairman of the Iowa Democratic Party, "Trump was the one who could help those without, as hard as that is to imagine."

He chuckled when he said it. Not because he thought that it was funny, but rather because he found that it was so ironic that some Iowans believed a billionaire egomaniac would care more about them than would a longtime public servant.

But Trump was more believable and inspiring, according to Kiernan. Clinton lacked candor and authenticity. She comes across as robotic, whereas Trump is all "piss and vinegar." This played well among a forgotten electorate, something the Clinton campaign totally missed. Too much time in New York and Washington, not enough time in Iowa, Wisconsin, Michigan, Ohio, or Pennsylvania, specifically the rural areas in Kiernan's estimation.

Kiernan knows what it is like to get tagged with that elitist label. "I became the elitist establishment!" Kiernan said after what he said he endured from some activists after he endorsed Clinton's 2016 campaign.

In Kiernan's mind, much of Clinton's problem specifically, and within his party overall, is a lack of trust. The "establishment" has lost trust with too many Iowans. Clinton was that establishment. "It's not a question always of what you don't do," he said of where Clinton failed to build that trust, "It's not even what you do. I'm not sure there was anything she could do or not do."

That was a pretty hopeless reality for Clinton, the way Kiernan sums it up. Clinton had almost 40 years of history in the public domain. That complicated history--which included commitments to education for children with disabilities, women's rights, marriage equality (eventually), rural broadband, expanded health insurance coverage, improved care for survivors of the 2001 terrorist attacks in New York--could get overshadowed with scandal, baggage and drama.

And that was not what enough Iowans wanted for their future. "It's the Clinton brand and what it stood for," he said.

Kiernan was one of the first Democrats who told me that he sensed trouble for his party. It was the Spring of 2016. Democrats salivated at the chance to destroy Trump at the polls, thinking-- foolishly at the time--that there was NO way he could become president of the United States. No way!

But Kiernan feared there was a way and it was because his party had lost its way, a problem he feared that had been growing for a decade and would last beyond 2016. Trust was gone.

Too many Iowans didn't trust that Clinton was the leader who could better their lives. Families who watched manufacturing jobs leave blamed NAFTA, the North American Free Trade Agreement that Clinton's husband championed as president in 1993. That eliminated nearly all tariffs and trade restrictions between the U.S., Mexico and Canada. Companies found it cheaper to set up shop in Mexico, in particular, where they could pay workers less and not have to worry as much about environmental and business regulations. Again, remember what happened in Newton when

Maytag left town. Why would they trust Hillary Clinton and the Democrats to make those manufacturing jobs return?

Most Iowa counties are shrinking in population. Younger people sought better economic opportunities elsewhere. The older residents who remained worried about what would happen to their towns. Clinton rarely visited smaller communities, rarely spent the night in Iowa (unless it was in Des Moines). Why would they trust her and the Democrats to understand their plight and their worries?

As Allen pointed out, at the end of the day, many of his neighbors (particularly those who live miles from a bigger city like Des Moines) care most about the economy. Iowans watched how the Clintons became tremendously wealthy after Bill Clinton's presidency.

Some worried the Clintons weren't as concerned about those who weren't the "one-percenters," those at the top of the income scale in the country. And people had questions about the Clinton Foundation (of course, others had concerns about the Trump Foundation, too). Sure, the Clinton Foundation undoubtedly did many good deeds--rebuilding after earthquakes, fighting HIV/AIDS and global poverty--but what about the foreign money that went to the foundation? Did those foreign leaders want to do good, or did they want access to President Hillary Clinton? What about the big money from leaders of corporate interests in the United States? What were their intentions with their dollars?

This was the first sentence in an Associated Press article about the foundation on August 24, 2016:

"More than half the people outside the government who met with Hillary Clinton while she was Secretary of State gave money — either personally or through companies or groups — to the Clinton Foundation. It's an extraordinary proportion indicating her possible ethics challenges if elected president."

The article also included this:
"Clinton was host at a September 2009 breakfast meeting at the New York Stock Exchange that listed Blackstone Group chairman Stephen Schwarzman as one of the attendees. Schwarzman's firm is a major Clinton Foundation donor, but he personally donates heavily to GOP candidates and causes. One day after the breakfast, according to Clinton emails, the State Department was working on a visa issue at Schwarzman's

request. In December that same year, Schwarzman's wife, Christine, sat at Clinton's table during the Kennedy Center Honors. Clinton also introduced Schwarzman, then chairman of the Kennedy Center, before he spoke.

Blackstone donated between $250,000 and $500,000 to the Clinton Foundation. Eight Blackstone executives also gave between $375,000 and $800,000 to the foundation. And Blackstone's charitable arm has pledged millions of dollars in commitments to three Clinton Global aid projects ranging from the U.S. to the Mideast. Blackstone officials did not make Schwarzman available for comment."

Really rich people gave money to the foundation while Clinton was secretary of state. It just made some Iowans uncomfortable. They weren't quite sure what to trust.

Then, there was the hierarchy of the Democratic Party. The Democratic National Committee's hacked emails showed a bias for Clinton over Senator Bernie Sanders. That didn't sit right with those who were already distrustful of the establishment. Again, in their minds, Clinton was the establishment. And the establishment was failing them.

"Middle class, working people," Kiernan said and he considered himself one of those as a kid growing up in Iowa. "People were sick of both political parties."

And some were sick of talking politics, Kiernan said, which was tough for a man who spent so many years working for campaigns, volunteering, door-knocking and speaking before activists.

"Some were too embarrassed to say (out loud) that they were voting for Trump. People didn't want to engage," he figured. "Citizens were feeling so low that there were no longer any options for them to have a voice in government."

It's all so troubling for Kiernan. As a boy growing up on a farm near Cumming in rural Warren County, the family hosted a yearly steak fry, a fundraiser for their good friend and politician, Tom Harkin. The family hosted the event for Harkin for 14 years. The final year, 1985, it attracted 2,000 people. The money helped Harkin's early career in the U.S. House and his transition into the U.S. Senate.

Kiernan believes that neighbors genuinely thought Harkin was one of them and had their best interests in mind. And they trusted Democrats to look out for their rural futures, as well. Over the years, for many reasons that we have already laid out in this book, that trust in the party eroded as the optimism in those smaller communities waned.

Kiernan considers some of the disconnect a contradiction in narrative. He cites one "between Iowa's agricultural economy and environmental supporters." Kiernan calls it "unfortunate."

He believes that it is possible to support both Iowa's vital agricultural sector, its workers and future, while still caring about the environment. Iowa's farms are getting bigger. It is just the reality. Democrats are too quick to say that these bigger corporate farms don't care about the potential damage runoff from pesticides and other chemicals inflict on the soil and water. Kiernan isn't trying to say there aren't legitimate concerns because he feels there are. But he also thinks his party needs to be more appreciative that those farms are still an indispensable cog in small town Iowa. Don't hate them. Work with them on better efforts toward conservation, environmental protection and climate change understanding. And, yes, that may sometimes mean tougher laws and regulations.

"I think most American farmers were the original stewards of the land," Kiernan says with optimism that his party will figure out how to better address the issue in the future.

"Trust is only built over time," Kiernan said.

That will be true about the environment, rural Iowa and leadership, he feels. "An important thing my mother (Joan, who was part of Democratic political campaigns for several decades) taught me was to understand your history. Understand that we're all here for the same cause. The old guard can make room for the new leaders but the new leaders have to understand the history from the old guard...the wins and losses. We have more in common than we don't."

Be genuine. Be honest. Be respectful of the past. Be understanding of what people want in the future. Kiernan feels then that trust Iowans once had with Democrats can return.

That is what Troy Price is trying to do...rebuild that trust. Price took over as his party's state chair in July of 2017.

Troy Price Bio

Chairman, Iowa Democratic Party
Senior Adviser, Hillary Clinton Iowa presidential campaign
Executive Director, Iowa Democratic Party
Political Director, Barack Obama Iowa presidential campaign

Executive Director, One Iowa
Deputy Communications Director, Iowa Governor Chet Culver

Price knew he had a lot of work to do as chairman. "The party is in trouble," he told me late in 2017.

(Note: I get this question occasionally, but Troy and I are not related. We do jokingly refer to each other as "Cuz," though, since inquiries about any family connection arise.)

Price should know about his party's troubles. He was part of campaign efforts that felt the impact of those troubles. Price worked for Iowa Governor Chet Culver. Culver got drubbed in his re-election bid in 2010 by former Republican Governor Terry Branstad.

Price served as the state party's executive director during the 2014 campaign cycle. Branstad got re-elected easily. Democratic Congressman Bruce Braley was defeated soundly in his U.S. Senate bid against Republican Joni Ernst.

And in 2016, Price served as Clinton's Iowa campaign senior adviser. "The message didn't connect," he said of the campaign's failed attempts in Iowa.

Of course, part of that was the fact that voters didn't always know what the message was. "Fighting for Us." "I'm With Her." "Stronger Together." Those were just some of the dozens the campaign hoped at one time or another would be *the* one that could lead to victory.

Obama had "Change We Can Believe In" and "Hope." It worked. Americans craved both of them. Clinton wasn't Obama. She didn't travel like him either.

Obama travel to smaller Iowa towns:

Knoxville: 7,181 people
Pella: 10,225 people
Missouri Valley: 2,649 people

(Population numbers from the Iowa State Data Center)

As one top Clinton supporter who didn't want a name attached to this simple-sounding but piercing take on the Obama vs. Clinton travel schedules said, "Barack spent the night in Iowa. Hillary would fly home."

Iowans pay attention to that. Price steered clear of the travel talk. He did acknowledge that Clinton's campaign became symptomatic of too many other Democratic campaigns in 2014 and 2016. "The message didn't connect," he offered.

"People were angry, upset," Price said, "Think Democrats don't get it. I think we turned a blind eye."

Democrats can talk to Iowans as much as they want. But if those Iowans don't feel like the Democratic candidates are listening, then the words are wasted. "There are a lot of people who felt like the party wasn't listening. And there's always going to be some of that," Price said.

But there was too much of that over the past decade.

Matt Paul, though, says don't just blame Hillary Clinton. "When people say, 'Oh, she didn't connect,'" Paul told me, "That's too easy. It was more."

Matt Paul Bio

Senior Vice President, Cornerstone Government Affairs
Iowa State Director, Hillary Clinton 2016 presidential campaign
Chief of Staff, Tim Kaine 2016 vice presidential campaign
Communications Director, U.S. Secretary of Agriculture Tom Vilsack
Vice President, LPCA Public Strategies
Press Secretary/Communications Director/Senior Adviser, Iowa Governor Tom Vilsack
Campaign Manager, Senator Tom Harkin 2008 campaign
Deputy State Director, Howard Dean 2004 Iowa presidential campaign
Executive Assistant/Speechwriter/Spokesperson, Cedar Rapids Mayor Lee Clancy and Mayor Larry Serbousek

Paul wasn't discounting what Price had said about Clinton's inability to connect with Iowans. Paul, a seasoned staffer, consultant and Democratic devotee, knows his party has failed in messaging when and where it mattered most. But he wanted to expound on what Price said and also, perhaps, make sure that the two of them weren't sounding like Clinton had ruined their party.

Paul grew fond of Clinton before the campaign and that fondness only increased while campaigning with her. Spending that time together gave him a deeper understanding of Clinton, the person, not just the politician.

"Part of it was...having spent some time with her family. She was the serious one. I think it had a profound impact on her," Paul explained. "She always told me to be out there and be tough but to keep your guard up. I think her father had a profound impact on her. More so than we ever knew."

Hugh Rodham was a demanding father, Paul grew to understand. Father expected his daughter to work hard and keep her head down.

And she did that in public. Perhaps, too much, too serious, especially when she faced comparisons to Bill, her gregarious, loquacious, two-term president-turned candidate's spouse.

"She was always compared to the presidents...her husband and Obama," Paul lamented.

And while Paul grew to understand Clinton's upbringing with a challenging parent, he struggled a bit to explain why Clinton failed to show more of herself--the real self that he witnessed in more intimate settings--in public. "I don't know..." Paul said, "She is such a funny, engaging, connected person to work for. She demonstrates that when she is one on one. She actually listens. There was always a difference when she was on stage."

But the constant barrage of complaints that Clinton was too robotic, too cautious, too formulaic, too much of a stiff politician, that's just a bit much for Paul. "It was unfair," he felt about the magnitude of the criticism.

Paul does acknowledge that the Iowa staff had some differences of opinion with Clinton's national campaign in Brooklyn, New York, a common complaint among presidential campaigns. The Iowa campaign wanted Clinton in the state more often, wanted her to get outside of the bigger cities more frequently, overnight more often in the state to help show she really wanted to be here and, yes, maybe bring in an Obama (maybe Barack and/or Michelle?) to help down the stretch when Clinton was failing to increase her support on her own. Bring along former Vice President Joe Biden, as well.

But it was also difficult to convince top leadership to increase resources, visibility and time in Iowa when the campaign's internal polls showed Iowa was becoming a lost cause for Clinton.

Paul felt like that happened for three main reasons.

1. Economic Message

"We did not follow the 'North Star' on the economy message as we should have." Donald Trump zeroed in on voters' angst about the jobs of yesterday disappearing today and worrying that there would be no jobs to replace them tomorrow.

2. The Affordable Care Act (A.C.A.)/Obamacare

"She (Clinton) was very loyal to President Obama. And I think tried so hard to run a campaign as good as his. But on the issue of healthcare...we spent so much time defending the A.C.A....and not enough time on co-pays and other things that would improve it. I think if she would have stood up and said, 'The A.C.A. was one step, but here's what we need to do to improve it.'"

The failure to acknowledge that Iowans' co-pays on their insurance kept going up and that many weren't saving the money on healthcare that candidate Obama had promised helped doom Clinton with some who weren't convinced that Obama's signature legislative accomplishment was as great as they had once hoped.

Clinton's loyalty to Obama definitely caught Paul's eye, though. "It's fascinating that after that nasty primary fight in '07 and '08 (between Clinton and Obama when they battled for the Democratic presidential nomination) and then eight years later, she would be so loyal to his healthcare plan."

"In a large part, that cost her the presidency," Paul said.

That, perhaps, but also the third major problem of the campaign.

3. The Emails

"We were playing defense from the get go," Paul said of what became the most talked about, most debated, and, yes, maybe the most over-hyped failure of Clinton's campaign: her decision to use her family's private, home server for her official email communications while she was the United States Secretary of State, instead of the secure federal system.

"I remember sitting in my office in the U.S.D.A...I had taken the job (with the Clinton presidential campaign) but not left U.S.D.A.," Paul recounted, "I remember watching the event she did at the United Nations."

At that event--which was actually about women's rights at a conference she attended as Secretary of State--Clinton tried to explain away her questionable decisions regarding her emails.

She failed. Badly.

Let's go back to what she said on that infamous day on March 10, 2015:

> "*There are four things I want the public to know. First, when I got to work as Secretary of State, I opted for convenience to use my personal email account, which was allowed by the State Department, because I thought it would be easier to carry just one device for my work and for my personal emails instead of two. Looking back, it would've been better if I'd simply used a second email account and carried a second phone, but at the time, this didn't seem like an issue.*
>
> *Second, the vast majority of my work emails went to government employees at their government addresses, which meant they were captured and preserved immediately on the system at the State Department.*
>
> *Third, after I left office, the State Department asked former Secretaries of State for our assistance in providing copies of work-related emails from our personal accounts. I responded right away and provided all my emails that could possibly be work-related, which totaled roughly 55,000 printed pages, even though I knew that the State Department already had the vast majority of them. We went through a thorough process to identify all of my work-related emails and deliver them to the State Department. At the end, I chose not to keep my private personal emails — emails about planning Chelsea's wedding or my mother's funeral arrangements, condolence notes to friends as well as yoga routines, family vacations, the other things you typically find in inboxes. No one wants their personal emails made public, and I think most people understand that and respect that privacy.*
>
> *Fourth, I took the unprecedented step of asking that the State Department make all my work-related emails public for everyone to see. I am very proud of the work that I and my colleagues and our public servants at the department did during my four years as Secretary of State, and I look forward to people being able to see that for themselves.*

Again, looking back, it would've been better for me to use two separate phones and two email accounts. I thought using one device would be simpler, and obviously, it hasn't worked out that way."

(Courtesy: Time Magazine)

Over the months that followed, Clinton's excuses for her decisions changed/morphed/evolved. But the answers only reinforced to some skeptics a reason not to trust Clinton...to believe that the Clintons play by their own rules...that the Clintons believe they are entitled to their own rules...and that they only talk about these things if they get caught.

Clinton wasn't really disciplined for her decisions. But she endured plenty of criticism. There was this, too, which became a headline across the country.

"Extremely careless."

That was how FBI Director James Comey on July 5, 2016, characterized Clinton's actions. "Although we did not find clear evidence that Secretary Clinton or her colleagues intended to violate laws governing the handling of classified information," Comey said, "there is evidence that they were extremely careless in their handling of very sensitive, highly classified information."

Clinton used her personal email system to send work email, some of which was classified. Comey said, while Clinton's actions violated laws, they didn't rise to the level of violations that should warrant criminal prosecution against her. Still, though, damage was done. The damage followed Clinton everywhere she went.

"Every event we did," Paul said, "that issue (email) never went away."

Clinton caused the problem, and her inability to fully take responsibility when she addressed it at the United Nations' event penalized her, regardless of Comey's decision not to punish her.

She downplayed it at the beginning, then tried to excuse it by saying that it was a matter of convenience to use one electronic device and one email for both work and personal matters, later got defiant trying to justify it and eventually--months after this became such a big deal--finally apologized for it.

"It was never put to bed. There was never a hard stop," Paul explained from a campaign messaging standpoint. "First, it was 'this is not important.' Finally, it became, 'I made a mistake.' There was never a hard stop."

I witnessed Clinton's reluctance during the middle of this mess to admit that she was the one who messed up. This was from July 26, 2015.

Me: "For the Democrats who really like you, I have heard some say, 'Why does this whole email thing have to be so complicated?'"

Clinton: "Yes, right. Well, actually it's not complicated. In fact, if you can cut through the efforts to make it complicated, it is pretty straightforward. I chose to use an email for convenience when I was Secretary of State."

She added, "Everything I did was legal."

"I never sent nor received any classified information." (She tried to claim that she didn't send anything that was classified at the time. Some material was retroactively deemed classified as she tried to explain).

Clinton closed her words on this topic with this, "I just regret that it's been confusing and, you know, somewhat concerning to people...because, there's as they say, no there, there."

No apology. No admitting that she caused this or that she broke the law. All we got from her at the time was that some people may have been confused, even though they shouldn't be confused. Her "no there, there" emphasis offered her final defense that she really didn't do anything wrong, so let's move on.

But enough of the public (and the media) didn't move on.

"It was a mistake," Paul summed up.

Clinton, the tactician, didn't just have style working against her campaign. She also had gender, in Paul's estimation. And that is something for future female candidates to remember in Iowa.

"You saw it at the state fair. I saw it at some of the union things," Paul said of the hostility and sexism he witnessed, "Some of the union guys...not so sure. We were asking people to replace an African-American president with a woman."

That was more diversity than some of these white men were ready to accept.

Remember the dedicated door knocker, Cindy Pollard, in Newton? She can't count how many times that she heard someone say or read someone post that Clinton was a b*tch on social media (others used even more derogatory terms). "Women were just as bad as the men...maybe worse," she said of the hostility she experienced toward Clinton.

Pollard had a female activist's take on Clinton. Paul provided a campaign assessment of the struggles of a female candidate. Dr. Dianne Bystrom has the research, analysis and insight to back up that women face additional hurdles to get into office. For 22 years, Bystrom served as the Director of the Carrie Chapman Catt Center for Women and Politics at Iowa State University in Ames.

To give you an idea of her background, just check out the names of some of the 19 books she has helped to write over the years:

"Media Disparity: A Gender Battleground"
"Women & Executive Office: Pathways and Performance"
"Cracking the Highest Glass Ceiling: A Global Comparison of Women's Campaigns for Executive Office"
"Gender and Elections"
"Legislative Women: Getting Elected, Getting Ahead"
"Gender and Candidate Communication"
"Anticipating Madam President"
"Women Transforming Congress"

That doesn't count her involvement in hundreds of other articles as the author or quoted authority. Although, as she points out, you don't need to be an accomplished clinician to see what Clinton was up against. She emailed me this:

"Let's not forget the Trump rallies – including those in Iowa. As was well documented throughout the election cycle, Trump's rallies were known for men and women advocating against Clinton with graphic messaging on signs, buttons and t-shirts, which subordinated and sexualized Clinton.

Some examples: 'Trump 2016: Finally someone with balls'; 'Life's a b*tch, don't vote for one' (with Clinton's face); 'Trump that b*tch"; 'She's a c**t, vote for Trump'; an image of a boy urinating on the word 'Hillary'; an image of Trump having knocked Clinton, clad in a clingy tank top, to the floor of a boxing ring; and 'Hillary couldn't satisfy her husband, can't satisfy us.'

Anger is known to provide a conduit through which perceived threats to masculinity result in a sexualization of the female target—which is viewed as either having or seeking more power and influence—in order to subordinate her and 'put her back in her place.'

Research illustrates that anger is one of several aggressive emotions—along with contempt and disgust—that yields backlash against female candidates who are perceived as power seeking. Researchers have theorized that many Trump voters engaged in such lewd communication about Clinton because she represented a threat to the masculine paradigm and they were unwilling to accept a woman holding a position of power over them."

People spewed that venom toward other female candidates, too. That included Patty Judge, an historic figure in the state. In 1998, Judge became the state's first female secretary of agriculture. In 2016, Judge--who also in her career served as state senator and lieutenant governor-- was the party's U.S. Senate candidate (she lost to Republican U.S. Senator Chuck Grassley by nearly 25 points). Judge told me that she had never seen it so bad in her nearly four decades in politics. "I've never seen such hostility, such crude and rude things hurled at me," Judge sneered, "It was just ugly."

Bystrom, the expert on women in politics, also felt that Clinton wasn't a typical "woman in politics." "Hillary Clinton has been in the national public eye since the 1992 presidential campaign," Bystrom said, "During which time she broke the mold of a 'typical' presidential candidate wife."

Breaking the mold meant changing the role of first lady. Clinton led a high-profile push to reform health care. It never made it through Congress. But the effort pushed Clinton into a much higher-profile role than her predecessors.

"Of all the first ladies, Clinton is considered one of the few activist first ladies. Eleanor Roosevelt was also an activist first lady," Bystrom said, "So, Clinton generated negative media coverage and public opinion when she stepped into the national limelight in 1992."

In other words, some people weren't ready or didn't approve of Clinton taking on a more public policy, rather than just mostly ceremonial role.

That's one academic's view. Here's additional scientific thought on this. RABA Research, a bipartisan firm based in Des Moines, asked a simple, but brilliant, question:

"Setting aside the current presidential candidates--do you think that Americans are ready for a woman to be president, or are they not?"

The poll sampled 1,076 likely voters in Iowa on September 6-8, 2016 (using traditional landlines, cell phones and online interviews). So this is two months before voters had to make their final choice on election day.

The results: 66 percent of those polled said Americans were ready for a female president. Obviously, that means about one-third of those who replied felt the country was not ready. That's a lot of people.

Some specific demographic breakdowns went like this about those who said the country was ready:

Men--63 percent
Women--70 percent

Not a huge difference here. I thought the gap would be wider.

Democrats--92 percent
Republicans--44 percent

Now, that's a difference.

Here are several additional numbers that stuck out to me that broke down respondents into age when asked if they believed the country was ready for a woman president:

18-29 year-olds--73 percent
30-64 year-olds--68 percent
65 plus--60 percent

It looks like Clinton's own age group (she turned 68 during that campaign) had the biggest concerns about a woman becoming the next president of the United States. And older Iowans are the most likely group to vote. That's an extra hurdle Clinton faced.

Those numbers are interesting. But I also have to wonder how many people had a hard time separating the question from Clinton? Clinton was the Democrats' nominee and well, she is a woman. So how much did that fact weigh on people's minds when they answered the question about whether they could support a woman president? Especially with Republicans?

Again, impossible to say. Either way, it was striking to me how many Republicans (56 percent) declined to say that the country was ready for a "Madam President."

Is that the main reason Clinton lost? Doubt it. There were additional factors, of course. What if those DNC emails hadn't been hacked and sensitive information became public that embarrassed Clinton?

What if the Russians hadn't been involved in the 2016 campaign by spreading false information through social media and actively working to get Trump elected instead of Clinton?

What if Comey hadn't alerted members of Congress just 11 days before the election that the investigation into Clinton's use of her private email server as secretary of state had uncovered additional emails "that appear pertinent" to that investigation?

Comey's decision dominated the national headlines at a time that undecided voters were making up their minds. It seems naïve to think that didn't influence some voters to turn against Clinton.

All of those factors, when combined, made it more difficult for Clinton. Yet, she still earned nearly 3 million more votes than Trump nationally.

Despite that accomplishment, it would stand to reason some people out there wouldn't vote for Clinton because she was a woman, right? Or that at least they were less inclined to vote for her because of her gender?

Back to something else Dr. Bystrom said, "I've studied her public opinion polls since 1992. In general, she gets very high marks when she is actually serving in office (U.S. Senator, Secretary of State) rather than running for office, particularly for president in 2008 and 2016. When she was first lady, she also had higher approval ratings at the end of her tenure and after Bill's affair with Monica."

I didn't doubt Bystrom's claims but wanted additional empirical perspective. Thankfully, the Pew Research Center made it easy. Americans clearly had different views of Clinton, depending on when it was, what was happening at the time and what role she had at the time.

May, 1993: 60 percent favorability

Clinton had just become the First Lady of the United States. People liked her.

February, 1996: 42 percent favorability

Uh, oh. "Travelgate" was soaring from shore to shore in the country, when Clinton was accused of improperly firing workers in the White House travel office. That was the Clintons' first real scandal of the first term. And the public didn't like it.

August, 1998: 63 percent favorability

Monica. Bill Clinton's dirty little secret was public. He, the 49-year-old married man, was fooling around in the Oval Office with 22-year-old Monica Lewinsky, a White House intern who wasn't even half his age. It was a brutal time for Hillary Clinton, no doubt, and her favorability with Americans climbed to its highest point thus far, thanks to people's sympathies.

After Bill left his second term, Hillary began her first as U.S. Senator of New York.

January, 2001: 60 percent

Clinton was back to where she started. Her approval rate at the beginning of her freshman year as senator mirrored her early days as first lady.

May, 2008: 48 percent

The public watched Clinton's first run for president, decided it didn't want her as the Democrats' nominee and also decided it wasn't a big fan of hers, either.

November, 2009: 66 percent

Look who's back! Clinton's first year as U.S. Secretary of State was a popular one with voters. She was more well-liked than ever on the national level.

December, 2012: 65 percent

America liked what it saw from Clinton traveling across the world at breakneck pace. Her numbers did fall after that, though, as reports continued about the four Americans, including U.S. Ambassador Christopher Stephens, who died during a September 11, 2012 attack by Islamic militants in Libya.

Clinton's numbers kept falling into her second presidential run, and she ultimately lost about a quarter of her support from her secretary of state high. Voters like Clinton more when she isn't a candidate, it seems.

"While I can't prove that gender worked against Clinton in Iowa, my opinion is that it did," Bystrom surmised.

One odd thing--at least to me--about Clinton's failings in Iowa, though, is the recent success of Republican women. Did gender not work against them? Iowa Republicans have achieved a series of historic firsts.

2013: Mary Mosiman appointed first female Iowa State Auditor (State Auditor David Vaudt resigned to become Chairman of the Governmental Accounting Standards Board)
2014: Joni Ernst elected first female U.S. Senator from Iowa
2015: Linda Upmeyer elected first female Iowa Speaker of the House
2017: Kim Reynolds became first female Governor of Iowa (ascended from lieutenant governor when Governor Terry Branstad became U.S. Ambassador to China)
2018: Reynolds became first woman elected Governor of Iowa

To be fair, Clinton was able to become the first woman to win the 2016 Iowa Caucuses. She did become an historic figure in her own right. But aside from that, most of the other recent, historic political firsts in Iowa went to Republican women instead.

CHAPTER 12

STATUS CHECK

Second District Congressman Dave Loebsack was the last Iowa Democrat standing in Washington, D.C. in 2018. The state's other five members serving in Congress were Republicans.

August 13, 2018 at the Iowa State Fair.

Photo by Dave Price

H illary Clinton became the figurehead of failure for the Democrats in 2016, mainly because she had been their presidential nominee. But she is one person and can't be blamed for nearly a decade of a declining disconnect for the party.

Before the 2018 midterm elections, I reached out to Democrats and Republicans for a status check. Where were the Democrats as the party in the minority? Where were Republicans with the mercurial President Donald Trump as the force of the party?

First, the Democrats. The 2016 presidential primary showed the split for the party: Clinton supporters and Bernie Sanders followers (no offense to the small but loyal Martin O'Malley contingent). And that Clinton-Sanders divide in political direction reflected what the party was up against.

Clinton had that trust problem with voters that may have been her greatest liability rather than the issues themselves. Her vice presidential running mate Tim Kaine, the U.S. Senator from Virginia, seemed to sidestep my question to him during the campaign about Clinton's problem of trust with the American people. Her email scandal and numerous others, including her husband's, throughout her decades in politics had taken a toll. How could she win if voters didn't trust her?

Here is what Kaine told me six weeks before the election when I asked him about polls that showed the public didn't trust Clinton:

"Hillary Clinton has a passion to serve families and kids and that's been the animating passion in her life...She is focused on others. Trump is focused on himself."

That's how he bypassed my question.

The Clinton campaign, in the months leading up to the caucus, worked to use people--small groups of them--to the candidate's advantage to overcome her issues of trustworthiness, access and relatability, like during that house party in Nancy Emanuel's home in Ottumwa.

"I think when she's in a smaller setting, she feels more relaxed and shows who she is," Emanuel said, "I'm assuming that's why she wanted to do more of these home visits...at ease, comfortable...not under the microscope."

And let's face it: Clinton WAS always under the microscope in the media, the public, everywhere. That happens when you are in politics for the past half century, no doubt.

So the Clinton campaign kept it small to try to win big later. Patty Judge, an early Clinton backer and former lieutenant governor of Iowa, told me after that house party that the strategy could work although she confided to me later that she may have just offered an answer back then out of blind party loyalty. "I was probably giving you a politically correct answer. But I think that she had to do those small parties because she needed to get some loyal people lined up."

Judge sensed back then that enthusiasm would be an issue for Clinton. It wasn't for Sanders. Why? Is socialism the way back to relevance for Democrats?

Few knew who Sanders was when he started campaigning for president in 2015. But he ended up pushing Clinton harder than most anyone could have predicted, both in the Iowa Caucuses and the national nomination process.

A few of the issues that Sanders championed give Judge pause, not because she doesn't believe in them but rather whether they should be major tenets of her party's priorities for 2020.

"I talked a lot about the minimum wage," Judge said of her own unsuccessful campaign for the U.S. Senate in 2016 against Republican long-timer, Chuck Grassley.

"I absolutely believe that it should be raised," she told me. Judge called it "the all boats theory." In other words, "a rising tide lifts all boats."

"If we do it over time," Judge said of raising the minimum wage, "It will raise everybody's salary."

However, Judge found that traveling the state, particularly in rural areas, pushing the idea of increasing the wage from the $7.25 minimum to $15 per hour as Sanders supported was just too much for too many people.

Judge said that her experience talking to people was that, "They think raising the minimum wage only shrinks the gap between what they make and what the illegal immigrant or the kid making minimum wage earns."

She felt people were more eager to hear the message Republicans sell on the matter. "They got a message from Republicans about just getting a better, good wage," Judge explained.

Judge's experience from talking to neighbors was that people thought the minimum wage could go up, but their own wages may not necessarily rise as much. In other words, the people who made $10 an hour or $13 or $14 before lawmakers raised the minimum wage expected that would just get bumped up to the $15 an hour level, like all the minimum wage earners. And the people already making $15 or $17 or $18 thought they would just stay where they were.

Judge's conversations told her that people feared too many individuals would all end up making essentially the same amount of money ($15 per hour), regardless of what they were doing. Businesses would likely raise prices and cut labor hours/positions. And in the end, the higher minimum wage wouldn't really be helping as many people as supporters hoped.

"In her heart," Judge said she feels like $15 an hour is a necessary wage for Iowans to make to try to support themselves. But she doesn't think that should be Democrats' main issue as they try to win back voters.

Tuition-free college was another one that gave her pause. No doubt it could reduce the debt load for college students. That could be particularly important in Iowa, where lawmakers have pulled back on funding for the past three decades, regardless of which major political party was in charge. That has meant students and their families have to pay a higher share of the costs, and that share has continued to escalate.

"Why should we pay for Donald Trump's kids to go to college," was Clinton's refrain on the campaign trail at the idea of tuition-free college that Sanders pushed. Tuition-free college may be an idea that sounds good in principle, but it's too costly and impractical for some, including Judge. Finding other ways to bring down the cost of college, particularly for low and middle income families is a better idea for Democrats in Judge's opinion.

Cathy Glasson disagrees. Glasson, a former nurse from Coralville, finished second in the 2018 Democratic primary for governor in Iowa. She often talked about the need for her party to be "bold." That became her campaign theme. And for her, being bold means hiking the minimum wage immediately (getting it to $15 per hour in three years) and making sure everyone can go to college by having taxpayers pick up the cost of college tuition. "Folks that are struggling to pay their bills, to put gas in their car, put food on the table, to pay rent, can't afford to wait any longer in this state."

Glasson laments the increasing gap between the "haves" and the "have nots." And she believes that minor changes like a small boost in the minimum wage or minimal increases in Pell Grants to help lower income families afford college won't do enough quickly enough. "Too many families are struggling," she said.

Glasson makes the case that more families who succeed instead of fail will benefit entire communities, not just that individual household. "That's what drives our economy," Glasson said, "People with money spending it locally."

That message did seem to connect with younger people, as evidenced by the visual makeup of the crowd at Sanders' 2016 crowds. Younger people weren't making as much money as they wanted after they graduated from college, had loads of debt and too often had to move back in with their parents. Not exactly the American dream.

However, Judge and Glasson's differing senses of the politically possible demonstrate a much deeper divide in philosophy for the party. The 2016 Clinton vs. Sanders squeaky close Iowa Caucus finish showed how split the party was on its future. These two septuagenarians got a lot of people thinking-- and arguing--over the future.

Those arguments continue. Peggy Huppert, an activist from Johnston, experienced them and still hears them. The "what if?" arguments. What if Sanders (she worked on his campaign) had won the nomination, instead of Clinton? Maybe he would be president? "He (Sanders) spoke to a lot of people," Huppert said, "I fear they ended up voting for Donald Trump."

Sanders, a career politician, came off as a non-politician with his disheveled look, embrace of Democratic socialism and disdain for big money, big corporations and traditional 10 second candidate sound bites, Huppert believed.

"It was just so interesting to see the random people who would just come into the office and volunteer. We had a bunch of inner city kids come from Chicago to canvas. Came in busses. Slept in sleeping bags and ate peanut butter sandwiches. We had one person from England, one from Canada," she marveled at the appeal Sanders had with voters who often had never been involved in a previous political campaign.

"The fact he was rumpled and unpretentious," Huppert surmised and agreed with the attraction. "I'll admit that I kind of liked his grumpy, rumpled persona."

But some friends didn't like her dedication to Sanders, rather than to the woman looking to become the country's first female president. "What's wrong with you?," Huppert said she heard, "You're a traitor to your gender!"

Huppert felt those attacks were misguided. Support the candidate because you believe in that candidate, not simply because of that candidate's gender. She knows the party has some serious work to do to mend itself.

Pete D'Alessandro, Sanders' state director for the 2016 Iowa Caucuses, would agree with that, but he also doesn't want to see Democrats abandon the far left of the party. "On the progressive side of things," D'Alessandro told me, "There's been a vacuum."

Sanders filled that vacuum. D'Alessandro tried to fill that void, too, when he made his first run for office in 2018 in what was initially a seven-person Democratic primary in Iowa's 3rd Congressional District. He finished third in what ended up being a three-person contest. But he doesn't think that means Democrats are rejecting the ideas that he and Sanders pushed...the anti-establishment, anti-big corporation, pro-worker Democratic socialist message. "People wanted to hear things that didn't sound like it was poll-tested," he said. Instead D'Alessandro said people crave talk, "Like it was real...I hate to say it this way, but it's kind of like the way Trump was able to do."

Trump connected with people but so much of the way he talks disheartens Joseph Jones. Jones, like D'Alessandro, has worked for politicians in the past (former U.S. Senator Tom Harkin and former Governor Tom Vilsack). And in 2018, *he* decided to run for office. And Jones won a seat on the city council in Windsor Heights, a town of about 5,000 people just outside Des Moines.

"People just felt emboldened to say whatever was in their head," Jones said of the political climate that Trump helped to create, "...all the things we teach our young kids what not to say...how to treat others...these American values were really being challenged."

It's not the civility that Jones preaches in his full-time job as Executive Director of the Harkin Institute for Public Policy and Citizen Engagement (the organization his former boss began upon retirement). "I think this was all a big siren call for people to say, 'Woah! Wait a minute. This is going too far. These people who say they don't trust the government and don't trust the media."

Jones can't stand it. He can't let people think they need to distrust anything that doesn't immediately echo what they initially think about an issue or person. So he got involved in the government to change that culture. He doesn't stand up and bad mouth anyone who might disagree with him. Keep it civil. That is what he urges other Democrats to do (although his city council seat is a part-time, non-partisan position). He wants them to get involved but not everyone needs to run for president of the United States.

Jones wants people to think about public service in whatever form works for them, whether it is city council, state legislature, Congress, school board or planning and zoning commission. Just do something.

Jones's bio on the Windsor Heights website reflects his commitment to get involved:

"Joseph serves on the Board of Directors for the Iowa Association of Business and Industry Foundation, Mid-Iowa Health Foundation, and Greater Des Moines Habitat for Humanity. Joseph is a Trustee on the American Council of Young Political Leaders Board of Trustees, is a graduate of Leadership Iowa, and was named to the Business Record's "Forty Under 40" Class of 2009. He is currently an active volunteer with Iowa Radio Reading Information Service (IRIS) and Everybody Wins! Iowa."

He feels Democrats are getting the message to get involved, in whatever form that may be. "In the past, you see people get angry about the presidential election and then it falls off," Jones said, "That hasn't happened this time."

Michael Libbie was another behind-the-scenes type who decided that 2018 was the time to be a candidate (although he did run for mayor of Fort Dodge three decades ago). Libbie's cause to run for city council in Windsor Heights was expanding senior housing opportunities. But he found out that what people really cared about were sidewalks. And many of them REALLY didn't want additional sidewalks through neighborhoods. "Angry people are resistant to change," Libbie realized.

Libbie, who owns his own marketing firm and hosts a radio show/podcast about business, said that his problem was running on policy. "I'm in the marketing business. I know people make up their mind on emotion, not fact. I should have known that."

So his advice to Democrats is to find better ways to connect with people on an emotional level. "Still pissed off!" he says of many people these days. Trump connected with those who had grown angry with politicians, the direction of the country and their own lives, Libbie said. Democrats need to figure out how to do that, too. "I don't want people telling me what to do," was what Libbie said people told him about those sidewalks.

Democrats need to understand that some people don't believe that government is the answer to their problems, Libbie thinks, so Democrats have to talk to them in a different way.

"Connecting with Iowans is rudimentary," said Deidre DeJear, also a first-time candidate in 2018. After working for Barack Obama's presidential campaign in Iowa, she decided it was time to get involved as a candidate and run for secretary of state. She lost her bid but won over scores of fans with her passionate commitment to the importance of getting active.

DeJear encourages her fellow Democrats to go meet people; don't wait for the people to come to them or their events. "The concept at its core relies on 'meeting the voter where they're at.' Whether that be an inbox, mailbox, senior living facility, school, civic organization, social media or union hall. Once making the connection, we then listen, in search of understanding who that person is and what's important to them."

Photo courtesy of Deidre DeJear

DeJear learned during her work as an organizer on the Obama campaign that people value feeling that someone was listening. It was something that became evident during Trump's successful run in Iowa, too. "Every person wants to know that their voice is heard, that their vote is valued and that they are a part of something bigger than themselves," DeJear said, "In today's climate, where so much seems to push us further apart, we need to find what knits us together rather than what sets us apart. We have more in common than not. And the first step will always be pulling up a chair, inviting someone to the conversation, and finding those shared values."

Get out there, even if it is uncomfortable is the advice of Iowa's only Democratic member of Congress in 2018, Second District Representative Dave Loebsack of Iowa City. Loebsack got elected in 2007. "I really believe a lot of the reason I have been able to win is my ability to get out and about," Loebsack told me by phone while driving from a trip to the Iowa Veterans Home in Marshalltown (It isn't in his district, but he wanted to make sure that veterans received proper care there he told me) and Mariposa County Park in Newton (This is in his district, and he checked on an ongoing restoration project).

"Getting out where people live, work and play," Loebsack said of his travel plans. But, he said, perhaps the most important thing he and other Democrats can do for the future is to make sure those travel plans include some uncomfortable stops, too.

"The easiest thing to do as a member of Congress is to avoid a place where you may not get a friendly reception," Loebsack explained. "It's easy. It's understandable. But it doesn't make any sense. I know that I need to go out to places where I may not feel entirely comfortable. Am I going to agree with everything I hear there? Of course not. But that's part of being a representative."

He may get chewed out from time to time. But Loebsack says that it builds a relationship with people--regardless of their differences--and he believes it will help the party rebuild. "I think politicians would be surprised. And I can't speak for the rest of the country," Loebsack said, "But I have found in Iowa that if I do that, those folks...more often than not...respect me for doing that."

Getting there is a big step but making use of the conversation is vital, too, Loebsack believes. He wants his party to talk more about the future. "I'm glad that the economy is doing well. But I think that was established by President Obama and Democrats in Congress (President Trump and Republicans who stormed to the majority in Congress when Obama left office in 2017 would disagree). We need to focus on expanding economic progress...making sure the economy works for everyone, not just the wealthy and well-connected," Loebsack advises.

"Whether it's education or job training, infrastructure, expanding rural broadband," he added, which he thinks should be part of the party's message to those who haven't benefited from the improving economic climate since the Great Recession hit in late 2007.

The value of the government should be part of that message to people, according to former Iowa Governor Tom Vilsack. Vilsack believes the message is critically important for Democrats to share in the rural areas. But he warns to pay close attention to *how* Democrats talk to people there. "Don't go there and say, 'I have a program for you!'" Vilsack cautioned.

"That's what Democrats do," Vilsack explained, "But that makes people say, 'Wait! I don't need you to give me something.' That again makes them feel like you are talking down to them. Talk instead about a partnership. Talk about what government does. We often don't talk about what government does well...whether it is coal in West Virginia or corn in Iowa. You gotta show up. You gotta sell government where you can...a compelling vision that shows that you understand the economy, the rural economy."

Vilsack probably spent almost 15 minutes making his point. That's how passionate he is about this and how frustrated he also is that too many Democrats didn't take his advice (yes, that included Clinton and her campaign).

Help people understand conservation, he says, and if necessary, incent them so they feel like they are part of a partnership with the government to promote cleaner agriculture. Vilsack thinks the same approach may work better for Democrats when it comes to regulation. "Fraud, waste and abuse," are what Vilsack says people hear about and convince them of the failures of government, so that feeds their inherent lack of faith in it. "People say, 'hell, yes, I want government out of my life!'"

So when Democrats push more regulations, that may instantly push people away from supporting them, at least some people. Vilsack says, instead, Democrats have to more patiently lay out the intentions of additional regulations and in some cases, "Might be better to incent changes sometimes rather than regulate."

Some changes, though, frighten people. And Vilsack believes some of that fear helped elect Trump. The world is changing quickly and people feel like that world is leaving them out or will soon. "The government needs to do a much better job of the future jobs...workforce. If driverless cars are going to replace professions, Amazon replacing malls...what are we going to do for all of these people? Are you preparing for that new day?" he said and urged Democrats to embrace the conversation with people about adjusting to the job market of the future.

Those were just a few of the examples Vilsack laid out. In the end, he underscored what he considers the most important facet of any of this for Democrats to reclaim relevancy: "Show up."

Get outside the big cities. Get everywhere. Don't just talk to reliable Democrats. Talk to everyone, even if it means intense debate (like Loebsack talked about) with those distrustful of what Democrats have done (or not done) over the past decade. Be sincere. Be thoughtful. Be patient. Be passionate. But show up. Doing those things, Vilsack believes, will help Democrats reconnect.

There is an eager audience out there, mainly because of the disappointment people are feeling from the Trump presidency, Vilsack maintains. "Want competence. Want someone who isn't yelling and screaming. Want less celebrity. But have to show they have the finger on the pulse. Show that they understand the tremendous transformation we're going through...that they can reduce the anxiety of the transformation," he said.

He continued, "Campaigns are often in response to previous campaigns. Folks, when they elected Barack Obama, wanted smart because they thought George W. Bush wasn't. Then with Trump...they thought Obama was cool. People wanted someone who wasn't."

Dave Kochel would not use the word "cool" to describe President Donald Trump. Mitt Romney, Lamar Alexander, George W. Bush? Kochel respected all of those Republicans and worked to get them elected president. In 2016, he preferred former Florida Governor Jeb Bush. But, Trump? No. Hell, no, in fact.

Kochel has worked for Republican campaigns for nearly four decades going all the way back to his college days at Iowa State University. Kochel led the students for Bob Dole for President in 1988 on campus.

But the 2016 campaign nearly killed him. Watching Trump take over his party tortured his soul. Cancer tested him more.

On October 10, 2015, Bush and the other Republican candidates were finding out how much of a force Trump would be in the presidential primary. Kochel's mind wandered to more pressing matters. His lack of energy, swollen lymph nodes and oddly colored tongue (it actually turned black) all led doctors to give him the grim diagnosis: he had acute lymphoblastic leukemia (ALL). It's a rare, aggressive blood cancer, especially rare.

The American Cancer Society estimates that just one half of one percent of all diagnosed cancers involve ALL. Kochel became one of the 3,280 men a year in the United States who became one of those one half of one percent.

Kochel had to put politics aside, the best he could. And it was time for him to be more aggressive with the cancer that, at one point, doctors estimated would only give him three more weeks to live. Three weeks.

F*ck you, cancer, would be his response.

Here is what Kochel wrote on his Caringbridge.org website where family and friends could track his battle:

"As for you, Leukemia, here is my message to you: I'm not just going to beat you, I'm going utterly humiliate you. You're going to be sorry. I'll burn your villages and your towns, and I'll embarrass you in front of everyone you care about. I'll smash you into pieces, and me and my friends will bury your dead parts across the seven continents. You'll never want to try me again. I promise. And when I'm bombing down the mountain at Vail next year on my new Burton snowboard — I'll let out a war whoop you'll hear from your graves."

He battled. The cancer lost.

Trump, though, couldn't be stopped.

Kochel was working with Bush's presidential campaign. He started as the national campaign manager and then, following a campaign shakeup, moved to senior strategist. Regardless of the title, it was tough.

Kochel had worked for Mitt Romney's 2008 and 2012 presidential campaigns. Romney had still been contemplating a 2016 run (which would have been his third try) when Kochel let him know that he would join the Bush team instead. "His family," Kochel said of the Romneys, "...I love them. It was difficult. It was heartbreaking."

It was so difficult because, while Kochel respected the man and his family so much, he also knew that another presidential run would ultimately end the same...defeat. Romney had already run for president twice. What would be different in a third run? Not enough, Kochel figured. And even Romney himself couldn't provide a convincing case for Romney 3.0. "You've run twice. You failed to get a nomination one time. You failed to beat Obama the second time. And I said, 'What's changed?'" Kochel recalled saying to Romney, "He didn't really have an answer."

In retrospect, Kochel wonders if Romney should have sat out for a while, noticed how Bush and his fellow Floridian, Senator Marco Rubio, both failed to flourish sufficiently enough and then swooped in as the final alternative to Trump? Perhaps. Who knows?

Instead, Romney stayed out, moved to Utah again and then got elected to the U.S. Senate in 2018.

But back to Bush. Trump mocked him as "Low Energy Jeb."

The campaign's exclamation point on the logo wouldn't change that image. Kochel thinks Bush could have changed it in a different way. "'Low Energy Jeb?'" Kochel wondered, "Fascinating because Jeb worked out all the time and could have kicked Trump's ass!"

I don't think he was kidding. I think Kochel wished it could have happened. Probably during one of those primary debates.

Bush during the campaign had called himself a "disruptor."

"A person or thing that prevents something, especially a system, process or event, from continuing as usual or as expected."

That is how the Cambridge Dictionary defines it.

Kochel felt like it meant someone, Bush, who could be "thoughtful and transformative." Someone who could come after a challenge in a unique way, not the standard, boring, safe way. He added this, "A no bullsh*t guy. Very disciplined. Super intelligent. Could defend conservative positions. Much more ideological than anyone gave him credit. Was the true ideologue in the Bush family," Kochel defined.

And while Kochel could tolerate the mocking of the "Jeb!" campaign slogan, he couldn't-- and still can't--handle the ridicule of Bush himself. "Of every Republican leader in the past 25 years, probably two stand out as the very best in talent," Kochel said, "That would be (Indiana Governor) Mitch Daniels and Jeb Bush."

Maybe Trump saw that, too. Maybe that's why he belittled Bush the way that he did. Bush couldn't shake the label of a "traditional" candidate, though, in Kochel's mind and he probably came across as "too polite" in those debates while Trump was far from it. "Probably an opportunity for Jeb to show some backbone...really give it to Trump," Kochel said that he wished would have happened, "He's always got his mom, Barbara Bush, over his shoulder, shaking her finger at him to behave, instead of going over to Trump and basically punching him in the face."

Now, 2 ½ years later, it's Kochel shaking his head instead. Trump is the most prominent member of his beloved Republican Party. But Kochel still doesn't consider Trump the head of the party. "Traditionally, the president is the head of the party," Kochel explained, "Trump is the head of the *movement*."

Trump's movement means keeping his base engaged and motivated on illegal immigration, tax cuts, cutting regulation and bashing the opposition. And he has been effective at all of those. Kochel gives him credit for that, even if he can barely stomach the vitriol that comes with much of that.

Kochel thinks Trump's success should be viewed as unique, though, not one that should be emulated by other aspirants. "You can't duplicate who and what he is. I just think the standards we attribute to him, you can't apply to anybody else," Kochel said.

"The 'bad boy brand' is already built into the 'Donald Trump brand'", Kochel figures.

Those divorces, tabloid headlines, lawsuits, etc., they are already there. That's the brand. "You can't apply these lessons equally to someone who is only known in the political context. To me, that's a huge inoculation to virtually every attack you can put on him. He's very unique in that way," Kochel said.

"Unique." The more he talks, the more you realize that the word isn't the quality Kochel wants emulated. "He's a cockroach when it comes to surviving. He could survive a political nuclear winter," Kochel said.

I have never heard Melissa Gesing or David Johnson call Trump a cockroach. But they both did view him as the annoyance that chased them away. Gesling quit her job. Johnson quit the party.

Gesing had been president of the Iowa Federation of Republican Women. As the name indicates, it is a group of Iowa women who support Republicans. Gesing still wanted to back Republicans, just not Trump, not after what he said and is alleged to have done to women over the years.

"I cannot in good conscience lead this organization or look at myself in the mirror each morning if I do not take a stand against the racism, sexism and hate that Donald J. Trump continues to promote."

That was part of Gesing's resignation announcement. She told me later that her decision to quit as the head of the organization cost her some Republican friends and it soured her feelings on politics. She left politics entirely for a while before finding what she considered to be a much better fit. Gesing took over in 2018 as the executive director of 50-50 in 2020. The group is non-partisan and aims to help women make up half of political officeholders by the end of the decade.

She will no longer be forced to try to fake loyalty to Trump.

David Johnson got elected to the Iowa House of Representatives in 1999 to represent Ocheydan, a town of about 500 (smaller than it was in the 1800s) in the far northwest corner of the state. Four years later, voters elected him to the state senate. Johnson proudly supported Republicans throughout his political career and was proud to say that he was one. But in 2016, he was so ashamed by one Republican, Trump, that he quit the party to become an Independent. "A bigot" Johnson called him. "Mark me down as never Trump!" Johnson declared.

Johnson, a follower of history, felt like Trump sounded too much like Germany's Nazi leader Adolph Hitler.

"Mr. Trump," Johnson said, "What he wants to do, is to make 'white male America' great again. This is very much a nationalist-driven campaign. I don't know why leaders in the Republican Party don't understand that."

Some of the leaders didn't seem to understand Johnson or Gesing's disgust with Trump. The Republican National Committee Chairwoman Ronna Romney McDaniel told me that Republicans should proudly run and follow Trump's leadership. "There is no problem running as the party of Donald Trump," she explained on November 8, 2017, during an event in Des Moines.

McDaniel made the case that members of the national media don't understand what is happening in too much of the country.

Republican Party of Iowa Chairman Jeff Kaufmann has been one of the most dedicated Trump supporters in the state. He is loyal to his party and its leaders and will scream until his voice gives out at rallies in their defense.

Although there was one night that stands out in contrast. It followed that "Access Hollywood" tape from 2005 with Trump seemingly bragging to host Billy Bush about his power over women.

"I better use some Tic Tacs just in case I start kissing her. You know, I'm automatically attracted to beautiful...I just start kissing them. It's like a magnet. Just kiss. I don't even wait. And when you're a star, they let you do it. You can do anything...Grab 'em by the p**sy. You can do anything."

It became a rather unfortunate situation for Kaufmann as he had to lead his party's annual Ronald Reagan Dinner in Des Moines on October 8, 2016. "I condemn those things when Bill Clinton did them and I condemn them now when Donald Trump says them," said Kaufmann.

Kaufmann also added that both candidates, Trump and Clinton, stood as far from perfect individuals before voters. "What we've got here in terms of the presidential election...we've got two flawed candidates," Kaufmann said, "Some people would say we have two seriously flawed candidates. Now Americans are going to have to make a choice."

But following Trump's election, Kaufmann made the choice with a full-throated support of Trump, at the expense of his voice at times. Kaufmann would make a habit of screaming into the microphone at rallies in defense of Trump by attacking opponents, critics, the media and use name-calling in ways I don't remember him doing during those years as a state legislator before becoming state party chairman.

"Are we proud of him?" Kaufmann asked at the party's July 20, 2018, fundraiser in Des Moines, "Absolutely!"

"Is he better than the left-wing nuts that they'd like to replace him with? Always!" Kaufmann roared with his voice straining.

Kaufmann also adopted Trump's style of name-calling. "Prince Frederick." "Sir Frederick." "The Prince of Polk County." Those were some of the names Kaufmann used during the 2018 Iowa governor's race to disparage the Democrats' wealthy nominee, Fred Hubbell, a retired businessman who grew up wealthy and became richer throughout his life. "Living in his own bubble," Kaufmann said of Hubbell.

The criticism was a bit rich from a party whose president benefited from his own father's tremendous wealth as a child. Nevertheless, Kaufmann used the insults as a way to portray Hubbell as out of touch with working families, a constituency that had proven to be vital to Trump's overwhelming 2016 election victory in the state.

Matt Strawn used a different style when he served as chairman of the Republican Party of Iowa for the 2012 cycle. Name-calling wasn't his thing. But Strawn did know what played in the state. He sensed Texas Senator Ted Cruz would do well in the 2016 Iowa Caucuses. "Iowa would be fertile ground for Ted Cruz," Strawn had told me months before the election.

Strawn was correct. Cruz won the Caucuses, successfully attracting the Christian conservatives like the two previous Caucus winners (Former Arkansas Governor Mike Huckabee in 2008 and former Pennsylvania Senator Rick Santorum in 2012, both of whom found virtually no traction as repeat candidates in 2016). But Cruz also "was running as an anti-establishment," as Strawn pointed out, a unique position for Cruz since he was a sitting member of the U.S. Senate.

But Cruz and Trump both sensed how annoyed the base was with Washington, D.C. and critics view of its continually hapless direction and failures to solve some of the country's most pressing issues.

Iowa Republicans wanted their own faith beliefs prominently respected in politics but they also wanted a leader who would give D.C. a hard kick in in the butt. Trump promised that and delivered. "Trump remains a brand more than an ideology," Strawn deduced, "...a brand of a style of politics and government the likes of which we haven't seen."

That doesn't mean Trump hasn't caused Strawn to squirm at times, particularly with his rhetoric on immigrants. But the way Trump talks and the issues he tries to champion will all cause Republicans to re-think what it means to be a Republican and what they want their party to be in the future, Strawn estimated.

"Establishment class versus anti-establishment class, social conservatism infused with a little Libertarian, Tea Party...we were finally going to settle that," Strawn had figured as he witnessed the debate during the 2016 campaign cycle overflowing with Republican primary candidates.

But Trump, the candidate who is so hard to define (Republican? Independent? Trump Party?), came out the victor in that. A truly unique force of his own. "Trump flipped over the table. Did Trump prolong that fight (for the future of the party) and that's a future fight that's just been put on ice?" Strawn wondered aloud, "Or will there be a fundamental transformation of the Republican Party and what becomes 'Trumpism?'"

For now, unlike Kochel's characterization, Strawn does consider Trump to be the head of the Republican Party nationally. "Absolutely," he told me, "When you look at the snapshot in time, the attitudinal change with Congress and the presidency."

Strawn accurately foresaw how much of the 2018 midterms would go. He knew that it would be a test for his party with Trump in charge. And it was. But he also knew that Trump could rally the base. And he did. "I believe that we are in an era of mobilization and not persuasion," Strawn had told me 11 months before the election, a theory that played out in 2018 as he predicted.

"Both parties will be talking to their bases," Strawn said, "The coastal media will be losing their minds over what Trump says. But if you have a few signature accomplishments, that can be enough to keep their base motivated and to show up (to vote)."

But Strawn, whose previous work also included state director for John McCain's 2008 presidential campaign, isn't so sure he would recommend that future candidates emulate Trump's style. "Be authentic and be true to who you are. It's trite to say. If you try to imitate Trump and it's not who you are, I don't think you're going to be successful."

Strawn does take a longer view on Trump's impact on the party, and he admits that he doesn't know what that will be. "In my neighborhood (relatively affluent and fast growing Des Moines suburb of Ankeny with a 2018 population of 63,000) many of those white collar families voted against Hillary Clinton," Strawn recalled of 2016 conversations with neighbors.

They voted for Trump but Strawn thinks it was more of a protest vote to support anybody but Clinton.

Going forward, though, Strawn is full of questions. Can Trump's blue collar populism that peeled Democrats away from

Clinton in 2016 resonate with white collar executives that have supported Republicans in the past? What about the college-educated couples? And those Independents and moderate Republicans, particularly women in the suburbs, can they stick with Trump?

The 2018 midterms showed suburban women especially turning away from Trump, a trend that particularly concerned Trump as he thinks of Trump's brand long-term. Younger people also ran away from Trump's party, another trend that is alarming to Strawn for the future.

Does that spell doom for Republicans again in 2020?

Strawn isn't so sure. Trump surprised many people once already in 2016 and he hasn't changed. "You can't say that Trump hasn't governed like he has campaigned!" Strawn summed up.

Don't count on Iowa's most prominent politicians to govern like President Trump, though, aside from western Iowa Congressman Steve King, whom voters narrowly elected to a ninth term in 2018, despite a whopping 70,000 registered voter edge that Republicans have over Democrats in the district.

King, whose comments degrading immigrants and diversity along with supporting white nationalists have irked party leadership, both in Iowa and in D.C., sounded Trump-like in his victory speech after the midterms. King used phrases like:

"Fake news"

"Never Trumpers"

"West Coast multi-billionaire leftists and East Coast multi-billionaire lefties" (blamed them for trying to beat him)

King told supporters, "My head is bloodied but unbowed. If they (his critics) think this is going to intimidate me, they are going to find out otherwise."

Iowa Governor Kim Reynolds has had to navigate supporting Trump with her public comments when she can, speaking out against him when her state's interests don't align with his words or policies plus keeping her thoughts to herself when she feels politically it would be wiser.

"He kept it simple," Reynolds said of Trump's success as a campaigner, "I mean, 'Make America Great Again.'"

"People were so frustrated. He really did speak to the working people. He resonated with them," Reynolds told me.

And much like other Republicans pointed out to me, she added, "So many new people to his rallies, not the people I have usually seen at the Republican rallies I had gone to."

Reynolds also appreciates the dedication of the throngs who endure hours of waiting in lines to get through security to enter Trump rallies and then sit or stand through a president who rarely seems at a loss for words when he stands at a microphone in front of thousands of riled-up supporters. Reynolds said, "He holds really long rallies and people would stay to the end."

The governor also added a comparison that, perhaps, the president wouldn't appreciate as much as she intended with the compliment. "Keeping the message simple. Kind of like (President Barack) Obama...connecting with people," she said.

Don't expect her to change her style to reflect Trump's, though. "I would take more from Governor (Terry) Branstad because we have similar styles."

Reynolds served as Branstad's lieutenant governor for six years before replacing him when he left to become Trump's U.S. Ambassador to China. "Talk, listen, work hard," she said she learned that from watching Branstad, "The honesty...be humble, be authentic...Iowans can smell a phony. The more they get to know you, they can trust you and understand you."

Why not emulate Trump's aggressive style on social media as a direct route to voters, away from the filters of traditional media outlets? "No," Reynolds laughed, "Not everyone can pull that off."

Reynolds called social media a mix of "a great media and a horrible media." It can be a great way to market a candidate and that person's positions, she believes, but the vitriol that can come along with it, she can do without. She has experienced that personally when trolls posted disparaging comments on her social media platforms, even though her posts had nothing to do with politics but rather included pictures of her grandchildren playing soccer.

"Disgusting," she called it.

And, no, Reynolds feels no obligation, need or desire to return the attacks. "I'm feeling no pressure to attack anyone on social media!" she told me emphatically, "I'm not compelled."

Reynolds' close friend, U.S. Senator Joni Ernst, who replaced her in the state senate in 2011 when Reynolds became lieutenant governor, seems to have a similar take on Trump, the candidate she once told in a private meeting in 2016 that she didn't want to be his vice president.

"I don't think airing grievances in public is the right thing to do," she said of Trump's attacks on Twitter, "I'm an eternal optimist. I want to believe in the best of people. I really think people come here (to Washington, D.C.) to do good for the people we represent."

And for the Democrats who don't share her positions? "Just because we believe differently doesn't make them a bad person," Ernst said.

Ernst clearly doesn't spend her evenings watching a lot of cable television where too many hosts seem to argue the exact opposite of what she was saying. In fact, her position likely costs her face time on cable television. But she doesn't much care. "I would rather be known as a person of substance not rhetoric, and not seize the headline of the day," Ernst said, "I don't immediately run to the camera."

Ernst stayed publicly neutral in the 2016 Iowa Caucuses. But she had been privately fond of Florida Senator Marco Rubio, a colleague who had impressed her. "His ability to inspire people was so important," Ernst said of Rubio. "...the fact that he had a very compelling life story...about his family and how they immigrated to the United States (from Cuba). They knew adversity. And that means you know what's it's like to overcome adversity."

The irony of her appreciation for Rubio's inspirational and, generally-speaking, even-keel mannerisms was that his inability to keep it that way brought Ernst her biggest disappointment in him.

"You know what they say about guys with small hands," Rubio had told a crowd at a rally on February 29, 2016, when he was still fighting Trump for the nomination (and after Trump taunted him by calling him "Little Marco," since he is about a half foot shorter than Trump).

Rubio's insinuation about Trump's small hands and an unstated correlation with his manhood was exactly the type of disparaging personal insult that repulses Ernst. "I think we should be above that. I didn't like any of that back and forth...we should be setting an example. We should be better than that," Ernst said and then added again for emphasis, "We should be better than that."

Ernst knows what it is like to be on the receiving end of mocks. As a candidate, she talked about her family's limited means growing up and that her mother would have her wear used plastic bread bags to protect her shoes, since she didn't have boots. Trolls ridiculed her and accused her of making up the story. Ernst admitted that she felt the sting of those cutdowns. "You always do take it a little bit personally. The point is to be a strong person," Ernst said, using similar words that she also uses to counsel others, "There are people out there--it doesn't matter what I say--they are going to be ugly. But it's because they are ugly to the core. I can't change that."

She realizes others, Rubio included, feel the pain of Trump's insolence. And Ernst still holds out (unrealistic?) hope that Trump will change his mean spiritedness. "Some people miss this," Ernst said of her private setting conversations with Trump, "But he's an extremely compassionate person. Sometimes we see that in a private setting. He actually has a big heart. I wish more people would see that."

Ernst pointed out that Trump deserves credit for his accomplishments, even if he has achieved some of them in ways that she would not have chosen. "President Trump is very unconventional, but that's okay. Does he sometimes exhibit what we want to see in a president? Probably not (i.e., the name-calling, mocking and ridiculing). But his voters support him for that," Ernst said.

And like many others also said to me, Ernst concluded, "He's not really any different than what he was in the campaign. I think if we focus on the policy, he's done a brilliant job."

Ernst's colleague, U.S. Senator Chuck Grassley agrees. The insults aren't the way Grassley has carried on during his nearly seven decades in public service. Neither is the reality TV theater that Trump brings to the daily stage, like when Trump held a live, prime-time event to announce his nomination of U.S. Circuit Court Judge Neil Gorsuch to the U.S. Supreme Court in 2017. "Every president is going to handle something different. I supposed he has that tradition on TV. It's pretty hard to separate a life's work from what you're doing as president of the United States," Grassley determined.

Another thing that Grassley determined was that he won't be copying Trump's style. "You couldn't away get away with that here in Iowa," Grassley said, "If I did that, I'd lose my reputation."

"Probably your wife, too?" I jokingly asked Grassley about his wife, Barbara, whom he married in 1954.

"Yeah!" he chuckled.

Tana Goertz isn't losing sleep over whether Iowa politicians are changing their behavior because of Trump. Trump inspired her to get involved in politics. Her familiarity with him after appearing as a contestant in 2005 on his NBC reality show, "The Apprentice," attracted her to his leadership skills. Although, after she got eliminated from the show, she did tell my television station in a live interview from New York that the process was "bulls**t!"

Nevertheless, Goertz said she became close to Trump and his family and decided that--for the first time in her professional career--which included a stint as a Mary Kay cosmetics salesperson, she would work in politics. "I'm only working on this because it's Donald Trump," Goertz told me in 2016, "That's really the only reason. I wouldn't work for anyone else."

Goertz thinks much of the blowback from critics about what and how Trump says things are due to a lack of understanding of the person he really is. "It does bother me that people are misunderstanding him." She uses this as an example:

"When Mexico sends its people, they're not sending their best. They're not sending you (referencing "you" as his supporters listening to him during this speech). They're not sending you. They're sending people that have lots of problems and they're bringing those problems with us. They're bringing drugs. They're bringing crime. They're rapists. And some, I assume, are good people."

Donald Trump, June 16, 2015

Goertz maintains that it is simply unfair to say that Trump is saying--either directly or indirectly--that Mexicans are rapists. Rather, what he is saying is that *some* Mexicans who come into the United States are rapists, drug dealers, etc. Critics misconstrue what Trump is saying, she argues. "He loves Mexicans. He hired Mexicans. He didn't say that they are bad Americans. We have rapists and drug dealers who live in our country, too," she said.

Trump is simply pointing out the obvious, even if it is difficult for some people to hear, Goertz says. And that is the sign of a true leader, in her opinion. "I witnessed firsthand what a real leader he is. I've seen him in action. I've seen that he's true to his word. I know how patriotic he is," she said.

That patriotism drives him, Goertz feels, not greed, ego, thirst for power as his critics claim. "I believe I know him better than anyone on the campaign. I've been in his home. I know his children. I know his favorite foods (pizza and bacon)," Goertz said, "You will never find a more loyal Iowan than me to Donald Trump!"

CHAPTER 13

WHAT'S NEXT

Kevin Lake of Jefferson, Iowa wore his confidence for Donald Trump's promise of a border wall at a campaign rally at Iowa Central Community College in Fort Dodge on October 27, 2016.

Photo by Dave Price

The 2018 midterm elections brought unique results that I hadn't experienced in Iowa in my time living here since 2001. Here is why 2018 was so different: the Republican governor won, her party lost a few seats in the Iowa House (but still held onto the majority), expanded its majority in the Iowa Senate but dropped two of its three seats in Congress.

Nationally, Democrats gained dozens of seats in the U.S. House to recapture the majority for the first time since 2011 (and made their largest gains since President Richard Nixon's Watergate-era scandal) but Republicans picked up two seats in the U.S. Senate. Overall, it was a strong election for Democrats but the midterms still brought mixed overall results.

Heading into the midterms, the majority of Americans disapproved of President Donald Trump's job performance. And that's despite an economy that grew at a strong pace during his tenure. On election day, RealClearPolitics found 43.5 percent of Americans polled approved of his performance, while 53.2 percent disapproved (RealClearPolitics aggregates national polls to compute its average).

Because of Trump's struggles with the public's acceptance and his acerbic nature, there had been speculation that Republican candidates would avoid campaigning with him in Iowa. The punditry figured that it would be too risky for them to be seen in public with Trump and doing so could turn off the political Independents who didn't like Trump as president.

However in 2018, Trump campaigned in the state on behalf of Governor Kim Reynolds and Third District Congressman David Young in the campaign's final weeks. Reynolds won. Young, the two-term incumbent lost. Mixed results. Trump wasn't the sole deciding factor in either race but he may have had a bigger role in Young's loss than Reynolds' win.

Trump was always a challenge for Reynolds, not his policies as much as his words. Reynolds had to push back when Trump said something outrageous (beat reporters asked her constantly about his most controversial comments) or when he instituted his trade war (primarily with China), which threatened the financial well-being of Iowa farmers. Agriculture, a cherished part of Iowa's economy, already struggled with strong global supplies of soybeans and corn, in particular, which depressed prices.

Smaller dairy farms also dried up as mechanization, for one, made those family-owned operations unable to compete with corporate competitors. Farm life has been strained for a while.

The trade war only added to that strain as it removed or greatly reduced overseas trading partners for Iowa goods. Producers had no way of knowing whether Trump's aggressive negotiating style with other countries would eventually bring longer-term benefits. For the short term, that style meant angst to an industry that had already been dealing with several years of financial anxiety.

Trump's language on immigration, for one, made the governor visibly uncomfortable when reporters pressed her on it. She would try to distance herself from the comments. Then Reynolds would attempt to redirect the conversation to decades of Congress' failed immigration reform, along with the need for better border security. It was never enough, though, for Democratic strategists and campaign operatives who would constantly try to make the case that Reynolds and Trump were one in the same.

Realistically, though, what more could the governor do politically? Could she speak out more forcefully and frequently about questions about his demeanor, falsehoods and questioned morality? Perhaps, if she thought that were the case. Maybe that could have demonstrated leadership as she established herself as the state's most prominent voice. But again, it's a political balancing act. The stronger she pushed back against Trump, the more she potentially risked also pushing away Trump's followers. And the more she strongly criticized Trump, the less chance she likely had of getting any assistance from him on policy matters. That is political reality.

Instead, Reynolds opted to keep a more business-like relationship with Trump and a closer relationship with his daughter. Ivanka did several events with Reynolds and called the governor following her election night win (the president and vice president offered messages of congratulations as well).

Reynolds praised the president during the 2018 campaign, especially when it came to the economy, tax cuts and eliminating regulations. Trump was the Republican president, after all. So she agreed with him on many prominent money matters. And with Iowa's unemployment rate falling near an historic low during her tenure and the lowest in the country, wages rising at nearly twice the rate of inflation and tax cuts on both the state and federal levels to trumpet, Reynolds saw good reason to praise the policies.

Reynolds needed Trump's political base to get re-elected. That base strongly remained in support of the president.

Other than when she once called the loudest critics from the political left "unhinged," I don't recall Reynolds ever copying Trump's harsh style when talking about opponents. That is a huge stylistic difference that she has maintained, which separates her from Trump.

Reynolds' method is more of engagement, one-on-one retail politicking, a very approachable style in interacting with the public. I can't count how many times I've heard Iowans call her "Kim." I don't think it is a lack of respect or reverence for her position as governor. I think it is the ease at which she puts people around her.

To me, that is one of the main reasons Iowans elected her in 2018. It is tempting to say voters "re-elected" her. But, again, this was her first time on the ballot as governor, after ascending from her role as lieutenant governor in 2017 when Governor Terry Branstad left to become U.S. Ambassador to China. But because she served as governor already by election time, perhaps she enjoyed the benefits of a "pseudo-incumbency" with some voters.

Leading up to the election, her inner circle constantly felt pressure about how to deal with Trump, though, and Fourth District Congressman Steve King (who narrowly got re-elected to his 9th term in 2018). Both men's words irritate and offend people. And Reynolds' staff--both her official administration staff and campaign staff--had to debate when, how and whether to disagree with comments the two men would make.

King's litany of remarks about immigrants, the dangers of diversity, his praise of Western European (primarily white) heritage and his support for Faith Goldy, a white nationalist running for mayor of Toronto, Canada (who ended up barely being a factor in that election) all reached a crescendo of discontent among some Iowa Republicans leading up to the 2018 midterms.

But history was on King's side, and the voters had been as well. Over the years, King had been intensely popular with voters in his district, controversies or not. They applauded his blunt talk and praised his commitment to traditional marriage and pro-life efforts. King generally won re-election by at least 20 points. Margins that big meant that he wasn't just getting Republicans to vote for him. Independents would come his way too.

But King's 2018 Democratic challenger, a previously unknown former journeyman, professional baseball pitcher, J.D. Scholten, pushed him in the election in ways few could have imagined.

Republicans held a staggering 70,000 registered voter advantage in the district over Democrats (Democrats had an advantage in each of the state's other three districts). Yet, despite that enormous apparent obstacle, Scholten lost by just 10,000 votes. That worked out to a less than three percent difference between the two. Stunning.

This political newcomer, with no experience at all, traveled the district's 39 counties multiple times--almost non-stop--in a used R.V. Aided by King's controversies, Scholten accomplished several things that shocked many observers. Some Republicans crossed party lines and voted for him (that included some who voted for the Republican Reynolds and the Democrat Scholten), and others just didn't vote for anyone in the race.

Reynolds had made the choice, despite the discontent building before the election, to hold her final campaign stop in King's district, in Sioux Center, in far northwest Iowa. And she allowed King to appear with her. It was clearly a political gamble. To win her race, she knew that she needed voters to come out in the Republican-rich 4th District. Strong turnout there could help her overcome expected weaknesses in stronger Democratic areas like Polk, Johnson, Story and Blackhawk Counties.

Reynolds had to weigh that reality with the alternative--as some close to her campaign had wanted--to shun King completely in the final weeks of the campaign, drop him as her ceremonial campaign co-chairman (the appointment is largely just a position in title only that is given in deference to a fellow, high profile party officeholders like King) and do her own thing without his baggage. Democrats constantly pushed the storyline that Reynolds should drop King if she disagreed with him. I have no idea if many voters paid much attention to it (Reynolds waited to sharply criticize King *after* the election).

Her decision to stick with King before the election may have paid off, though, or maybe it played no real role at all. It's hard to tell. But voters turned out in droves in that 4th District, allowing her the victory in the state, despite losing to her Democratic challenger (wealthy, retired Des Moines businessman Fred Hubbell) in the other three Congressional districts. And in Sioux County, where she did that election eve rally in Sioux Center, Reynolds received more than six times as many votes as Hubbell. That county alone netted her about 11,000 more votes than Hubbell.

Hubbell had a tough task before him as the Democrats' great hope to reclaim the governor's mansion for the first time since 2011 and offer the nation a public demonstration that, despite Trump's overwhelming 2016 election success in the state, Iowa was firmly ready to take a stand against him and the party that had largely stuck with him.

To do that, Hubbell had to convince Iowans that the economy wasn't really as strong as Reynolds and Trump made it out to be. He needed Iowans to take a deeper look into the numbers, he told me. Hubbell tried to remind them that too many Iowa families were still struggling with jobs that paid too little, housing that costs too much and that they were hampered by a widening divide between those with true economic opportunities and others with too many obstacles that would never allow success. Republicans were underfunding health care and education, Hubbell argued.

In some ways, the gubernatorial campaign became the always optimistic economic message of Reynolds vs. the more pessimistic, somber tone of Hubbell. If the two candidates were meteorologists giving forecasts, Reynolds called for more sunny skies, Hubbell predicted storms ahead.

Nearly 36,000 more Iowans preferred Reynolds. Her message resonated. Some may have cringed at her failure to fully distance herself from King and Trump. But, in the end, what she did worked. She greatly outperformed King in his district in their respective races.

Sioux County, where Reynolds and King shared the stage during that election eve rally, illustrates the difference. Final results from the secretary of state's office show that King defeated his Democratic opponent by about 50 percent in that county. Reynolds beat her Democratic challenger by a staggering 73 percent. Reynolds proved to be the superior Republican candidate.

Nationally, Democrats may have enjoyed that "Blue Wave" they craved, since they took back the majority of the U.S. House by flipping more than three dozen seats. However, I understand how some felt that Democrats could only truly attain that "Blue Wave" if they took back the U.S. Senate, too, which the party failed to do. Accomplishing that will be a challenge for the future until Democrats better connect in rural America.

Regardless, I'm not sure "Blue Wave" really fits in Iowa. It's not like Democrats had a bad year in 2018, but I don't think that I would call it a great one for them. The party was able to flip two

Congressional seats held by two-term incumbent Republicans. That is substantial. Iowans routinely re-elect incumbents. And to boot out two in one cycle is highly unusual.

Democrats last accomplished this feat in 1974 when Tom Harkin and Berkley Bedell (two men who became revered Iowa politicians from their party) defeated Republican incumbents. And in both cases, they were rematches from 1972 (thanks to the progressive blog, Bleeding Heartland, for researching the achievement).

Harkin defeated William Scherle in the Fifth Congressional District in 1974. Bedell beat Wiley Mayne in the Sixth Congressional District. Familiarity may have helped the Democratic challengers in their second attempt. But the fallout from Watergate in 1974 surely helped, too. Regardless, it took the party another 44 years to duplicate their accomplishment.

Trump and his administration tried to help Republicans hold onto the two seats in 2018. The president held campaign rallies in both the First and Third Congressional Districts. But Republican Congressman Rod Blum lost his re-election in the First by five points (17,000 votes) and Young lost in the 3rd by two points (8,000 votes).

Two years earlier, it seemed Iowa Democrats kept trying to tie any Republican candidate to Trump, assuming that there was no way Hillary Clinton would lose to him (and assuming that the public would never take Trump seriously enough to elect him). But it didn't work as Republicans ended up having a good year in 2016 with Trump the victor at the top of the ticket.

In 2018, Democrats had a better game plan. They weren't going to repeat their mistake--as tempting as it might be--to link Republicans with an unpopular president all the time. To be sure, they still tried to tie Reynolds to Trump when they felt they should. Of course, Reynolds did a campaign rally with Trump four weeks before the midterm, so the connection wasn't too difficult for Democrats to allege. Reynolds did it for them.

But the Democrats' winning Congressional challengers--two-term State Representative Abby Finkenauer of Dubuque in the First and West Des Moines small business owner Cindy Axne in the Third--largely avoided Trump in their campaign ads.

They knew that voters already knew about Trump. Instead, healthcare was much more prevalent in their campaign messaging, particularly their commitments to making sure health insurance providers cover people with pre-existing health conditions. They knew what they were doing. It was one of the top issues on voters' minds.

The Affordable Care Act, a.k.a. Obamacare, may not have delivered the savings President Barack Obama promised, allowed people to remain with their doctors as described or become as popular as Democrats would have hoped, but it did make Americans realize how important protection for their pre-existing health conditions was. Democrats campaigned vigorously that Republicans would take away that guarantee.

The Kaiser Family Foundation found that in 2016 about one in four Iowans had some type of pre-existing health condition that could make that person uninsurable if it weren't for Obamacare (the number was almost identical compared to the rest of the country).

Democrats knew that Republicans campaigned intensely ever since 2010 when Obama signed the Affordable Care Act, that they would repeal and replace it. Republicans failed again and again to actually accomplish that. The irony was that in 2018--after failing to deliver on their promise to repeal and replace Obamacare, despite their majority in Congress with a Republican president-- some Republicans tried to campaign on protecting the provision about pre-existing conditions.

Young tried that. Voters didn't buy what he was selling, though.

Obamacare may have been initially unpopular with voters. Perhaps, if Democrats had allowed time for a national debate on this massive change instead of rushing through the vote in Congress, the program could have been more popular? That aside, Americans wanted the pre-existing condition protection, regardless of other issues with the new healthcare plan.

The politicians sensed this. NBC News exit polls found that healthcare was voters' top concern at the midterms, with twice as many people citing it compared to the economy or immigration. Democrats capitalized on this. Republicans had no real answers in their defense. Healthcare was a winning issue for Democrats.

The 2018 midterms also showed that Iowans wanted Democrats as a public check on the president. For the most part, voters liked the economic direction of Iowa and they sent Reynolds back to the governor's mansion for state matters. But they didn't want Republicans Young and Blum headed back to D.C. to support Trump. They wanted more Democrats over there with the unpredictable president. So they did a flip. That's why I earlier stated that I think Trump hurt Young more than he helped Reynolds.

Following the 2016 election, Iowa had three Republican members in the U.S. House and one Democrat. But in 2018, voters decided that they wanted three Democrats and one Republican instead.

What does all of this mean going forward? It means a lot of Democrats contemplated the chance to take on Trump. They saw how controversial he was. They saw how unpopular he was overall. And they presumed the country's long economic recovery that began in June of 2009 when the Great Recession ended was bound to slow down, perhaps, during the 2020 presidential campaign. Where would Trump be without the roaring economy that he promised voters?

Both before and after the midterms, I reached out to 33 Democrats who had been mentioned as potential 2020 presidential candidates. Yes, 33! A lot of Democrats considered running for president or allowed speculation that they were thinking about running.

I wanted to ask a simple question about the future of the country and see how they would respond. Would they respond with criticism about Trump? Would they offer something visionary? Would they get specific or keep their response generic? Would they be positive? Would they be fiercely partisan? Would they respond at all?

Some declined to answer the question. Others either never responded or didn't follow through with a response. Nineteen offered their thoughts, either in person or through email.

Here was the question:

"What should our country's biggest priority be as we head toward 2020?"

I asked those Democrats who responded to keep their thoughts to between 200-300 words. Here is what they said:

U.S. Senator Cory Booker
New Jersey
Elected in 2013

"We are looking for simplistic solutions. I was a mayor. Do you want to know what's important to public education? Yeah, we need to fund public education. But do you know what's also important? It's that my kids can't show up with lead poisoning or a thousand jurisdictions where kids have twice the blood lead levels than Flint, Michigan. They can find unleaded gasoline easier than they can find unleaded water. That's an education issue, as well. Think about this: it's not only an education issue that we are an industrialized nation that leads planet Earth in infant mortality and maternal mortality because in rural areas, they have to travel hours and hours and hours just to see an OBGYN.

You think that there is one thing? That we just need to fund teachers more? We need to increase teacher salary. But if that's where we stop and we don't understand the inter-relatedness of the environment, infrastructure, education, economics...all of this coming together. And that's why I say we cannot solve these complicated problems if every day we turn on the news and we try to demonize somebody from a different party."

(Responded in person)

Michael Bloomberg
Former Mayor of New York City
Business Owner/Philanthropist

"We have just got to have a government that faces the issues. You can't have a government that doesn't believe in science. For God sakes, if you get sick, do you really want to go to a witch doctor? I don't think so. You want the best science there is. So to sit there and say 'I don't believe science,' when you have something that a vast majority of science thinks is happening...you just have to assume that that is right. And people say, 'Well it is not 100%.' Nothing is ever 100%. But we have to face climate change.

We have to face guns...30,000 people commit suicide or get shot with illegal handguns. Nobody wants to take away anybody's guns. But we should have background checks so we don't sell guns to minors. We shouldn't sell guns to people with psychiatric problems. We shouldn't sell guns to people with criminal records.

And the vast majority--85 to 90% of NRA members who are gun owners-- would agree with all three of those things. There's Opioids. 70-odd thousand people in 2017 died. There will be a lot more this year (2018). Tobacco is still...after all of our work...still kills an enormous number of people."

(Responded in person)

U.S. Senator Sherrod Brown
Ohio
Elected in 2006

"When you love this country you fight for the people who make it work – all people. Too often I hear pundits say we must choose between fighting for workers or fighting for our progressive values. That's a false choice. We can and we must do both.

That means fighting for workers' rights and civil rights, voting rights, women's rights and LGBTQ rights. It means standing up to Wall Street, drug companies, big oil and the gun lobby.

It means fighting to make hard work pay off for everyone, no matter who they are or what kind of job they do - whether they punch a clock or swipe a badge, earn a salary, or make tips; whether they're raising children or caring for an aging parent; regardless of their race or gender; whether they live in a big city or small town or whether their family has lived in that same Midwestern city for seven generations or they immigrated to this country in just the past few years.

It means fighting for all the people Donald Trump has betrayed and belittled while he's used the White House to sow division and enrich people like himself. President Trump doesn't respect the dignity of work. We must. When work has dignity, everyone can afford healthcare, education and housing. They have power over their schedules and the economic security to start a family, pay for daycare and college, take time off to care for themselves or their families when they are sick and save for retirement.

When work has dignity, our country has a strong middle class and everyone has the opportunity to build a better life for themselves and their families.

That's our priority heading into 2020 and beyond."

(Responded by email)

Governor Steve Bullock
Montana
Elected in 2012

"Whether you live in Ohio or whether you live on the East Coast, most people want and value the same thing. They want a decent job. They want a roof over their heads, a safe community, good public schools, clean air and clean water, the belief you can do better for your kids and grandkids than you. When I was growing up, 90% of 30-year-olds were doing better than their parents were at age 30. Today, it's only half. So folks don't feel like they're getting a fair shot in getting ahead. The economy is broken. The political system is broken. You look at that and there's nowhere to go.

You don't believe that the political system actually represents the will and interest of most Americans. As Democrats, going forward, we ought to be talking about that not everybody is getting ahead in this economy and we're going to work and fight to make sure that you can get ahead. And the way to actually bring the country forward isn't through the divisions that we're seeing under the current administration, when we expect, quite candidly, less out of our President than we do of our preschoolers. That doesn't help the overall lifting of the representative democracy that we expect."

(Responded in person)

Mayor Pete Buttigieg
South Bend, Indiana
Elected in 2011

"In one word: security. But there is a lot more to security than the traditional concept. Helping Americans to live a good life in the 21st century means understanding that national security begins with personal security in getting through everyday life. The times demand a new level of resiliency to new security challenges headed our way. That means not only familiar issues like military and border security, but new ones like cybersecurity and election

security. Securing our democracy is imperative, and yet we are already behind in this regard.

Modern security means facing that there is such a thing as climate security, and our communities must prepare for the gathering impacts of climate change even as we fight to slow its effects. And we must better understand what economic security means in the face of accelerating automation and the rise of artificial intelligence. Our entire national economic structure of compensation, benefits, and safety nets must be adapted for an age in which my generation, the millennial generation, will have to change careers more often than our parents' generation changed job titles. Government doesn't decide whether or not people live rich, fulfilling lives—but it can succeed or fail in creating the basic conditions for a good life.

Only if we understand security in its broadest sense—from securing access to health care to securing our neighborhoods with common-sense gun policies—will we succeed in delivering for a new generation."

(Responded via email)

Julian Castro
President Barack Obama's Secretary of Housing and Urban Development
Served from 2014-2017

"The national priority has to be that everybody has goods and opportunity. I believe that President Trump is riding the coattails of President Obama. And his (Trump's) erratic decisions--whether it's on tariffs or other things--are going to catch up with our country. So we need a vision for the future.

We need a vision that's based on what it takes for people to thrive in the 21st century, not the 20th century. Treasury Secretary Steven Mnuchin was asked about the impact of automation. He literally said, 'Well, we'll think about that in a few years.'

We have to be thoughtful about what it's going to take to succeed in the 21st century, how we're going to deal with automation, how we're going to deal with the fact that you need more of an education, more skills today than ever before. And then we have more people living longer than ever before. The extent of giving tax cuts to wealthy corporations and wealthy individuals...we need to be putting that into the bread-and-butter safety net for seniors because we have more of them living longer than ever before."

(Responded in person)

U.S. Representative John Delaney
Maryland
Served from 2013-2019

"We've got to get back to putting country ahead of political party, heal the wounds of divisiveness and start preparing our citizens for the high-tech, globally-connected economy of the future. The time for fighting is over and we must start working together to get real things done for the American people that make their lives better, create good jobs for them and their children, and build a future that is more prosperous, secure and just.

In ten years, no one is going to remember much of what dominates the news cycle on a day-to-day basis, but they're going to remember whether or not we took action to prepare the country for the future. It's correct that globalization and technology have brought big changes to our economy in the last three decades, but what people are missing is that those changes are just beginning, especially as it relates to technology. AI (Artificial Intelligence) is going to be incredibly impactful, because automation is going to cut across multiple industries, blue collar and white collar.

The American people understand what the President is, truly. How could they not? As Democrats it's our job to make it clear to people what we're going to do to help them and their kids live a better life. We have to build a more just and inclusive capitalism where more people benefit from innovation. We need a new social compact that provides universal healthcare coverage, moves education from outdated K-12 to pre-K-14, and expands the EITC (Earned Income Tax Credit).

We need to make transformative investments in infrastructure and research and create incentives for private sector investment capital to flow into all of our communities. Silicon Valley is going to keep booming, but the real question is how can we make sure that everywhere else starts to benefit as well. And we need to reassert our leadership position on the global stage and work with our allies to build the new world order for peace and security."

(Responded via email)

U.S. Representative Tulsi Gabbard
Hawaii
Elected in 2012

"One issue that often gets pushed aside, yet is vital to 2020 and beyond, is protecting our electoral process. We have seen and continue to see vulnerabilities in our electoral systems and technologies. The ball is in Congress' court, but to date, no action has been taken. Every American, regardless of political ideology, should agree that faith in our voting process is critical to our democracy.

Politicians speak out with vagaries about other countries 'meddling in our elections,' yet fail to focus on the very specific and solvable vulnerabilities threatening the security and integrity of our voting process—which is necessary to restore voter confidence in our elections and our democracy. The fact is, for generations, foreign countries have been trying to influence America's elections and public opinion in one way or another. The United States has done the same to other countries. This must be addressed separately.

For these reasons and more, I introduced the Securing America's Elections Act, which mandates paper ballots or voter-verified paper backups for electronic systems. This legislation focuses specifically on correcting weaknesses in our electoral infrastructure—vulnerabilities that should be addressed before the 2018 election, but sadly, won't be. The bill has been sitting in Congress for months without a vote.

Some politicians say they worry about the integrity of our elections, using dangerous rhetoric to serve their own political agenda, but when it comes down to it, many don't do anything to fix the problems right in front of us. My bill is a big part of the immediate solution—and its passage would put us on the path to restoring people's trust in our elections in 2020 and beyond.

In 2020 we have to reverse this alarming trend. That starts with reclaiming our 'We the People' democracy. We must break the corrupt cycle that has let the powerful and privileged call the shots for too long. If we remake our democracy into one that is responsive to the interests of working, blue-collar families like the one I grew up in, we can invest in good jobs, reliable healthcare, affordable housing, and quality education for all. Shouldn't middle-class families sitting around their kitchen tables feel excited, not anxious, about the future?

I want a child growing up in a blue-collar family today to feel the same hope and excitement as I did, here in America, regardless of which side of the train tracks they were born on and regardless of their race, religion or family makeup. That's what America means to me—and that's a vision worth fighting for."

(Responded via email)

U.S. Senator Kirsten Gillibrand
New York
Appointed in 2009

"Remembering who, and what we're fighting for. As a mother of young sons, I'm committed to fighting for America's kids as hard as I fight for my own. As we look to the future, we need leaders with the compassion, courage, and determination to take on the tough fights and win.

We must prioritize expanding health care for all Americans through Medicare For All, rewarding hard work by passing paid family leave, bettering education across all communities, and getting big money out of politics. For future generations to get ahead, it means tackling student debt, training for jobs of the future, and taking bold action on climate change. It means taking on the systems of power that keep our political system broken and put shareholders ahead of America's hardworking families.

We must also do more to elevate women's voices. 2020 will mark 100 years since women were granted the right to vote. It is a reminder of the courage of the women who came before us, determined to break barriers and create opportunity. There are already five women running for president who are making history in their own right. I'm so inspired by their leadership and the diverse field of candidates who are adding their voices to this debate.

Our Party is unified in our vision of restoring integrity to the White House. It is one of hope and compassion, and of our shared belief that we must expand opportunities for every family, regardless of zip code. I believe our country's best days are ahead of us, and no matter what, I'll always remember who and what I'm fighting for."

(Responded via email)

Governor John Hickenlooper
Colorado
Served from 2011-2019

"A good job is a key to a good life. I remember what it felt like to be laid off from my job as a geologist in 1986. After a while, you start to see a different person in the mirror, a less confident person. A lot of Americans feel they've been left behind economically, while others are thriving. We need to focus on how we can work together to ensure that our economy can benefit everyone.

The Democratic Party is the party of social justice. It always will be. There's still this tired idea that Republicans are the only ones who care about jobs and reducing red tape. That's just not true. In Colorado we cut or modified half of our 24,500 rules and regulations.

We built the number one economy in the country by going out to all 64 counties and learning how they wanted to grow. We worked together, and we didn't sacrifice our values. We expanded health care coverage and prioritized clean air and water. Our goal from the beginning was to be the most business-friendly state, with the highest ethical and environmental standards. We weren't going to compromise one for the other - and we haven't had to. Our country shouldn't either.

Politics today is so often defined by opposition. Liberal vs. Conservative. Urban vs. Rural. Rich vs. Poor. If there's one thing I learned after 15 years in the restaurant business, it's that there's no margin in enemies. There's more value in knowing what you're for, and how to work together to achieve it, than just sitting around and repeating what you're against."

(Responded via email)

Eric Holder, Jr.
President Barack Obama's U.S. Attorney General
Served from 2009-2015

"Since January 2017, there has been an awakening amongst our fellow citizens, a 'New American Engagement.' I have been inspired by, among others, the actions of concerned women, teachers, LGBTQ Americans, those in still distressed minority communities, and students devastated by gun violence who have marched and organized to demand fairness, opportunity, and justice. But in too many places, regardless of political affiliation, age or race, people feel that our system of government is breaking down. For too many, our democracy is not working. As a result, the issues that are of greatest concern - income inequality and stagnant wages, climate change, immigration, personal freedoms - are not meaningfully addressed.

Dark money corrupts our campaigns and influences how politicians vote. Discriminatory voter ID laws and gerrymandering diminish voting power and allow a party with minority support and views to hold a majority of power in Congress and in state legislatures. The proponents of an extreme ideology seek to drown out the voices of an inherently reasonable people. Politicians use inflammatory rhetoric and "alternative facts" to divide us even though average Americans have more in common with each other than those who always side with the rich and powerful.

At this moment, when the American system is being tested, we can't take our democracy for granted. But this is not a time for despair -- our history has shown that we should never underestimate what is possible when Americans come together to shape the fate of our nation. We need even more people to stand up for our values and our rights, and to use consistently the most powerful tool we all have as citizens – the vote. Together, we the people can bring about a new era of change and progress and stay true to our founding ideals. America is both exceptional and a work in progress. We can and must commit ourselves to constructing a nation that stays true to the ideals that have always defined us."

(Responded via email)

U.S. Senator Jeff Merkley
Oregon
Elected in 2008

"I grew up in a blue-collar family. My dad worked as a mechanic. Back then, in the decades after World War II, workers shared in the wealth they created—and we had a solid, middle-class life. My parents owned their own home; put food on the table; even took a modest camping vacation every so often. Back then, in the decades after World War II, a lot more workers shared in the wealth they created.

I was the first in my family to go to college, and my parents thought that the American dream would be even more incredible for my generation than theirs, although we know that wasn't always the case for all families in our nation.

But instead, a group of rich and powerful Americans have taken over our economy and our democracy. And working Americans are paying the price.

Most middle-class families worry about the same basic things— what I call the four sides of the kitchen table.

Healthcare. Education. Housing. And of course, jobs.

Over the past few decades, good living-wage jobs have become ever harder to come by. Meanwhile, the cost of good health care, education, and housing has soared out of reach for millions of middle-class Americans."

(Responded via email)

U.S. Representative Seth Moulton
Massachusetts
Elected in 2014

"To change this country, we need to change our leaders. That's never been more evident than on February 15, 2018, the day after the Parkland shooting. Across the country, Democrats, Republicans--Americans--were pleading with Congress to do something to stop these tragedies. But instead of enacting any straightforward, bipartisan, common-sense gun reforms, Republican leadership voted on HR 620: a bill to gut part of the Americans with Disabilities Act.

Seventeen Americans had just been killed, and Congress started the next day by making life harder for people in wheelchairs. People often ask me why votes like this happen, why Congress is so broken, or why Congress is 'so stupid.' The truth is that what's missing in Washington isn't intelligence--it's courage. Most Members of Congress know that climate change is real, that automation--not immigration--is the real threat to our workforce, and that families need a break from skyrocketing healthcare costs. But they're more worried about getting re-elected, so they vote along party lines to protect their base rather than do the right thing for the country.

That's why it's time for a change. We can build a safe and strong America where everyone has a job that matters, and where our leaders solve problems instead of creating them. But we won't build it by sending the same old people to Washington to think the same way about a different world.

Americans deserve elected leaders they can trust. It's time for those who will live with the consequences of our policies for the next 50 years to have a hand in shaping them. It's time for the generation that fought in Iraq and Afghanistan to replace the generation that sent us there. It's time to elect a new generation of leadership in America--leaders who have the courage to be honest about the problems we face, and the resolve to go out and do something about them. Then we can stop trying to go back in time to 'make America great again,' and get to work making it better than it's ever been."

(Responded via email)

Governor Martin O'Malley
Maryland
Served from 2007-2015

"Our economy is not money, it is people — all of our people. Therefore the biggest issue facing our country is the economy and jobs of the future — in short, whether we will be able to give our kids more opportunities than our parents gave us. This is the social compact of the United States — a country where everyone who works should get ahead.

But right now, the anxiety and depression being experienced across our country is grounded in a fear of worthlessness. Unemployment has never been lower, and yet, white male suicides have never been higher. Far too many of our people are working harder and falling further behind. In the absence of a national story for success, 'change' has become a word that many Americans fear. It doesn't need to be this way. Wage stagnation, growing income inequality, monopoly concentrations, a national government starved by tax cuts for the wealthy — these are all political choices.

The entire world is fast moving into a Third Industrial Revolution — a coming together of new technologies in energy, transportation and communications. Renewable energy. The Internet of Things. Autonomous travel. Whole systems will change. Some skills will become obsolete, others will be needed. Making our children winners in this changing economy rather than victims of it, requires a country that works, a country strong enough to take advantage of change for the benefit of all of us, a country that provides its workers and its next generation the skills they need to seize and hold the new jobs of this Third Industrial Revolution."

(Responded via email)

U.S. Representative Tim Ryan
Ohio
Elected in 2002

"2020 will be the most consequential election of our lifetime. I, like so many Americans, can feel the sense of urgency in the air. With political polarization at an all-time high, and a trust deficit between the American people and our intuitions of government wider than any time since at least Watergate, it can be tempting to withdraw into our respective political "tribes" and all the partisan trench warfare that comes with it. We must resist those temptations and urge our citizenry to strive for national healing, instead.

It is not surprising that passions run so high. The election and subsequent presidency of Donald Trump has been a traumatic experience for many. Immigrants have been demonized and harassed by emboldened xenophobes, hate crimes against LGBTQ+ individuals have skyrocketed, African Americans striving for equal justice under the law have been rebuffed by the Administration, a woman's right to make her own reproductive choices is under threat, and Unions are seeing their right to organize for a fair wage hamstrung at every level. These are issues that strike at the very core of a person's being.

What we lose when we get too caught up in the day-to-day rage of this Administration is that our fellow citizen is not our enemy. More unites us than divides us. The President relies on fear and division to prevent progress and we cannot allow him to do that. All of us must strive to find common ground and forge a consensus that improves the lives of hardworking people in every community across the United States. If we are to do this, it will take all of us. We can't afford to write off any single person."

(Responded via email)

Tom Steyer
California Philanthropist/Political Activist

"Donald Trump might have been impeached by the time you read this. If not, then our most pressing and urgent task for the United

States in 2020 is voting him and his Republican enablers — out of office.

But our larger task is to reclaim American values to build a society in which respect and dignity for everyone is the norm. If we want a government that serves everyone, rather than the self-serving interests of powerful corporations and the wealthy, we need to expand our electorate. Roughly 40 percent of eligible voters did not cast a ballot in 2016.

Not only is that unacceptable in a democracy, it's part of the reason we have Donald Trump endangering America from his chair in the White House.

Our only course of action is to put power back in the hands of everyday people, to increase the number of voices with a say in their future. This means investing time and resources to organize in every community, and encouraging everyone — especially young people and people of color — to cast their ballots.

Every potential voter has to understand their stakes in this election. The destructive and corrupt Trump agenda has nothing to offer the 43 percent of our households struggling to afford the basics they need to prosper in today's economy. 2020 is an opportunity for the American people to demand better from the wealthiest, most powerful country in human history.

We must elect dedicated democrats—with a 'small d'— who will fight for the rights of Americans that have been under assault from corporate interests and their powerful lobbyists for far too long: The right to a decent living; to a safe and healthy life; to learn; to a just and equal society; and to a fair democracy. These five rights are essential to restoring the American Dream in the 21st Century. Guaranteeing their protection would fundamentally shift the assumptions of how America governs itself, away from serving just the powerful.

A life of dignity and respect should not come with a price tag. It's time to take back the institutions that Donald Trump and the Republican Party are exploiting to attack working Americans and vulnerable communities. Only by expanding our democracy, and electing representatives who are committed to serving the people, can we create an America that works for us all."

(Responded via email)

U.S. Representative Eric Swalwell
California
Elected in 2012

"I was raised to believe that hard work in America means something – that if we work hard, we do better for ourselves and dream bigger for the next generation.

I learned that from my dad who worked as a cop and from my mom who raised four boys and worked every odd job imaginable to make sure I was the first in the family to go to college. Hard work should be a path to success, but today that's no longer true for everyone. That's what threatens Americans most – not the tweets, not the chaos in the Oval Office, not the corruption of cashing in on access to the White House. Americans are hurting because they're working as hard as ever but making less while costs rise, and the next generation doesn't have careers they can count on.

The priority for 2020 and beyond is to change that by investing in modern schools for every neighborhood in America. We should make sure every kid can aim beyond high school and afford to do so. Healthcare costs eat too far into most Americans' take-home pay, so it's time for a Medicare-for-All guarantee. And we need to create a tax code that helps small businesses succeed instead of making the biggest corporations bigger and the richest Americans richer. Tax cuts should be tied to profit- or equity-sharing; if a company does better because of lower taxes, it shouldn't just be the top floor of the company that tastes the success. If the CEO gets a raise, so should the janitor."

(Responded via email)

U.S. Senator Elizabeth Warren
Massachusetts
Elected in 2012

"I think our priorities should be to make democracy work and that's what today is all about. It's about all the people who volunteer, raise their voices and say they want an America that reflects their best values...an America where every kid gets a fighting chance to build a future."

(Responded in person)

Andrew Yang
New York City Entrepreneur

"We can all sense that America is entering the fourth inning of a massive crisis, but most politicians are misidentifying the problem. The Trump administration is a symptom of our democracy breaking down, not the cause. It's time to acknowledge that the average American is under attack. GDP is booming, but middle-class workers are suffering. New technologies and automation have already displaced millions of workers in manufacturing and retail, and if we do nothing, the coming wave of job loss will be catastrophic. This must be our top priority in 2020.

My plan is to implement a series of policies to guide us through this next phase of our economy, centered around the Freedom Dividend, a form of Universal Basic Income that would put $1,000 per month, no strings attached, in the pocket of every American between the ages of 18 and 64. This would permanently grow the economy by around 13%—or about $2.5 trillion by 2025—and allow Americans to relocate for job opportunities, go back to school, start a business or care for their loved ones. The Freedom Dividend would be supplemented with universal healthcare, a robust infrastructure spending bill, affordable higher education, and a plan to address climate change through geoengineering, among other innovative policies. A just, democratic, abundant future is within our grasp—in 2020, we must commit to building it together."

(Responded via email)

The sheer number of potential candidates, along with their varied responses on this one question that I asked about the country's future priority, set up a fascinating 2020 landscape. Should Democrats try to "out-Trump Trump" by nominating someone who can provide the same verbal barrage of insults and attacks? Show that Democrats aren't wimps and that Trump can't just bulldoze over them? Could the public even stomach a presidential race like that? I'm not so sure.

Or should Democrats instead nominate someone who can provide the opposite--someone who is more of a visionary? Barack Obama sold Iowans on "hope and change." What is the 2020 version of that? "Opportunity for all?" And which Democrat is most able to not just deliver that theme but make Americans believe in it like Obama in 2008 and 2012 and Trump in 2016?

Hillary Clinton tried a host of slogans, seemed too rehearsed (not the genuine person Iowans close to her claim she really is) and failed to rally Iowans on her historic bid as the nation's first female president. Bernie Sanders inspired a more passionate, vocal following, both during his rallies and the digital conversation. But is socialism (or Democratic socialism) the direction Democrats want to point the country? No doubt that Millennials seemed to gravitate to his message.

There was real energy at his rallies and younger voters brought that enthusiasm. Sanders made it obvious where he stood on major issues. Clinton wasn't always so clear. But, of course, she earned the nomination. He didn't. So what does that say about the Democratic electorate? How far left politically does the party really want to go?

Should the nominee run on a "Medicare for all" concept, and take the private (for profit) insurance industry completely out of the business? Raise taxes on the rich? Tuition-free college?

Democrats seem to be searching for a plan on at least two big issues: the economy and immigration. Maybe 2018 will show that they are figuring it out. Or perhaps since they didn't get the gains that many wanted--both in Iowa and nationally--it shows that they have much work to do on this.

Scholten performed impressively in rural Iowa in that Fourth District race, but the same can't be said about Democrats in most rural legislative districts. Democrats face a major challenge going forward, unless they only want to just be the party of the state's urban areas. How Democrats engage with Iowans about money matters will be key to overcoming that challenge.

Economic Priorities

What is the economic vision for Democrats? The Republicans' tax plan, "The Tax Cuts and Jobs Act of 2017," didn't turn out to be overwhelmingly popular with the public. Democrats frequently trashed it. But many were hesitant to lay out specifically how they would change the tax code. Whose taxes will go up if Democrats had their way? Whose tax breaks will go away? Which businesses should start paying more or receiving less in subsidies? Specifics. Democrats were too often reluctant to offer them.

President Trump's policy to separate migrant children from their parents in 2018 revolted the general public. He had to reverse course, realizing how hugely unpopular his decision on this was. Increased border security, building a border wall and making sure people are in the country legally--while controversial with some people--weren't nearly as repulsive to the masses like forcibly removing children from their parents with no guarantee that they would ever be reunited.

Immigration Reform

But what will the Democrats' immigration plan be? They, too, failed to pass an immigration plan when they were in the majority in the past. Should anyone be allowed to come into the country and stay here, essentially a true "open border" policy? Isn't that dangerous for our country?

Is it fair to let everyone who is already in the U.S. illegally have the right to stay here legally and then say after a new immigration policy that anyone who tries to do it tomorrow, though, can't? Does that make any sense? Should there be exceptions based on how those in this country illegally lived while they have arrived here? They get to stay, but those who committed crimes should leave? And how serious should those crimes be to get a person deported? These are deep, serious and vexing questions. But shouldn't Democrats have a specific plan on all of this so that Trump can't say they all just want to open the borders and let any potential terrorist or gang member freely walk into the U.S.? Specifics.

Emerging Power

What role will women play, not just for Democrats, but in the nation's politics? Women ran for office in 2018 in record numbers and they won like never before. Clinton's two presidential runs and defeats likely inspired some of that, right? So, too, I presume did the #MeToo movement where female victims went public with sexual misconduct and harassment allegations against well-known members of entertainment, the media and politics. The lengthy list of female accusers of President Trump added fuel to that movement, as well, regardless of his denials.

Female activism soared. Candidates spoke out against harassment but also became leading voices on healthcare, education, economic opportunities and fairness. Women proved that there remains no doubt they can win in Iowa. Sure, they likely still face additional barriers. But, perhaps, it's finally a small minority of voters who refuse to believe that women should be elected leaders. The 2018 election saw Iowa's first elected female governor, its first two women sent to the U.S. House, and more women to the state senate and house. A record year indeed. Clinton won the 2016 Iowa Caucus and then lost overwhelmingly in the general election that November. But other women have fared incredibly well since then.

The overall increased prominence of women in politics will no doubt impact campaigns and policies in 2020, both in terms of female candidates and prominent campaign positions.

Hatred and Racism

How, too, will a very ugly, disturbing trend play a role in political conversations going forward? What is behind the rise of hate? National attention focused on white supremacists who rallied at the "United the Right" gathering in August 2017, in Charlottesville, Virginia, and the supporter who authorities say intentionally drove his car through a group of protesters, which killed a woman.

Iowa saw its own hateful acts. High profile incidents over the past two years included racist graffiti and phone calls targeting African American students at Drake University in Des Moines, two radio broadcasters fired for racist remarks during a high school basketball game in Forest City and five Creston high school football players removed from the team after video surfaced of them wearing white hoods and standing next to a burning cross.

What ignited all of this? Has the explosive state of politics fueled this somehow? And why now? How will this impact the electorate as the state and nation look to the 2020 presidential election?

Donald Trump

President Trump has been a remarkable combination of controversy, reality TV and political theater that has engaged many who rarely, if ever, have engaged in politics. He made people in rural Iowa--where jobs have disappeared, schools have closed and families have moved away--believe that he will restore life as it once was. Trump's promise to "Make America Great Again" resonated with their sense of nostalgia, back when they felt their towns had a more obvious future and their children and grandchildren would be there to share that future with them. Some Democrats are too quick to assume that Trump's appeal is all based on race, a pitch to whites who resent people of color's push for equality.

It would be naive to think that wasn't a factor with some people. But it's also too much to say that racism is entirely the reason Trump became president.

Trump's "America first" themes also resonated with blue-collar patriots who don't like that the rest of the world has been taking away jobs and their economic opportunities. Trump has been the eternal campaigner-in-chief. Every speech seems to be a campaign rally, regardless of whether he is at the White House or somewhere on the road.

He managed to hold support with Evangelicals, despite his foul language and numerous allegations of infidelity and hush money payments to former lovers. He can be at his best with inspirational, passionate speeches that speak of American dominance in the world, mixed in with a little self-deprecation that can make people think, for a moment, that even he knows that he can become a Hollywood caricature of himself. His sly smile seals the deal.

Trump is at his worst when he belittles and mocks those he feels stand in his way, challenge or disagree with him. He seems to show no reasonable limits to his attacks...war veterans, the physically challenged, immigrants...all can be his targets. He routinely spews untruths and conspiracy theories in ways that no other modern U.S. leader ever has before. The professional fact checkers can't keep up with his unfounded claims. And he sews distrust of the media, his own law enforcement and the court system in ways that threaten public confidence and the core of the country's beliefs in itself.

The national news media covering Trump frequently provide a stream of breathless, "breaking news," non-stop coverage of his latest comments, policies or misstatements that rattle political norms. And despite (maybe because of?) Trump's claims of "fake news" when the media don't report something the way he demands and his baseless attacks that the media are "the enemy of the people", trust in the media is actually going back up.

A Gallup national poll of adults released on October 12, 2018, found that Republicans, Democrats and Independents all had an increased level of trust in the media since Trump's election in 2016. Overall, 45 percent of people trusted the media. That's still not good, obviously (it was 68 percent in 1972). But it represents a 13 percent increase in two years.

(Source: "Americans' Trust and Confidence in the Mass Media")

Why? Trump's presidency makes the public pay attention and it makes people seek out media sources for information about him.

While Trump has failed to increase support in Iowa, he still has fervent followers. Trump fills arenas for campaign rallies with thousands of devotees that could make a rock band envious.

Some supporters discount his vitriol as just an attention-grabbing flashpoint to make sure everyone is paying attention. But others support his White House behavior like they did during his campaign to get there. Trump is the person who isn't loyal to tradition, customs, political norms or parties. He is a unique force. He is loyal to the spotlight of that moment and to govern by chaos. He demands and craves the public's engrossment. He will do things *his* way and attempt to destroy those who get in his path.

Investigations into virtually every aspect of Trump's life (business interests, charity, alleged payouts to lovers, relationship with Russia) will ensure that Trump remains one of the most divisive figures in the country. The outcomes of the those investigations could significantly impact the legacy of the Trump presidency.

Whether people revere or despise him, though, one of Trump's greatest legacies could be forcing people to have uncomfortable conversations. His policies, actions and words force people to look deeper into themselves about their feelings about immigration, security, race, taxes, healthcare, education, faith, sexual orientation, government, media, military, values and the country's role in the world. The country could and should be better for the future because of those conversations.

In 2020 (if Trump runs for re-election as he said that he would), Iowans will help decide whether Trump's incendiary methods will make the country better than it has ever been, to "Make America Great Again" as he promised, or whether they will realize that a second act of this reality TV star's leading role is one that the United States of America may not be able to withstand.

ABOUT THE AUTHOR

D ave Price has reported from the depths of the Atlantic Ocean inside a nuclear submarine and high above the Rocky Mountains while co-piloting a Navy T-34 Mentor single engine plane. But it's his connections in Iowa politics that make this book one of his greatest adventures --- with a former reality TV star the ringleader of the caucus circus.

Dave is the political director at WHO-TV in Des Moines, Iowa, and has spent more time with presidential candidates over the past 17 years than nearly any local TV reporter in America. His access to those seeking the highest office in the land provide a front row seat to the greatest show in presidential politics: the Iowa Caucuses. And Iowa's traditional status as a "purple state" always adds to the intrigue about which party's nominee will capture the state's imagination.

Iowans have preferred the Democratic presidential candidate in six of the past eight general elections. But the state had been trending more toward Republicans this decade. The 2020 Iowa Caucuses look to be another unpredictable collision course.

Caucus Chaos Trump goes deep inside the Iowa landscape, where Donald Trump built a following that few expected. Interviews with dozens of activists, party insiders and top state and national leaders reveal how Trump has changed politics and how Democrats hope to defeat him in 2020.

Dave did much of his best writing for this book in his family's basement at a big, old wooden desk rescued and refurbished by his father-in-law. The occasional interruption by kids Hayden, 8, and Lyla, 3, drew out the book launch a little longer than he (and his wife Emily) would've liked. Those kids are behind every good story though –like when Dave left the hospital to interview candidate Hillary Clinton when Lyla was just 16 hours old or when Hayden raced up the stairs (slipped and split his lip) to let his mom and sister know Trump was headed to victory on election night.

The Prices live in Clive, Iowa.

Made in the USA
Columbia, SC
16 March 2019